AGILE AND BUSINESS ANALYSIS

BCS, THE CHARTERED INSTITUTE FOR IT

BCS, The Chartered Institute for IT champions the global IT profession and the interests of individuals engaged in that profession for the benefit of all. We promote wider social and economic progress through the advancement of information technology, science and practice. We bring together industry, academics, practitioners and government to share knowledge, promote new thinking, inform the design of new curricula, shape public policy and inform the public.

Our vision is to be a world-class organisation for IT. Our 70,000 strong membership includes practitioners, businesses, academics and students in the UK and internationally. We deliver a range of professional development tools for practitioners and employees. A leading IT qualification body, we offer a range of widely recognised qualifications.

Further Information
BCS, The Chartered Institute for IT,
First Floor, Block D,
North Star House, North Star Avenue,
Swindon, SN2 1FA, United Kingdom.
T +44 (0) 1793 417 424
F +44 (0) 1793 417 444
www.bcs.org/contact

http://shop.bcs.org/

AGILE AND BUSINESS ANALYSIS
Practical guidance for IT professionals

Lynda Girvan and Debra Paul

Published by BCS Learning & Development Ltd, a wholly owned subsidiary of BCS, The Chartered Institute for IT, First Floor, Block D, North Star House, North Star Avenue, Swindon, SN2 1FA, UK.
www.bcs.org

ISBN: 978-1-78017-322-1
PDF ISBN: 978-1-78017-323-8
ePUB ISBN: 978-1-78017-324-5
Kindle ISBN: 978-1-78017-325-2

British Cataloguing in Publication Data.
A CIP catalogue record for this book is available at the British Library.

Disclaimer:
The views expressed in this book are of the authors and do not necessarily reflect the views of the Institute or BCS Learning & Development Ltd except where explicitly stated as such. Although every care has been taken by the authors and BCS Learning & Development Ltd in the preparation of the publication, no warranty is given by the authors or BCS Learning & Development Ltd as publisher as to the accuracy or complete-ness of the information contained within it and neither the authors nor BCS Learning & Development Ltd shall be responsible or liable for any loss or damage whatsoever arising by virtue of such information or any instructions or advice contained within this publication or by any of the aforementioned.

BCS books are available at special quantity discounts to use as premiums and sale promotions, or for use in corporate training programmes. Please visit our Contact us page at www.bcs.org/contact

Typeset by Lapiz Digital Services, Chennai, India.
Printed at Hobbs the Printers Ltd, Hampshire, UK.

CONTENTS

List of figures ix
List of tables xii
Authors' biographies xiii
Foreword xiv
Preface xvii

1. **BUSINESS ANALYSIS IN AGILE ENVIRONMENTS** 1
Introduction 1
The rationale for business analysis 3
Business agility 5
The agile business analyst 6
The agile business analysis book 8

2. **AGILE PHILOSOPHY AND PRINCIPLES** 11
Introduction 11
The origins of agile 12
The Agile Manifesto 16
The 12 agile principles 19
Agile approaches 20
Agile practices 21
Conclusion 22

3. **ANALYSING THE ENTERPRISE** 24
Introduction 24
The business analysis perspective 25
Agile Manifesto for buiness analysts 31
Agile business thinking 32
Conclusion 39

4. **ADOPTING AN AGILE MINDSET** 41
Introduction 41
Relating the agile principles to business analysis 41
Collaborative working 43
Self-organising teams 46
Continuous improvement 49
Iterative development and incremental delivery 52
Planning for and building in change 55
Doing the right thing and the thing right 56
Conclusion 57

5.	UNDERSTANDING AGILE METHODS AND FRAMEWORKS	59
	Introduction	59
	Key elements in agile methods	59
	Popular agile methods and approaches	61
	Scaled agile approaches	73
	Conclusion	75

6.	MODELLING THE BUSINESS CONTEXT	78
	Introduction	78
	Organisational agility	79
	Using modelling techniques	82
	Modelling at a business level	86
	Conclusion	94

7.	WORKING WITH STAKEHOLDERS AND ROLES	96
	Introduction	96
	The nature of stakeholders	96
	The multi-skilled team	99
	Customer categories	103
	Stakeholder engagement	106
	Stakeholder categories, roles and perspectives	110
	Conclusion	119

8.	DECOMPOSING GOALS	121
	Introduction	121
	The relevance of goal-based analysis	121
	Goal and functional decomposition	123
	Understanding goal levels	126
	Using goals to achieve business agility	128
	Using goals to define iterations and releases	128
	Conclusion	129

9.	PRIORITISING THE WORK	130
	Introduction	130
	The importance of prioritisation	130
	Prioritising requirements	131
	Applying prioritisation	137
	Prioritisation decomposition	138
	Prioritisation issues	139
	Conclusion	144

10.	DECIDING THE REQUIREMENTS APPROACH	145
	Introduction	145
	The requirements engineering framework	145
	Planning the requirements approach	149
	Issues with requirements engineering	151
	Agile requirements engineering	152
	Requirements elicitation techniques	154
	The role of business analysis in elicitation	156
	Conclusion	158

11.	**MODELLING USERS AND PERSONAS**	**159**
	Introduction	159
	Benefits of a modelling approach to requirements	159
	Modelling users and functionality	161
	Analysing users and roles	164
	Analysing personas and misuse characters	168
	Analysing the system context and scope	172
	Visualising user journeys	178
	Conclusion	179
12.	**MODELLING STORIES AND SCENARIOS**	**180**
	Introduction	180
	Modelling system usage	180
	User stories	182
	Scenarios	193
	Behaviour driven development	195
	Story mapping	197
	Conclusion	202
13.	**ORGANISING TASKS AND REQUIREMENTS**	**204**
	Introduction	204
	Types of requirement	205
	The requirements catalogue	208
	The itemised backlogs	209
	Requirements catalogue or solution backlog?	213
	Recording non-functional requirements	214
	Hierarchy of requirements	216
	Conclusion	221
14.	**ESTIMATING AGILE PROJECTS**	**222**
	Introduction	222
	Agile estimation approaches	222
	Why and when to estimate	223
	Estimation techniques	224
	Conclusion	231
15.	**PLANNING AND MANAGING ITERATIONS**	**233**
	Introduction	233
	The iteration	233
	Iterations and goals	236
	Planning the iteration	238
	Managing and monitoring the iteration	249
	Reviewing the iteration	253
	The role of business analysis in agile iterations	256
	Conclusion	258

16.   **CONSIDERATIONS WHEN ADOPTING AGILE**   **259**
         Introduction   259
         Agile adoption   260
         The business analyst role in an agile world   265
         Conclusion   269

         Index   271

LIST OF FIGURES

Figure 1.1	Business Analysis Maturity Model™	3
Figure 1.2	Business analysis activities	5
Figure 2.1	Waterfall development approach	12
Figure 2.2	The main elements of agile	15
Figure 2.3	The manifesto for agile software development	16
Figure 3.1	Three BA perspectives	26
Figure 3.2	Pre-project analysis work	27
Figure 3.3	POPIT™ model	28
Figure 3.4	Pre-project business analysis	29
Figure 3.5	An Agile Manifesto for business improvement	31
Figure 3.6	Aspects of systems thinking	33
Figure 3.7	Principles of Lean thinking	35
Figure 3.8	The '8 wastes'	36
Figure 3.9	Organisation versus customer value perception	38
Figure 4.1	Six core agile values for business analysts	42
Figure 4.2	Mehrabian's elements of communication	44
Figure 4.3	Tuckman's stages of group development	48
Figure 4.4	*Kaizen* PDCA cycle	51
Figure 4.5	Iterative development adapted for process improvement	53
Figure 4.6	External and internal sources of change	55
Figure 5.1	Example of a Kanban board	71
Figure 6.1	The iterative nature of business environment and strategy analysis	81
Figure 6.2	Informal model of a business situation	83
Figure 6.3	The FMM	85
Figure 6.4	The Simplified FMM	87
Figure 6.5	Value chain for training service	88
Figure 6.6	BAM of a training business system	89
Figure 6.7	Business process model for bespoke course development	90
Figure 6.8	Business use case model	92
Figure 6.9	Example of business epics	93
Figure 6.10	Template for a business epic card	93
Figure 7.1	The T-shaped BA professional	100
Figure 7.2	Example of different types of T-shaped professionals in a development team	103
Figure 7.3	Types of business customer	104
Figure 7.4	Organisation versus customer value perceptions	106
Figure 7.5	Stakeholder wheel	107
Figure 7.6	Power/interest grid	108

Figure 7.7	The relationship between stakeholders and roles	111
Figure 7.8	Business/governance roles on change projects	112
Figure 7.9	Architectural domain roles on change projects	114
Figure 7.10	External stakeholder roles on change projects	115
Figure 7.11	Stakeholder roles within the development team	117
Figure 8.1	Organisational chart showing a high-level business process	122
Figure 8.2	Functional decomposition of the goal, 'Open a café'	123
Figure 8.3	Goal decomposition of the goal, 'Open a café'	124
Figure 8.4	Decomposed goals for the 'Serve hot drinks' goal	125
Figure 8.5	Cockburn's levels of goals	127
Figure 8.6	Examples of different goal levels	127
Figure 9.1	Calculation for WSJF	133
Figure 9.2	Prioritised list of requirements or work items using MoSCoW	136
Figure 9.3	Release schedule showing MoSCoW priorities	138
Figure 9.4	Decomposed requirements/goals with priority levels	139
Figure 9.5	Questions used during prioritisation	141
Figure 10.1	Requirements engineering framework	146
Figure 10.2	Slices of requirements engineering applied iteratively	149
Figure 10.3	A suggested FMM plan for the requirements approach	150
Figure 10.4	Traditional approach to requirements engineering	151
Figure 10.5	An agile approach to eliciting requirements	153
Figure 10.6	A low fidelity throwaway prototype	156
Figure 10.7	Business analyst standing between customer and development team	157
Figure 10.8	The business analyst role in facilitating collaboration	157
Figure 11.1	IT systems and processes in 'the simplified FMM'	160
Figure 11.2	The value of modelling	161
Figure 11.3	Using models to provide context from business to iteration	162
Figure 11.4	User analysis matrix	165
Figure 11.5	Approach for user role development workshop	166
Figure 11.6	Role card description	169
Figure 11.7	Personas for customers of a holiday company	170
Figure 11.8	Persona for a customer of a training provider	170
Figure 11.9	Misuse character card	171
Figure 11.10	Context diagram for course booking system	173
Figure 11.11	Showing 'use' on a context diagram	173
Figure 11.12	Use case levels	174
Figure 11.13	Discovered use case	175
Figure 11.14	Briefly described use case	175
Figure 11.15	Fully described use case	176
Figure 11.16	Activity diagram for use case	177
Figure 11.17	'As is' user journey	178
Figure 12.1	The simplified Functional Model Map	181
Figure 12.2	Example user story	189
Figure 12.3	Example user story 'confirmation'	192
Figure 12.4	Approach to developing scenarios	194
Figure 12.5	BDD collaboration	196
Figure 12.6	Story map backbone	199
Figure 12.7	Story map populated with decomposed stories	200

Figure 12.8	Using the story map to define deliverables	202
Figure 13.1	Types of requirement	205
Figure 13.2	Three different views of the backlog	210
Figure 13.3	Example requirements catalogue definition of access requirements	215
Figure 13.4	Visible non-functional requirements and constraints	216
Figure 13.5	Hierarchy of requirements	217
Figure 13.6	Decomposed business use case into system use cases	218
Figure 13.7	Decomposed business use case showing external actor component	219
Figure 13.8	Hierarchy of use cases leading to user story development	220
Figure 14.1	Estimation cycle	223
Figure 14.2	Relative sizing using jelly beans	225
Figure 14.3	Planning Poker® cards	229
Figure 14.4	Planning Poker® process	230
Figure 15.1	Cycle of an iteration	235
Figure 15.2	Iteration activities	235
Figure 15.3	The layered approach to iterations	236
Figure 15.4	The relationship between iterations, releases and goals	237
Figure 15.5	Calculating team velocity	240
Figure 15.6	Backlog refinement activities	245
Figure 15.7	Agile board	246
Figure 15.8	Example of a burndown chart showing story points	250
Figure 15.9	Example of a burndown chart showing remaining effort	252
Figure 15.10	A burnup chart showing progress of iterations	253
Figure 15.11	Common retrospective questions	255
Figure 16.1	Scott Ambler's 'Software Development Context Framework'	263
Figure 16.2	Levels of influence when adopting agile	264
Figure 16.3	Key characteristics of an agile business analyst	266
Figure 16.4	BA role in agile	267
Figure 16.5	Main elements of agile	269

LIST OF TABLES

Table 1.1	Structure of this book	9
Table 2.1	Agile development methods	14
Table 2.2	The 12 agile principles explained	19
Table 2.3	Agile work practices	22
Table 4.1	The three elements of communication	43
Table 5.1	Key elements in agile methods	60
Table 5.2	Four key Scrum events	63
Table 5.3	Three Scrum roles	64
Table 5.4	Three Scrum artefacts	65
Table 5.5	Five rules of XP	66
Table 5.6	DSDM life cycle phases	68
Table 5.7	Roles defined within DSDM	69
Table 5.8	Four phases of the UP	70
Table 5.9	Agile toolkit of Lean software development	72
Table 6.1	Strategic analysis techniques	80
Table 6.2	Three perspectives of the FMM	85
Table 6.3	Cockburn's levels of goal	86
Table 9.1	Prioritisation techniques	137
Table 10.1	Techniques for evolving requirements iteratively	154
Table 11.1	Techniques to analyse users and usage	163
Table 11.2	Guidelines for brainwriting	167
Table 12.1	Techniques for modelling stories and scenarios	182
Table 12.2	Levels in a user story hierarchy	183
Table 12.3	Patterns for splitting compound user stories	187
Table 12.4	Guidelines for writing user stories	190
Table 12.5	Scenario formats	195
Table 12.6	BDD structure and example	197
Table 14.1	Commonly used estimation units	226
Table 16.1	POPIT™ analysis of agile adoption	260
Table 16.2	Key factors for adopting or scaling agile	261

AUTHORS' BIOGRAPHIES

Lynda Girvan is a principal consultant and trainer for Assist Knowledge Development (AssistKD). Lynda has over 25 years' experience in business analysis, agile development, agile coaching and transformational change programmes across both public and private sectors. Lynda developed and leads the agile business analysis training portfolio for AssistKD and was a key contributor during the creation and development of the Advanced Diploma in Business Analysis. Lynda is a co-author of the BCS publication, *Developing information systems* (2014) and has spoken at European and international conferences on agile and business analysis. Lynda is a member of BCS.

Debra Paul is the managing director of Assist Knowledge Development. Debra has worked in business analysis (BA) and business change for over 30 years and has experience in a range of sectors and organisations. Debra is the editor and co-author of the best-selling BCS publication, *Business analysis* (2014), and co-author of *Business analysis techniques* (2014) and *The human touch* (2012). Debra has extensive knowledge and expertise in applying a range of BA tools, techniques and best practices and is a regular speaker at conferences and seminars. She was the chief architect for the Advanced Diploma in Business Analysis. Debra is a Chartered Fellow of BCS and a founder member of the BA Management Forum.

FOREWORD

I thought I would begin with an agile foreword:

1.   Buy this book.
2.   Read it.
3.   Follow the advice in it.
4.   Recommend it to your colleagues.
5.   Repeat steps 2 through 4 as appropriate.
6.   If it's a print copy, store it on your shelf to show to everyone how smart you must be.

And now for a more traditional foreword 😊.

Analysis is so important for agile teams that we do it every single day. Every. Single. Day. The implication is that we need one or more people on the team who has analysis skills; the more people the better in my opinion. Agile analysis skills are critical in the agile world.

But do agile teams need people who are just analysts? Sometimes yes, but very often no. In most situations, agile teams need people who are generalising specialists, people with strengths in one or more specialities (such as agile analysis); a broad understanding of the software process and the domain they're working in; and the willingness to learn new skills and share their own with others. This is a different staffing strategy from that which is typical of organisations still taking a traditional approach to IT.

This begs the question of when do we need people who are specialised in agile analysis? The answer is 'at scale'. When a team faces a complex domain, it is common to see one or more people who focus on exploring, understanding and then communicating the inherent complexities to the rest of the team. In other words, an agile analyst. Similarly, when a team has geographically distributed stakeholders, then having analysts at the various locations makes a lot of sense. When a large agile team, or agile programme, is organised into a collection of smaller subteams it is common to put analysts on the team who work closely with the programme's product owner to communicate the requirements to their subteams. These analysts working on geographically distributed and/or large teams are referred to as 'junior product owners' in some organisations or business analysts in others. The point, contrary to what you may have heard, is that some teams need agile analysts.

I'm the guy behind the agile modeling (AM) method (see AgileModeling.com), which was the first serious look at how modelling and documentation activities fit in on agile teams. I led a group of people, several hundred from around the world, to develop the initial version of AM in the 2001/2002 time frame. It's evolved since then of course, capturing collaborative lightweight strategies for analysis, architecture, design and even documentation activities for agile teams. Needless to say I'm excited that this book has been written.

What should you hope to gain from reading this book? Here are my suggestions for what you want to learn:

1. **Discover the agile mindset:** whenever you think, 'that won't work for me because I'm in a different situation', the best thing to do is to assume that you're completely and utterly wrong about that (you very likely will be) and therefore need to work things through. Being agile, having the mindset to collaboratively work in an agile manner, can take a long time to truly learn.

2. **Keep analysis light yet sufficient:** when it comes to 'doing agile' the biggest change is often the focus on keeping your work and the artefacts that you create as light as possible. In agile modelling, we promote strategies such as working with the audience of an artefact to learn what they really need, preferring direct communication with others as opposed to documentation hand-offs, and capturing requirements in the form of executable tests.

3. **Focus on working collaboratively with others:** modelling is something you should do with others, ideally using inclusive tools such as whiteboards and sticky notes. Many heads are better than one.

4. **Embrace an evolutionary approach to analysis:** as I said earlier, analysis is so important that we do it every single day on an agile team. This is because of the agile philosophy of embracing change – we accept the fact that our stakeholders' requirements will evolve over time, necessitating an ongoing and evolutionary approach to analysis (and architecture, and design and all other aspects of solution delivery).

5. **Seek active stakeholder participation:** one of the more radical ideas in agile modelling, one that we adopted from usage-centred design, is that the people who are best suited to perform requirements-oriented modelling are your stakeholders. If we can find ways to get our stakeholders actively involved in our modelling efforts, something that inclusive tools (whiteboards, paper) and inclusive techniques (such as the simple model types described in this book) enable, then we are much more likely to find out what our stakeholders actually need.

6. **Continuously improve:** part of the agile mindset is to regularly reflect on what is working well, and what isn't working so well, so that we can potentially learn from and address the challenges we face. Similarly, the Lean mindset tells us to experiment with potential improvements, study their effectiveness, and then adopt new ways of working accordingly. We can always get better.

7. **Constantly expand your intellectual toolkit:** there are some great modelling techniques described in this book, including many common ones such as user stories, epics and personas. These techniques are of course the tip of the iceberg – there are hundreds of strategies out there that you should

experiment with and learn when (and when not) to apply them in practice. The more techniques you have in your intellectual toolkit, the greater the chance you'll choose the right one for the situation you face.

8. **Be enterprise aware:** one of the hallmarks of working in a disciplined agile manner is to recognise that your team is only one of many within your organisation. You need to work with other teams to accomplish your goals; few agile teams are rarely whole, regardless of the rhetoric you may have heard, and that's OK. Furthermore, your team should strive to do what's right for your organisation, not just what is convenient for you. All teams should work towards a common vision, should follow common conventions and should strive to work together effectively.

I believe that this book captures critical ideas and skills for anyone wanting to improve their agile analysis skills. This is critical for all agile team members, but is particularly important for anyone in the role of product owner or agile analyst. Your investment in reading this book will be time well spent. Enjoy!

Scott Ambler
Author of *Agile modeling*
Co-author of *Disciplined Agile delivery*
November 2016

PREFACE

Our idea for a book that looked at business analysis from an agile perspective, and agile from a business analysis perspective, arose following many discussions with colleagues and customers. We were concerned that the development of business analysis, and the inroads made in appreciating the benefits it can offer, were in danger of being eroded if agile was adopted by organisations and projects without consideration of the business analysis world view. A review of available publications highlighted that business analysis was not widely explored within agile and the application of agile principles to business analysis (and, conversely, the application of business analysis to agile projects) were not clearly defined anywhere.

Therefore, the topics in this book aim to address this gap and provide comprehensive and practical guidance, enabling business analysts to understand how and when they can support agility at an enterprise, programme and project level. To do this, we needed to provide sufficient details of the agile philosophy, methods and practices plus the relevant business analysis approaches and techniques. The more we considered how these two disciplines would work in combination, the more we felt it was a 'marriage made in heaven' that had significant potential to improve information systems activity and outcomes and, consequently, the efficiency and effectiveness of organisations.

In order to provide the coverage we felt necessary, the book forges a path from the origins of agile, through the different levels and aspects of information systems work and, ultimately, looks at how agile might be adopted by an organisation. We felt it was important that all these dimensions were explored if the landscape of business analysis was to be represented thoroughly. Similarly, it was important to encompass the agile world across this landscape.

One of the key aspects we think important, is the need to tailor the approach adopted to information systems work in the light of the organisational context and the scope of the problem to be addressed. Given that agile originated as a software development approach, adapting it to business improvement projects requires careful consideration. Comments made to us about 'following the Scrum method' do not align with our world view, which is to always consider the most appropriate way of achieving the desired outcomes that will benefit the enterprise. This is reflected throughout the book as we have described various approaches and techniques in order to support business analysts, and any other IS professionals interested in this topic, in building a toolkit and applying it in an informed way.

The extensive coverage of this book was an ambitious undertaking. As a result, we needed help and support from a number of people. In particular we would like to thank the following two people.

Simon Girvan: Simon is a Fellow of the BCS and a Chartered Engineer, who has over 10 years' experience working in agile teams in the UK and Australia. He is currently in a technical director role within UK Government, leading several agile teams working on complex bespoke software projects.

Simon's experience implementing agile principles with non-software projects, and within traditional governance contexts, gives him a perspective on agile development that aligns well with business analysis.

Simon wrote the book sections on estimation, iterations, methods and the history of agile. He was also a reviewer of many chapters and created most of the diagrams used in the book.

Alan Paul: Alan has over 30 years of experience of change programmes and software projects, and has worked in a range of roles including analyst, project manager and technical strategy director.

Alan has worked on projects that have applied various methods and techniques, including structured and agile approaches; this has given him unique insights into the issues that can arise during information system development.

Alan reviewed every chapter in the book and contributed to the sections on analysing the enterprise and estimating.

We were also very fortunate to have colleagues and friends who supported us by reviewing several chapters and suggesting changes to the narrative: Martin Pearson, AssistKD Marketing Director, conducted a thorough and detailed review of several chapters as the book neared completion. James Cadle, AssistKD Director, and Terri Lydiard, Teal Business Solutions Ltd., reviewed the narrative for particular chapters in order to ensure clarity and correctness. Julian Holmes, ThoughtWorks Ltd, worked with us over several meetings to define the initial structure for the book. Carol Christmas undertook a full and thorough review of an early draft of the book.

The BCS publishing team provided ongoing support and encouragement and we would particularly like to thank Ian Borthwick, Becky Youe and Florence Leroy.

This book was a labour of love because we felt it was such an important topic. It required many conversations, coffees and cakes before we felt it offered a valuable contribution to the business analysis and agile domains. We hope all readers will gain insights and useful guidance that will support them in their professional work.

Lynda Girvan
Debra Paul
February 2017

1 BUSINESS ANALYSIS IN AGILE ENVIRONMENTS

This chapter covers the following topics:

- the rationale for business analysis;
- business agility;
- the agile business analyst;
- the agile business analysis book.

INTRODUCTION

All businesses have to be on constant alert for changes that may cause problems or offer opportunities for them. These changes may originate from industry factors such as competitor actions, or may involve broader developments such as demographic or technology changes. In addition to these external forces, there can also be internal drivers for change including new ideas raised by executive managers. While some drivers for change are highly visible, others can be very subtle and easy to overlook so identifying change drivers may not be straightforward. However, making the changes happen is often where the real challenge begins.

For several decades, change has been enabled by technological developments and has involved the introduction of new or enhanced software products. Initially, changes to software were seen as sufficient and the broader context into which the new software was to be released tended to be overlooked; the computer system was seen as offering sufficient new features to generate the efficiencies and improvements needed by the business. This approach began to change in the late 1980s when greater awareness of the need to ensure that new software was accompanied by the relevant changes to processes and jobs came to the fore.

Challenges have persisted, though, and the intervening decades have continued to be marked by highly publicised information systems (IS) project failures. As a result, there have been many initiatives to introduce methods and techniques that will improve the quality of the delivered change solution including structured analysis methods, the Unified Modelling Language (UML), systems thinking and business process re-engineering. There have also been attempts to move away from the more traditional, linear methods for systems development and business change projects. Instead, there has been an increasing adoption of iterative and incremental development approaches that offer a greater emphasis on 'just in time' delivery; these approaches align with, and have contributed to, the development of the agile philosophy.

The last few years have been marked by the widespread adoption of agile methods within the IS industry. This may be seen as a response to the traditional and structured software development methods, which have been challenged as not meeting the needs of today's fast-moving business environments. While the original agile philosophy was focused upon the development of software, it has become apparent that software development projects need to ensure that they are 'business relevant' if they are to support the activities conducted to perform the business work. To do this, the application of agile principles needs to move beyond software to encompass the entire business system if benefits are to accrue for organisations.

Three particular issues have been identified:

1. **The rush to adopt agile in recent years:** it has often seemed as if many organisations and individuals wanted to jump on the agile 'bandwagon' just to make sure that they weren't left behind, but did this without giving due thought to the adoption of Agile.

2. **The cynical response to agile from some:** this has been rooted in previous experiences with initiatives that had promised to avoid IS project failure – structured methods, object-orientation, governance, to name but a few. However, as IS professionals, it is important that we reflect on the agile philosophy, tools and approaches in order to consider how they could improve and extend business analysis work in order to deliver increased benefit to organisations.

3. **The software focus:** the Agile Manifesto (explored in Chapter 2) is clear that the agile philosophy and principles are concerned with software development. However, this has been recognised for several decades as only one element of the business improvement domain. Business analysis is concerned with resolving business problems and, typically, these need the people, organisation, process, information and technology aspects to be considered, not just the technology element. Although the original Manifesto and philosophy focused on 'working software', it is important that business solutions are holistic; this is at the heart of business analysis. Failing to take a holistic view raises the risk of solving the manifest symptoms rather than the root causes of problems, and of investing in technology and applications that provide only partial solutions.

Consequently, we feel that the valuable ideas that have been developed within the agile domain should be explored within the context of delivering business outcomes rather than software products. The role of the business analyst, with its focus on defining the problem to be solved and evaluating the options to do this, needs to be considered within this context. Accordingly, this book examines agile work practices through the business and business analysis lenses, discussing the use of agile methods and techniques within a business context and the role of the business analyst in conducting this work.

THE RATIONALE FOR BUSINESS ANALYSIS

It is instructive to consider why we need business analysis within IS projects. Business analysis originally developed as a discipline responsible for analysing requirements where the analysis activity was firmly located within the organisational context and analysts were familiar with the jargon, rules, standard practices and business processes of that context. Although systems analysis had been a key activity within the IT systems development process for many years, problems had arisen because of an identified lack of understanding on the part of the systems analysts about the broader context beyond the IT system. There were criticisms that systems analysts focused solely on specifying the system requirements and failed to consider what the organisation actually needed. For example, sometimes the organisation needed business system – rather than solely IT system – change, but this was not within the remit of the systems analyst. Accordingly, the broader role of the business analyst emerged, which had both a business and system focus, and approaches such as requirements engineering were developed to ensure that both business and solution requirements were identified, prioritised and delivered.

The maturation of business analysis

The increasing maturity of business analysis over the last two decades gave rise to the creation of the BA maturity model in Figure 1.1. This model captures the trajectory of the development of the business analyst role as the scope of the role expanded and business analysts gained in authority.

Figure 1.1 Business Analysis Maturity Model™

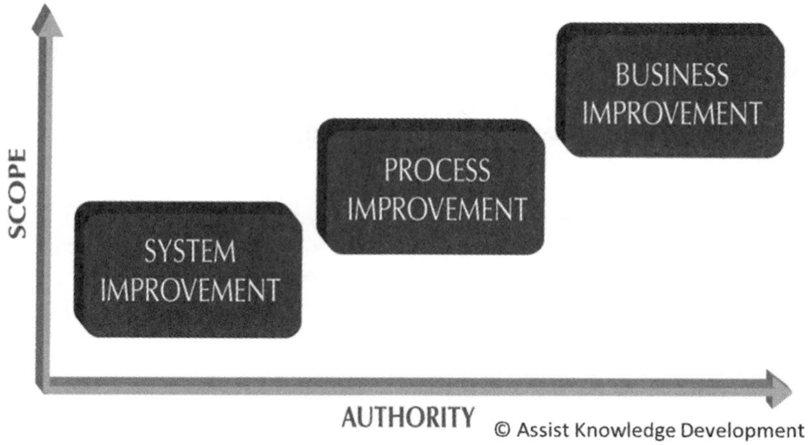

© Assist Knowledge Development

The three levels shown capture the different flavours of the business analyst role as follows:

- the initial focus on defining requirements as a basis for IT system development or enhancement;

3

- the extended focus to include process improvement plus the attendant impacts on people and organisational structure;

- the movement into a role of trusted advisor on business improvement, with a focus on asking **'What problem are we trying to solve?'** and establishing the best means of addressing the problem.

Many change programmes and projects begin with an idea or initiative. This idea is formalised by the programme initiation, which includes a definition of the objectives, deliverables and timescale. However, sometimes, the idea is weak and may offer limited benefits, or may not improve the organisation at all. A typical example involves the purchase of a software package (or possibly an enterprise-wide suite of software packages) because it is felt that this will deliver benefit to the organisation. Without any analysis of the problem to be solved and the options available to the organisation, there is a high risk that the desired business outcomes will not be achieved and the project will fail. In the worst case, such an initiative could absorb a lot of (wasted) money and possibly cause damage to the organisation.

The maturation of business analysis has led to an increasing recognition that an initiating idea needs to be investigated to ensure that the genuine problem is addressed, and the available options are identified and evaluated before setting off down a path of no return. Business analysts have a toolkit of techniques and approaches that help them to analyse often vague and ambiguous business situations such as, 'we need to be more efficient', 'the processes are a bit clunky', 'we have to improve our capability'. Therefore, they are well placed to take on the work of uncovering the root causes of problems and clarifying the issues to be resolved. One of the key aspects of business analysis involves recognising that there are different perspectives on any business situation and without the development of a shared understanding and consensus view, it is going to be difficult to find a solution that will be acceptable to the key stakeholders. Business analysis also takes a holistic view, ensuring that all aspects of the business situation are considered during investigation and solution definition. The IT system may be at the heart of the solution, enabling the business improvement, but without consideration of the people, their processes, work practices and information needs – and the organisational structure and culture – the solution will not deliver the promised benefits.

The business analysis landscape

In recent years, business analysis has become a broad discipline with professional business analysts working in advisory roles helping to ensure that IS investment funds are spent wisely. A good definition of the role of the business analyst has been defined by the UK Department for Work and Pensions:

> The role of the BA is to ensure the vision and services are realised, to challenge and act as the critical friend, to represent the needs of all users and to translate the needs of the whole of DWP.
> (Defined by DWP BA Community, reproduced with permission)

The range of activities required to conduct business analysis is shown in Figure 1.2. These activities focus on ensuring that the problem situation is understood before moving towards the desired outcomes. They emphasise the need to analyse the business needs and to evaluate the range of potential options, before defining the detailed requirements for change. While the model shows the overall direction of the work, it does not dictate a strict linear sequence. In practice, there will be iterations between and within many of the activities.

Figure 1.2 Business analysis activities

Source: Paul et al. (2014)

Business analysts need an extensive toolkit of skills and techniques if they are to carry out these activities effectively. Adding the agile approaches and techniques to this toolkit will help business analysts to conduct these activities more effectively and support the delivery of timely, effective solutions. It is important to recognise that this is not only within an organisation that has adopted agile software development; some of the agile tools, for example, MoSCoW prioritisation (see Chapter 9) can be extremely useful in a range of situations.

BUSINESS AGILITY

The term 'business agility' is often used these days. All businesses recognise that they need business agility but there are two questions we need to consider; 'What is business agility?' and 'How is it achieved?'

Let's look at the first question: 'What is business agility?' It is the ability of an organisation to be responsive to forces within the business environment and to be adaptable when change is required. Agile organisations are able to act when the environment changes and are able to adopt new ideas. They have flat structures, with processes and systems that embrace change. Their cultures are open and adaptable, their people empowered and flexible.

Systems thinking incorporates the concept of self-regulating business systems that can monitor the business environment through feedback loops and adapt to the changes encountered. To do this, the business system – or department, division or even entire organisation – needs to understand the rationale for its existence. Why does it do what it does? What are its values? Simon Sinek (2011) expounded the importance of understanding why an organisation exists before exploring the what and the how of the organisation's operations. This is at the core of the organisation with business agility. If the staff need to constantly ask how they should respond to situations or have to request approval for everyday decisions, the organisation is not displaying agility – it is as simple as that.

How then is business agility achieved? To return to Sinek, it has to start with a clear understanding of the underlying rationale and values of the organisation. This should drive how the organisation operates and should provide the employees with a basis for decision-making. Empowerment should be embedded within the organisational culture and should be observable at all levels. Processes should not involve tasks with a primary focus on 'ticking the box' – the work should have a real purpose and, fundamentally, that should be concerned with delivering the organisation's products or services in line with meeting the needs of customers. The customers should be at the heart of the agile organisation. This is not always the case, however. For example, one of the most disliked innovations in recent years has been the introduction of the self-checkout in supermarkets. However, as most customers welcome anything that makes it quicker and easier to pay for goods, why is this the case? A brief foray into the 'bagging area' soon provides the answer. The systems are set up to meet the needs of the organisation rather than the customers. As a result, at any moment, the system could lock up and demand the attendance of a store employee, whether because the customer was too slow putting a scanned item into the aforementioned bagging area or, even worse, putting the item in a bag that is being carried rather than in the designated bagging area.

Some organisations focus on defined targets such as those encapsulated in their service level agreements (SLAs) and believe that 'fulfilling the SLA' is sufficient to ensure good customer service, even if this has just involved sending an email during the designated time period to confirm that the situation is still under investigation. Continually calling to say that no action has been taken is of no use to a customer, even if the internal communication target can be ticked as achieved!

How can the agile approach help with business agility? If we apply the agile philosophy as a basis and understand the nature of adaptable business systems and the realisation of value from service, we have a basis for developing business agility. Business analysts who understand Lean, systems and service (Chapter 3) and adopt the core agile values (Chapter 4) will be able to support their organisations better, as they can introduce relevant techniques and philosophies into their business change work.

THE AGILE BUSINESS ANALYST

There are two distinct aspects where the agile approach is relevant to business analysis:

1. the role of the business analyst in enabling business agility through the use of the agile philosophy and approaches;
2. the role of the business analyst in supporting the use of agile techniques during business improvement and software development projects.

Let's look at these in more detail.

Business analysis enabling business agility

The underlying premise of several philosophies – agile, lean thinking, systems thinking, service thinking to name a few – is that any business system or process has an underlying rationale for its existence. In other words, we need to be able to state the reason why the system exists. Understanding the underlying rationale enables us to determine what needs to be in place to make the business work more effectively. These philosophies are covered in Chapter 3 of this book; understanding and applying them is key to being an agile business analyst.

It has been said (by one of the authors!) on numerous occasions that the role of the business analyst should be the most agile of the business improvement roles. This is because business analysis can apply the agile philosophy and techniques in a number of contexts or situations:

- by challenging ideas, views and issues raised by business managers and staff in order to determine their relative importance and ascertain whether or not they align with the organisational strategy and tactics;
- by ensuring that different customer perspectives about a situation are understood and supporting the development of a shared perspective;
- by using techniques that allow the business stakeholders to provide relevant, timely information;
- by ensuring that options are always considered to determine where the best business outcomes can be achieved;
- by prioritising proposals and requirements at different levels of decomposition and focusing on the achievement of business goals;
- by aligning the different elements of the holistic view to ensure that change projects do not separate into individual silos.

The adoption of an agile mindset, when undertaking business analysis, helps to generate business agility within an organisation. Agile business analysts should understand why the use of agile is of benefit, what agile work practices are available and how they should be used. They also need to extend their toolkit to encompass agile approaches and techniques.

Agile business analysts should support business agility both before the inception of a programme of change and during a change project, helping to ensure that change initiatives are focused on meeting the needs of the organisation and delivering the desired outcomes.

Business analysis on agile software projects

Several agile software development methods have emerged since the late 1980s, including Rapid Application Development, Dynamic Systems Development Method (DSDM), Extreme Programming, Scrum and Disciplined Agile 2.0. These methods and more are discussed in Chapter 5. However, one of the factors common to these methods is that they do not recognise the business analyst role. So, does this mean that the use of agile methods removes the need for business analysis? To answer that question, let's revisit why business analysis was originally developed. It was to address an issue that had afflicted systems analysis – the communication gap that existed between technical and business staff. That's not to say that all systems analysts had communication problems, but it was an issue that business staff often complained about. And so the concept of a more business-focused analyst role was created.

The agile principles, discussed in Chapter 2, include a principle that identifies the importance of a face-to-face conversation between a developer and a business user when uncovering requirements. Highlighting the importance of a conversation to clarify requirements means that business analysis is needed, even if the work is done by someone with a different job title.

Within agile teams, the concept of a generalising specialist (discussed in Chapter 7) is often used where an individual may possess cross-functional skills in addition to the area within which they specialise, and utilise these skills at the point that they are needed. This would seem to imply that the developer may take on the business analyst role – which is fine as long as they have the requisite business analysis skills, knowledge and attitude, and provided the conversation is at an individual project team level and not spanning multiple business areas.

Is this the best way to do this though? Business analysts have extensive toolkits of techniques and approaches that they have often developed over several years; this is also the case for other roles within software development such as developers, testers and so on. Therefore, in practice, the answer is 'it depends'. Often, it is useful for a developer to analyse the information being provided by the business user as part of a conversation. However, where there are more extensive business analysis activities to be conducted – such as determining business requirements or developing business models – then greater skills may be needed and a specialist business analyst will probably provide a more efficient and accurate service.

THE AGILE BUSINESS ANALYSIS BOOK

This book was written with three aims in mind:

1. to help business analysts understand how agile works and their role in software development projects;
2. to enable business analysts to apply the agile philosophy, principles and techniques during their business improvement work;
3. to help anyone engaged in developing software without the participation of business analysts to understand the relevance and application of business analysis.

To achieve these aims, we decided that we needed to ensure that agile was presented clearly for a business analysis audience and that the links to business change projects were clarified. As a result, this book covers a wide range of topics that are included in order to support business analysts as they work on projects using agile and deliver skills that will enable their organisations to work with agility. The chapter breakdown is set out in Table 1.1 below.

Table 1.1 Structure of this book

Chapter 1: Business analysis in agile environments	The development of business analysis and the rationale for applying business analysis within an agile world.
Chapter 2: Agile philosophy and principles	The origins of agile and the fundamental philosophy and principles upon which all agile activities are based.
Chapter 3: Analysing the enterprise	The analysis and business thinking approaches that can help when applying agile to organisations.
Chapter 4: Adopting an agile mindset	Adapting the core agile values to business analysis.
Chapter 5: Understanding agile methods and frameworks	The evolution of agile methods, and the characteristics of the methods and frameworks used in agile software development.
Chapter 6: Modelling the business context	Techniques to model the business context to enable the application of agile on business change projects.
Chapter 7: Working with stakeholders and roles	The range of stakeholder roles encountered on business change projects, including the variety of customer roles. The stakeholder roles specified by Scrum and DSDM.
Chapter 8: Decomposing goals	The technique of goal decomposition, how it is applied within business and the relevance to agile business analysis.
Chapter 9: Prioritising the work	The need for prioritisation and the range of techniques that may be used on agile projects. The relevance of prioritisation to an agile mindset.
Chapter 10: Deciding the requirements approach	The project characteristics and planning the relevant approach to the requirements work.
Chapter 11: Modelling users and personas	Techniques used to analyse and model the user community.
Chapter 12: Modelling stories and scenarios	Techniques to analyse and model the features and functionality required by system users.
Chapter 13: Organising tasks and requirements	The approaches used to organise and manage requirements on change projects. Comparing and contrasting the requirements catalogue with the solution backlog.
Chapter 14: Estimating agile projects	Techniques used to estimate the work on agile projects, including estimating for iterations.
Chapter 15: Planning and managing iterations	The ceremonies and techniques used to govern iterative development.
Chapter 16: Considerations when adopting agile	The implications of adopting and adapting agile in complex business environments, and the role of the business analyst on agile projects.

The range of topics covered in this book is extensive and includes the agile philosophy, and the popular agile methods and techniques, viewed through a business analysis lens. These topics are intended to provide business analysts with a toolkit that will enable them to contribute effectively to agile projects and enhance the agility of their organisations.

REFERENCES

Paul, D., Cadle, J. and Yeates, D. (2014) *Business analysis: 3rd edition*. Swindon: BCS.

Sinek, S. (2011) *Start with why: how great leaders inspire everyone to take action*. London: Penguin.

2 AGILE PHILOSOPHY AND PRINCIPLES

This chapter covers the following topics:

- the origins of agile;
- the Agile Manifesto;
- the 12 agile principles;
- agile approaches;
- agile practices.

INTRODUCTION

Agile is a lightweight software development approach that evolved in the mid-1990s and resulted in an Agile Manifesto and an accompanying set of '12 principles of agile software' published in February 2002. Since then, it has grown in popularity and is now an extremely common and fashionable umbrella term for a number of methods and processes. It is used by thousands of development teams across the world, and is the subject of numerous books, papers and training courses. In that time, it has evolved and changed, and is not only applied to software products, but also to other types of development.

There are many synergies between agile and business analysis. Agile favours highly collaborative working between the customer and product development team; a focus on the early and frequent delivery of tangible solutions; and an iterative approach that is highly responsive to changing requirements. While the major focus of the agile approach is on the development of software, the concepts can apply to business analysts working on change projects, where the project focus is on business rather than technology changes. However, to do this successfully, business analysts need to understand the rationale and philosophy that underpin the agile approach.

While the rest of this book will focus on how it may be applied to business analysis, this chapter explains how agile has developed and provides an introduction to the agile philosophy, principles and methods.

THE ORIGINS OF AGILE

Before the term, 'agile' was coined, software had been successfully created for decades. Until the early 1990s, linear planning techniques were commonly used, which isn't surprising, given that software development originated from computer systems engineering. These linear systems are commonly referred to as 'waterfall', due to the way that they were drawn in Winston W. Royce's influential article from 1970, 'Managing the development of large software systems'. Interestingly, Royce did not actually use the term 'waterfall' in his paper; however, he is renowned for developing this approach and its resulting use ever since.

Royce represented a common approach to developing complex software systems, as shown in Figure 2.1.

Figure 2.1 Waterfall development approach

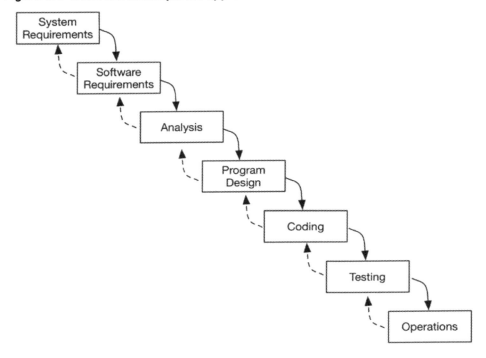

Unfortunately, Royce's paper was widely misunderstood. He presented the above model as **'risky and invites failure'**, and was proposing modifications to make it much more iterative and incremental. However, that element of his work is largely forgotten, and his waterfall picture remains in common use, although the names of the stages have changed a little over time.

As discussed in the BCS publication *Developing information systems*, the waterfall method and its variations are effective for some types of development. However, as

Royce himself stated, it is less suitable for many types of project, as capturing and baselining all the requirements early in the development life cycle, and expecting them not to change, is a significant drawback for many, if not most, projects.

The evolution of iterative methods

New methods began to emerge in the 1980s and 1990s as a response to some of the challenges that developers faced when using a waterfall approach. One of the first to become popular was Rapid Application Development (RAD), which involved creating prototypes and using them to elicit requirements, validate designs and evolve toward usable solutions. RAD began at the New York Telephone Company and was refined by IBM in the 1980s. A book, *Rapid application development*, by James Martin, with contributions from several others, was published in 1991.

Although RAD is a method in its own right, it also spawned a number of alternative approaches that are based on some of the same principles. One popular example is the Spiral model, developed by Barry Boehm (1988), one of James Martin's collaborators. This model introduced the concept of incremental planning, definition, design and development of software so that each time around the spiral the risks are reduced and the end result is more predictable.

A different iterative development method emerged in the late 1990s that combined some of the rigour and whole life cycle elements of the waterfall life cycle, with incremental delivery and a particular focus on modelling. It was based on the research of three men who originally collaborated to create their most famous work, a modelling notation known as the UML. James Rumbaugh, Grady Brooch and Ivar Jacobson (known as 'The Three Amigos'), developed 'The unified software development process' in 1999 with Philippe Kruchten, who provided the overall architecture for the iterative approach.

At the time, they were working for the Rational Software Corporation and their process therefore became available as the Rational Unified Process (RUP). RUP is risk driven, iterative and takes a use case- and architecture-centric approach.

The founding agile methods

Through the 1990s, a number of alternative ways to organise and structure the development of software products began to emerge and shape the thinking that eventually evolved into 'agile' in 2001. These approaches were referred to collectively as 'Lightweight Methods'. The key developments are described in Table 2.1 below.

The Agile Alliance

It was Kent Beck who first sowed the seeds of the agile movement, with the publication of his book in 1999 and his invitation to various leaders in XP to join him at a retreat in Oregon. Significantly, he didn't just invite XP thought leaders, but also several other people who had similar interests. These included Alistair Cockburn (Crystal), Jim Highsmith (ASD) and Dave Thomas (co-author of *The Pragmatic Programmer*) (2000). At this initial meeting, they discussed the similarity of XP with other methods and decided to meet again, with a broader range of people, to explore common ground.

Table 2.1 Agile development methods

Year	Name of method/approach	Description
1992	Crystal	Alistair Cockburn started the Crystal family of methodologies, which advocated co-located developers, frequent delivery of usable code to users and reflective improvement.
1994	Dynamic Systems Development Method (DSDM)	The DSDM consortium was founded to provide some structure to the emerging RAD movement that was gaining in popularity at the time, but was proving difficult for companies to adopt.
1995	Scrum	Jeff Sutherland and Ken Schwaber introduced the 'Scrum Development Process' at the OOPSLA (Object Oriented Programming, Languages and Applications) conference. Scrum is now the most widely practiced agile methodology.
1997	Feature Driven Development (FDD)	Emerged when Jeff de Luca was working on a large software development project for a bank in Singapore. He had hired Peter Coad, who had a particular focus on using fine-grained features to plan and drive the project, to lead on the overall modelling. This approach, together with other processes that de Luca had developed, captured the attention of his peers and he was persuaded to write it down and publish it.
1999	Extreme Programming (XP)	In the mid-1990s, Chrysler began a programme to replace the many legacy payroll systems written in COBOL. The team responsible, led by Kent Beck, pulled together all the practices that became known as XP; this was published in Beck's book of the same name in 1999.
2000	Adaptive Software Development (ASD)	This concept was coined in a book published by Jim Highsmith in 2000. The approach grew out of RAD and proposed a collaborative approach, with repeated cycles of *Speculate, Collaborate, Learn* to deal with complex and fast-changing problems.

On 11 February 2001, a group of 17 people met at 'The Lodge' at Snowbird Ski Resort in Utah to talk, ski, relax and try to find common ground between their thoughts on software development. They represented the leading thinkers from XP, Scrum, DSDM, ASD, Crystal, FDD and Pragmatic Programming, along with others who wanted a viable alternative to heavyweight, documentation-driven development processes.

Two days later, they had agreed on a name to replace the term 'lightweight' (which had been used up to that point but was not well liked), a manifesto that embodied the values they all believed in and a set of guiding principles. The Agile Alliance was born.

The agile mindset

One of the remarkable things about those two days at the ski lodge in Utah is that 17 people with very different backgrounds and perspectives managed to reach agreement on what agile means. They were applying different approaches, and had different ways of achieving similar outcomes. Yet, they were still able to agree a set of principles and values that they could all sign up to.

This is why agile should be regarded as a mindset – a way of thinking, and not a method to be learned. This mindset should be supported by methods and techniques that help projects to adhere to the principles and values, as shown in Figure 2.2.

If agile is thought of in this way, it is possible to see why there are different agile approaches and methods that can all support the same principles, even though they differ in execution. Unfortunately, this also means that it is not possible to instruct someone in how to be agile; they have to adopt the mindset. While you can teach a process, you cannot teach a way of thinking, and just applying an agile process or technique will not mean that you are applying the agile principles and values.

Agile is a philosophy to be felt and comprehended, such that it guides the way in which work is approached. It is not a method to follow.

Figure 2.2 The main elements of agile

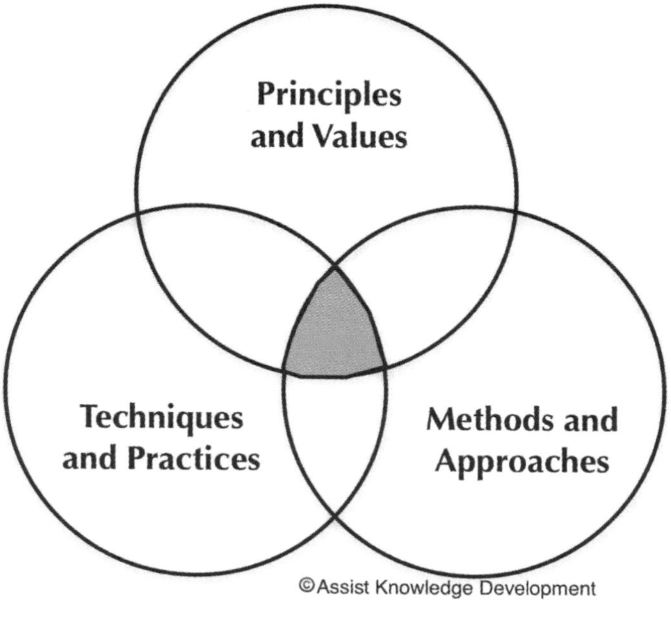

©Assist Knowledge Development

Although this is not a universally held view, it is held strongly by the authors of this book. While it can be possible to treat agile as a recipe to be followed for straightforward projects, as complexity increases this becomes less and less likely to succeed. In practice, projects are not simple, and in order to succeed with an agile approach, the team must have or gain an agile mindset.

THE AGILE MANIFESTO

The most important and most visible result of that meeting in Utah, shown in Figure 2.3, was the publication of the manifesto for agile software development.

Figure 2.3 The manifesto for agile software development

Manifesto for agile software development

We are uncovering better ways of developing software by doing it and helping others do it. Through this work we have come to value:

Individuals and interactions over processes and tools.

Working Software over comprehensive documentation.

Customer Collaboration over contract negotiation.

Responding to Change over following a plan.

That is, while there is value in the things on the right, we value the items on the left more.

The manifesto for agile software development (often shortened to **the Agile Manifesto**) is short but powerful; in a few words it manages to encapsulate a wide range of concepts, ideas, prejudices, values and experiences of software development. Although the key focus is on software development, once unpacked, there is very little that is actually software specific. That's why various commentators over the years have proposed amendments and changes. Indeed, in Chapter 3, we shall propose our own version, reflecting a business perspective and more applicable to business analysts. However, the original words remain unchanged on the website, and, for the most part, still hold true for many situations.

Although simple, the Agile Manifesto is often misunderstood. In particular, the final clause is often forgotten or ignored: **'That is, while there is value in the things on the right, we value the items on the left more.'** It is really important to remember that agile projects still require processes, tools, documentation and plans; it is just that these are not the **most** important artefacts or deliverables. It is the outcome delivered by the project that is the actual value.

Let's look at the individual statements of the Manifesto in greater detail.

Individuals and interactions over processes and tools

Creating solutions is a team sport. Team members need to communicate with one another. They need to ask questions, discuss ideas, debate ways forward and support one another. Particularly with more complex problems, the ancient adage that **'two heads are better than one'** still holds true. Of course, tools and processes are also important, sometimes critical. They can help teams be consistent, encourage the right things to be done in the right order and optimise repetitive tasks. In fact, without tools, some common agile practices like continuous integration or version control would be much harder. But, on balance, agile teams should get the people parts right first.

Working software over comprehensive documentation

The perspective of a software development team is that it exists to produce working software, that has been tested and delivers an expected outcome to the users to a desired level of quality. Good software should also be properly documented, of course, and poor documentation can diminish or nullify the value offered to the customer. For example, if the customer isn't able to set up the software because they don't understand the controls, they will not realise any value from it. Similarly, ongoing maintenance and further development of the software will require the relevant documentation.

Having said this, no matter how good the documentation, at the end of the day it is the software, or a working solution, that the customer needs. An important word in the Manifesto value is **'comprehensive'**. There can be a tendency in some teams to generate huge volumes of documentation in great detail. It is often as if there is a feeling of comfort in producing documentation – if we analyse and document everything, we won't be caught out! Similarly, where a method permits tailoring (as many do), inexperienced or cautious project managers have a tendency to include more artefacts than required. Does an architectural prototype intended to help the customer understand how the interface might work really require a test plan and a support guide? Probably not. When it comes to documentation, as with most other elements of agile development, teams should aim for **Just Enough, Just in Time**.

This is just as true for non-software solutions. Overly focusing on the word 'software' can be dangerous, particularly for larger, more integrated solutions, or when trying to solve business problems with a holistic solution. Business analysts often work at higher levels of abstraction, where IT or technology is only one aspect of the solution, and may use models like POPIT™ (discussed in Chapter 3) to explore how people, the organisation or processes also need to be changed.

Business analysts may find that this value challenges some of their work within project teams, particularly with regard to requirements documentation. However, experienced business analysts are skilled in deciding the requirements approach, and this includes determining the artefacts that will best deliver the project objectives. To achieve this, the Lean principle of **Just Enough, Just in Time** should be borne in mind. The requirements should provide sufficient detail to allow working solutions to be created; there should be a much lighter touch for requirements that are not to be implemented within the current release.

Customer collaboration over contract negotiation

This value is based upon the premise that the people who know best what a system should do are the customers who will be using it. They will know what business outcomes they are trying to achieve, and, as your system takes shape, they will be best able to judge whether it looks like it will help them. Since most projects are complicated and have to encompass numerous requirements of different types and of varying complexity, it is hard to define exactly what those needs are in advance. This is the fundamental problem encountered when applying the Waterfall development life cycle, where requirements must be agreed and signed off before design and implementation begin.

Inevitably, at some point, there will be changes made to the requirements or an earlier misunderstanding about what is needed will emerge and require clarification. Under the Waterfall model, this would require a formal change request process to be followed, with all the consequential effort this would demand. Since this situation is common, agile teams like to pre-empt it with contracts that are less prescriptive and with high levels of engagement and collaboration with customers.

This presents many problems. Customers are often very busy or they may be located at different, or dispersed locations. There may also be different types of customer (explored in Chapter 7), all of whom may have a different perspective on the system under development. This is where business analysis can be invaluable. Business analysts are able to analyse and manage stakeholders and as they will typically hold knowledge of the business domain, can help the customer to better understand the potential the software will offer and the real business needs to be met. The level of collaboration is expected to be much greater on an agile project and, as a result, business analysts can expect to have a different kind of relationship with customers.

Responding to change over following a plan

This is probably the single most important element of agile software development; the expectation that things will change, and the adoption of processes, practices and principles that not only expect change but embrace it.

This is also the element of agile that causes the most angst, and challenges orthodox development methods the most. It is inherently **logical** to want to know what you can expect, when and for what cost. Most project management and systems engineering approaches aim towards delivering a certain set of things, on a certain date, with a certain amount of budget, in the hope that this will reduce risk. Senior stakeholders want to be able to make promises to others about what they can expect, and it seems perfectly sensible to want to be able to give them an answer.

In reality the only certainty is that things change: technologies, business strategies, competitors, personnel. Solution development methods that expect, anticipate and deal with change will be more likely to navigate those changes with the least impact and the highest chance of succeeding; that's why agile teams value responding to change.

This does not mean that plans are bad. On the contrary, plans are essential, but they must be able to change when the environment that affects them changes.

THE 12 AGILE PRINCIPLES

The Agile Manifesto is supported by a set of 12 principles, drafted during the original meeting in February 2002 and finalised over the following few months. Table 2.2 shows the 12 principles, and briefly describes why they are important.

Table 2.2 The 12 agile principles explained

Our highest priority is to satisfy the customer through early and continuous delivery of valuable software.	The customer is the most important stakeholder, and what is most important to them is knowing that you will solve their problem for them. It is even better if they can receive something of value early.
Welcome changing requirements, even late in development. Agile processes harness change for the customer's competitive advantage.	Requirements change for all sorts of reasons. Agile teams expect this and anticipate it.
Deliver working software frequently, from a couple of weeks to a couple of months, with a preference for the shorter timescale.	The best way to know if something is right is to see it in action. This helps to refine requirements for future releases, raises customer confidence in the software development team and offers the potential to realise value early.
Business people and developers must work together daily throughout the project.	Most projects are too complicated to assume that written down requirements will capture every detail. Being able to ask questions and clarify understanding throughout the project is essential – the best way to do that is face to face.
Build projects around motivated individuals. Give them the environment and support they need, and trust them to get the job done.	People build solutions, and people do better work when they are motivated, empowered and have the right tools for the job. The impact on quality and productivity caused by not doing this should not be underestimated.

(Continued)

Table 2.2 (Continued)

The most efficient and effective method of conveying information to and within a development team is face-to-face conversation.	While other forms of communication are important, for many things, face to face is by far the best.
Working software is the primary measure of progress.	It is better to measure progress in terms of the actual thing you are delivering, rather than other factors (like effort spent) since that's what the customer really cares about.
Agile processes promote sustainable development. The sponsors, developers and users should be able to maintain a constant pace indefinitely.	People build solutions, and people don't do good work when they are overworked, stressed or neglecting other parts of their life. Good agile teams don't rely on a hero culture.
Continuous attention to technical excellence and good design enhances agility.	Delivering quickly is not an excuse for poor engineering. In fact, good design can make it easier to add new capability quickly.
Simplicity – the art of maximising the amount of work not done – is essential.	It is easy to make things hard, big and complex. Often, it is harder, but far more valuable, to make things simple.
The best architectures, requirements and designs, emerge from self-organising teams.	A self-organising team that is fully focused on the goal will offer more relevant answers than those imposed upon them.
At regular intervals, the team reflects on how to become more effective, then tunes and adjusts its behaviour accordingly.	No team is ever perfect and the environment it operates in is never static. The best teams identify regularly the adjustments they should make in order to improve.

The agile principles are largely self-explanatory, and although seemingly heavily weighted toward software development, in the main, may be applied to other types of project or solution. They embody the values in the Manifesto and provide concrete examples about how the values should be demonstrated.

The principles describe not only how an agile team works, but how its members should think, behave and feel. Compromising these principles, perhaps when changing a process to suit a particular project, can cause inconsistency and a lack of coherent focus; this will often lead to problems at a later stage.

AGILE APPROACHES

As discussed earlier, several 'lightweight' development processes existed at the time the Agile Manifesto was created; additional such methods have emerged since. They are now described collectively as 'agile' methods. Chapter 5 will describe some of the more popular methods in detail. However, in overview, the key methods are:

- **Scrum:** a very popular method that borrows its title from the rugby scrum, and uses it as a metaphor for the daily progress update meeting. Scrum has short iterations (sprints) that each focus on delivering working software, a tightly prioritised 'backlog' for both the sprint and the product, and specifies a 'Product Owner' role who sets the priorities.

- **XP:** the source of many popular agile practices, and the key founding method. A disciplined approach with high customer involvement, continuous planning, continuous testing and rapid delivery in very short intervals.

- **DSDM:** provides project governance and scaling around XP or RAD approaches. It has three main phases called pre-project, project and post-project and includes defined formal stages within the project phase. **Fitness for Business Purpose** is the primary criteria for delivery and acceptance of a system and MoSCoW is used for prioritisation.

- **RAD:** both an umbrella term for a range of agile and iterative approaches, and a method described by James Martin (1991) in its own right. RAD takes the analysis, design, build and test phases and repeatedly iterates through them developing prototypes and versions of increasing functionality.

- **Unified Process (UP):** an iterative and incremental framework, with several implementations including the RUP, OpenUP and AgileUP. A highly tailorable framework that takes a RAD approach that is architecture-centric and risk-focused. The phases of the UP are called Inception, Elaboration, Construction and Transition, and each has a different focus.

- **Lean:** originating in manufacturing in the 1970s, the principles of Lean were applied to software development by Mary and Tom Poppendieck (2003) in their book, *Lean software development*. Lean focuses on the delivery of value to the customer and on eliminating waste from the process.

- **Kanban:** an approach that originated in Lean manufacturing and has been further developed by David Anderson (2010). Kanban is based on workflow visualisation, typically on a physical board, addressing issues that cause problems, limiting the team's work in progress and balancing the demands on the team.

There are many other agile methods in use today. This includes hybrid methods such as ScrumBan and numerous in-house customisations that individual companies have developed.

AGILE PRACTICES

Given the popularity and widespread adoption of agile, and the profusion of different approaches, it is not surprising that there are numerous agile practices and techniques. The Agile Alliance maintains a guide to these agile practices on their website. Some of the most commonly used practices are listed in Table 2.3 below and are explored throughout this book.

Table 2.3 Agile work practices

Requirements practices	• Backlog: a prioritised list of requirements or work items that is frequently updated • Definition of done/definition of ready: setting acceptance criteria for a requirement • Personas: a way of identifying and describing users of the system • User stories: a way of capturing requirements • Story mapping • Story splitting: breaking down stories that are too big • 3Cs: a way of structuring user stories: Card, Conversation, Confirmations
Estimation practices	• Planning Poker • Point estimates • Relative estimation • Velocity: a way of predicting how much work the team can do
Team leadership and organisation practices	• Iterations/timeboxing • Daily meeting (Scrum) • Burndown chart: a measure of progress in this iteration • Task board/Kanban board • Retrospective: a review meeting to identify things to change in the next iteration • Scrum of scrums: a way to manage multiple teams working on related projects
Software development practices	• Pair programming • Test driven development (TDD) • Behaviour driven development (BDD) • Refactoring
Testing and release practices	• Automated build • Continuous integration • Version control

CONCLUSION

This chapter has discussed the history and development of agile, and has described the values and principles at its core. Having originated from a software development base, the Agile Manifesto and principles have a strong software focus. However, agile may be applied to a much wider context and can be beneficial if used on other types of change project such as process improvement or skill development.

REFERENCES

Anderson, D.J. (2010) *Kanban: successful evolutionary change for your technology business*. Washington, DC: Blue Hole Press.

Beck, K. (1999) *Extreme programming explained: embrace change*. Canada: Addison Wesley.

Boehm, B.W. (1988) *A Spiral Model of software development and enhancement*. ACM SIGSOFT Software Engineering Notes, August. Available from: http://csse.usc.edu/TECHRPTS/1988/usccse88-500/usccse88-500.pdf [6 December 2016].

Cadle, J. (ed.) (2014) *Developing information systems: practical guidance for IT professionals*. Swindon: BCS.

Highsmith, J.A. (2000) *Adaptive software development: a collaborative approach to managing complex systems*. New York: Dorset House Publishing Co. Inc.

Jacobson, I., Booch, G. and Rumbaugh, J. (1999) *The unified software development process*. Reading, MA: Addison Wesley.

Martin, J. (1991) *Rapid application development*. USA: Macmillan.

Poppendieck, M. and Poppendieck, T. (2003) *Lean software development: an agile toolkit*. Boston, MA: Addison Wesley.

Royce, W.W. (1970) Managing the development of large software systems, *Proceedings of IEEE Wescon*. Available from: www-scf.usc.edu/~csci201/lectures/Lecture11/royce1970.pdf [6 December 2016].

FURTHER READING

Agile Alliance. Available from: www.agilealliance.org [6 December 2016].

Ambler, S. (2009) *The Agile Scaling Model (ASM): adapting agile methods for complex environments*, IBM Rational. Available from: www.webfinancialsolutions.com/wp-content/uploads/2011/10/Adapting-Agile-Methods-for-Complex-Environments.pdf [6 December 2016].

Ambler, S. and Lines, M. (2012) *Disciplined Agile delivery*. New Jersey: IBM Press, Pearson.

Hunt, A. and Thomas, D. (1999) *The pragmatic programmer*. Reading, MA: Addison Wesley Professional.

Interview with Jeff de Luca (2007) 'Jeff de Luca on Feature Driven Development – interview April 2007'. Available from: www.it-agile.de/fileadmin/docs/FDD-Interview_en_final.pdf [6 December 2016].

Paul, D., Cadle, J. and Yeates, D. (2014) *Business analysis: 3rd edition*. Swindon: BCS.

The Agile Manifesto. Available from: http://agilemanifesto.org [9 January 2017].

3 ANALYSING THE ENTERPRISE

This chapter covers the following topics:

- the business analysis perspective;
- Agile Manifesto for business analysts;
- agile business thinking: systems thinking; Lean thinking; service thinking.

INTRODUCTION

Agile is usually mentioned and applied within the context of software development but the underlying philosophy and principles can – and should – be applied much more widely. However, to do this requires the adoption of a mindset that aligns with the agile philosophy and then for this to be applied to business needs; for some this will require fundamental change in the way they think and behave. Where an agile mindset is applied within an organisation, it will enable greater adaptability and the delivery of business changes that have the potential to bring early benefit to the organisation.

A good example concerns the development of a new product: this may be a new service to be offered, such as a training course, a software application or possibly a physical item such as a piece of furniture. When developing different types of product, many ideas and requirements may be put forward but some of them may not enhance the product at all or may not be worth the expense or delay required to incorporate them. In some situations, there may be requirements that can be deferred. For example, a company may offer an item of furniture in a limited range of fabrics initially, with the intention of extending the range of options at a later point. Similarly, there may be a possibility of providing additional features, such as extra reading materials to extend the learning from a training course, additional software functionality or even extending the geographical area in which a product or service may be offered. Enabling early delivery of an initial version of the product requires the project team to adopt an agile way of thinking, ensuring that the required features are prioritised and recognising that some requirements do not need to be fulfilled at the outset – or even at all.

Some organisations associate agile working practices with the use of a particular method, such as Scrum, or certain techniques, such as user stories, without fully adopting an agile mindset. This can limit the potential of agile and diminish opportunities for achieving business benefits because the use of agile is focused on software development rather than business improvement. While this is the case for many organisations, others are beginning to recognise that it may be applied more broadly and can offer benefits to business change initiatives. This broader, more holistic view, with a focus on business rather than software, opens up the agile landscape and provides an opportunity for further business value to be realised.

This is where business analysts should have a central role, changing the focus from the IT system to more holistic business improvement initiatives that may or may not involve the use of technology. It is important to recognise that we don't need to use a specific agile method or technique in order to adopt an agile mindset, and that user stories and sprints are not compulsory. It is more important to think and behave in line with the agile philosophy and principles, prioritising ideas and requirements, focusing on the most beneficial aspects and understanding when a particular feature should be delivered.

This chapter explores the evolving role of business analysis in an agile landscape and sets out an Agile Manifesto for business analysts that introduces a new way of thinking.

THE BUSINESS ANALYSIS PERSPECTIVE

The formal responsibilities of the business analyst role are well defined where a linear approach is adopted on a software development project. There are likely to be clear stages covering the pre-project or feasibility study, detailed requirements engineering, business acceptance testing, change implementation and benefits realisation. Each of these stages will require the involvement of business analysts as the project moves through a waterfall or V model life cycle. When a business analyst is working within an agile environment, it is still important to carry out this work but the likelihood is that it will be conducted differently. Essentially, there are three business analysis perspectives that are relevant to an agile change project:

- the Enterprise BA conducting pre-project business analysis;
- the Programme BA working across the change programme;
- the Project BA working within the development team.

These three roles and perspectives are reflected in Figure 3.1.

The Enterprise BA: pre-project business analysis

New initiatives tend to arise frequently within organisations. This may be because of factors within the external business environment or as a result of new ideas generated by internal stakeholders. Whichever is the case, it is important to assess the feasibility of a proposed project or initiative because it helps to determine three things:

1. why a project has been proposed and whether it is viable and will meet the business need;
2. what the solution should comprise – the combination of changes to the POPIT™ aspects of processes, organisation, people, information and technology;
3. how the solution should be developed – for example, is an agile approach relevant and, if so, are there likely to be any difficulties in adopting agile?

Figure 3.1 Three BA perspectives

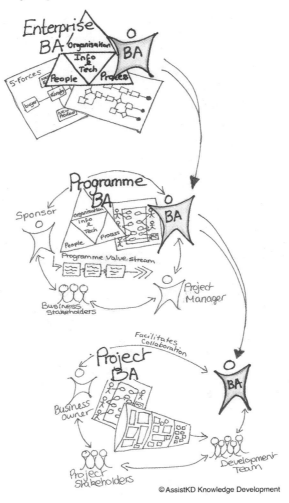

© AssistKD Knowledge Development

This work is sometimes called pre-project analysis and requires business analysis involvement to consider the areas shown in Figure 3.2 below.

Too often change projects are initiated that are not well founded. Typical examples are:

- where a solution has been identified without there being sufficient understanding of the problem or opportunity;

- where an idea has been allowed to evolve into a project without any evaluation of the situation or the available options.

Figure 3.2 Pre-project analysis work

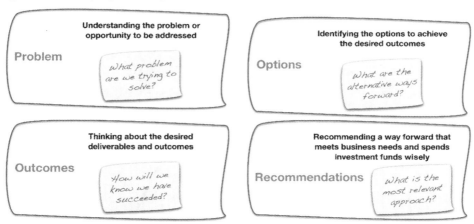

Early business analysis work is essential if an organisation is to be assured that a proposed investment is well founded and the project is relevant. And, this is the case whether we adopt a linear or agile approach to the work. In a similar vein, Scott Ambler, in his Disciplined Agile Framework, highlights the importance of an Inception phase to determine the basis for a development project, including the need to discuss the vision for the work with stakeholders and assess the feasibility of the proposed project. Ambler and Lines comment

> we recognize the need to point the ship in the right direction before going full-steam ahead.
>
> (*Disciplined Agile Delivery*, 2012, page 14)

The goals of this stage include clarifying the business problem to be addressed and identifying the approach required to complete the work; the achievement of these goals requires the application of business analysis to the particular situation.

Business analysis skills are essential for the successful conduct of this work. An analytical approach is at the heart of working with stakeholders to define a consensual vision; a feasibility assessment is only possible if a holistic view of the situation is taken and options are analysed.

The recommended solution is likely to require changes to several of the elements shown in the POPIT™ model in Figure 3.3.

The POPIT™ elements are:

Figure 3.3 POPIT™ model

Process	The definitions of the processes, how they are communicated to the business staff, the level of IT support, the documentation used when carrying out the processes.
People	The skills of the people, their motivation levels, their awareness of the business objectives they are required to support.
Organisational context	The management structure and governance approach, the definition of job roles and responsibilities, the lines of communication and authority, the working relationships across functional boundaries.
Information and Technology	The information needs for the business, the technology support that delivers the information and supports the processes.

Changes to any combination of the POPIT™ elements will result in a programme of business changes. The holistic view provided by business analysis is necessary to define which changes need to be made. The software development project is typically just one element of a change programme and, as indicated by the interfaces of the POPIT™ model, needs to be aligned with the other areas such as revised processes, working practices and roles. Figure 3.4 reflects the pre-project work that a business analyst working at the enterprise level performs, helping to ensure that the right problem is addressed, the rationale for change is understood, relevant options are evaluated and the solution addresses all of the required POPIT™ elements within the business system.

Figure 3.4 Pre-project business analysis

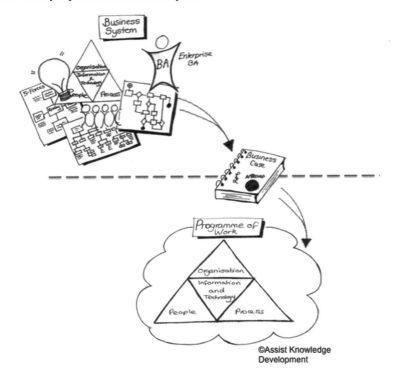

©Assist Knowledge
Development

The programme BA: business analysis and the change programme

A change programme is likely to encompass many interrelated and dependent change projects. While the programme manager will be responsible for coordinating the projects, it is the business analyst that ensures that the solution development work continues to focus on the business outcomes. For example, there will be a need for business analysis to ensure the changes are understood and that there is alignment between the different elements. Early delivery of working software alone is unlikely to offer the value anticipated by the organisation; it needs to be accompanied by the other changes that will make the solution holistic and viable.

However, where an agile approach is to be applied to a change project, any business analysts working on the broader business changes can apply the agile philosophy and principles (set out in Chapter 2) to all aspects of the programme. For example, by:

- working collaboratively with the stakeholders to elicit and analyse the business and system requirements, and to support the iterative development of the new features;
- clarifying the priorities of the required features;

- taking a programme-level view of the business changes;
- ensuring that any increment delivered to the business staff has been considered holistically and offers a complete unit of change;
- supporting the deployment of the incremental changes to the business system.

When working at the programme level, the business analyst is required to support key stakeholders in making informed business decisions. This is achieved through the business analyst choosing and applying a wide range of practised analytical techniques that the key stakeholders are often not aware of, or practised in.

The project BA: business analysis within the development team

The work of the software development team requires business analysis work to be conducted if a business-relevant solution is to be delivered. This work is likely to include activities such as stakeholder engagement, process modelling and requirements analysis, all of which may be necessary to ensure that the development work is aligned with the needs of the business. Investigating the rationale for requests made by the business users is one of the key responsibilities of a business analyst and helps to ensure that effort is not wasted developing features that are unlikely to offer benefit to the organisation. While one of the agile principles states that a face-to-face conversation is the most effective means of conveying information within the development team, it does not necessarily follow that this will result in the most useful information being communicated. Sometimes, a conversation with business users that explores the rationale for a suggested requirement is necessary in order to ensure that there is a genuine business need to be addressed. Similarly, many business analysts have encountered the situation where a proposed 'requirement' is actually a perceived solution, which requires further investigation in order to explore the possibilities that improved processes or technology might be able to offer if the underlying requirement is clearly understood and expressed.

While it is the case that business analysis work will be required within the development team, does this mean that a designated business analyst is needed? It is possible that other members of the development team may take on some of the business analysis work and act as proxy business analysts. However, care needs to be taken to ensure that business analysis skills are available within the team in order to avoid problems. For example, without skilled business analysis, there can be a tendency for all customer suggestions to be accepted at face value and assumed to be necessary, regardless of whether they align with the needs of the business. The history of information systems projects demonstrates that incorporating stated requirements without considering the underlying rationale can be a recipe for a lot of unnecessary work. The application of business analysis skills helps to ensure that solutions align with business needs, uncovers tacit knowledge and confirms that investment funds are spent wisely. Achieving this requires a range of business analysis skills and experience in applying business analysis techniques. Assuming that these are readily provided by professionals from other disciplines is at best naïve and, at worst, highly risky.

Business analysts bring a unique skill set to agile development teams. They are able to look beyond stated requirements to challenge assertions, consider wider impacts and evaluate proposed solutions. They have the skills to engage with a range of stakeholders and have knowledge of the business domain, and this helps to facilitate collaboration with both customers and developer colleagues.

AGILE MANIFESTO FOR BUSINESS ANALYSTS

While the original Agile Manifesto stated which aspects of software development work were of a higher priority, the statements need to be updated if there is to be a manifesto for adopting agile within a business analysis context. While working software is important in the business analysis domain, it is rarely the entire solution and sometimes software is not required at all. Additionally, while working software is of value, it is the outcome or improved experience produced by the working software that is the domain of business analysts.

The original focus on software is relevant for IT projects but needs to be extended if it is to reflect the holistic nature of business change programmes. There needs to be greater emphasis on improving the entire business system and recognition that the realisation of business benefits results from business changes, not software delivery. Whereas the original Agile Manifesto focused on software development, this is too limited for business analysts who need a modified manifesto that offers a broader view and has the potential to inspire agile business change.

A modified version of the Agile Manifesto, which is intended to work as an extension to the original manifesto, is shown in Figure 3.5 and reflects a business analysis perspective. This version embraces the Agile Manifesto and philosophy, but also encapsulates a world view that is relevant to business analysis and the broader business change context.

Figure 3.5 An Agile Manifesto for business improvement

Flexibility of approach over methods and processes

Holistic Solutions over working software

Relevant Artefacts over comprehensive documentation

Team Collaboration over directive governance

The modifications shown in Figure 3.5 reflect the way in which the agile philosophy is now applied within business contexts. It emphasises that an IT system is not as important as ensuring that there is a holistic solution. It also reflects the widely held view that adherence to a method or approach is less relevant in today's business world than adapting the tools to the situation.

However, this requires broader thinking and a focus on business needs and improvement. It also requires a good understanding of prioritisation approaches (see Chapter 9) to ensure that the features that will contribute to the delivery of early benefits are identified. In short, it needs the involvement of specialists who can marry the business requirements with the solution development work – the business analysts.

AGILE BUSINESS THINKING

There are several schools of thought that are beneficial to anyone working to improve how organisations operate. Different ways of thinking are required if we are to focus on delivering outcomes with the potential to offer value to the customer. Three philosophical schools of thought are helpful when conducting business analysis within an agile environment:

- systems thinking;
- Lean thinking;
- service thinking.

These approaches offer relevant insights that have the potential to enhance the business analysis work and thereby enrich the business outcomes.

Systems thinking

Systems thinking offers an approach to viewing an organisation and its component areas as a hierarchy of business systems. A great deal of research has been conducted into the different aspects and applications of systems thinking. One particularly relevant development is the Soft Systems Methodology (SSM), which was defined by Checkland in 1981. Although much of this research was conducted several decades ago, systems thinking and the SSM are extremely useful in today's business (and business analysis) world. They ensure that the underlying rationale for a business system is always kept in mind, thus reducing the potential for unnecessary work and keeping a focus on changes that would be beneficial. They also offer a means of viewing business situations holistically and considering the interdependencies between systems and sub-systems. The nature of systems thinking was summarised by Peter Senge in *The fifth discipline* (2006).

> Systems thinking is a discipline for seeing wholes. It is a framework for seeing interrelationships rather than things.
>
> (Peter Senge, 2006)

There are three key elements considered within systems thinking:

- the underlying rationale for the system under investigation: Why does this system exist? What are the values it applies? What priorities does it address?
- the interrelated elements that conduct the work of the system: What are the activities, dependencies, rules and so on that enable the work to be carried out?
- the properties that emerge from the formed system: What is achieved by the system as a result of all of the elements working together?

These elements are summarised in Figure 3.6 below.

Figure 3.6 Aspects of systems thinking

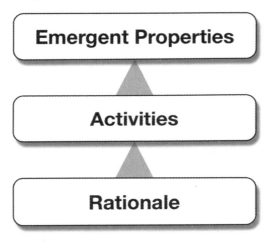

These three areas are extremely important to understand when analysing business systems. Let's look at them individually.

First, they tell us that we need to be cognisant of the underlying rationale – the 'why' of a system. This principle is well established in numerous frameworks, including the SSM, Zachman's Framework and the OMG Business Motivation Model, and helps analysts to understand where the primary focus of the work should be placed. Without understanding the rationale for a system, the analysis work can often be too concerned with the detail of how things are done rather than trying to understand the relevance of the system to the organisation. Exploring the rationale for a system also helps analysts to understand the problem they are attempting to address in order to ensure that the system objectives are achieved. Recognising the rationale for a system is invaluable when adopting agile thinking. If we understand the problem to solve and know why the solution is relevant, we are much more likely to produce something with the potential to offer value to the organisation.

Second, the activities and supporting tools, rules and information. Any system is made up of parts – the elements that make it work – so this is a principle that is very familiar to most analysts. Historically, we have had a separation between the IS practitioners and the rest of the organisation, which has caused the term 'system' to become synonymous with 'IT system'. Systems thinking broadens that understanding and causes analysts to think holistically about business systems and identify how the elements of a system need to work together to deliver the outcomes that align with the system rationale. The application of systems thinking helps analysts to enable organisational agility by ensuring that change releases provide holistic solutions, rather than focusing solely on software.

Third, additional properties emerge from the synthesis of the elements of a system. The car is often used as an example. It is made up of many parts, but only as a whole can it actually move and transport passengers from one location to another. So, the ability to transport those sitting in the car is the emergent property and all of the elements of the car have to be working together in order for this property to be provided. It is also the case that the emergent property may be negative. In the car example, a car's radiator can overheat if another working part is not functioning correctly. It is vital that business analysts understand that systems have emergent properties and these need to be harnessed if solutions are to be valuable to customers.

It is the responsibility of the business analyst to look beyond stated problems to find the underlying root causes and to define a holistic solution. Systems thinking and the techniques within SSM are invaluable when doing this. They also align with agile thinking, as the focus is on understanding which areas within the business system are of the highest priority and, therefore, where there is the potential for the delivery of benefit at an early stage.

The POPIT™ model, shown above in Figure 3.3, was developed in order to provide a framework for thinking holistically about solutions so is also useful when used with the systems thinking approach. Business analysts can apply the agile philosophy and principles in all of the four dimensions. So, if considering the processes, the business analyst might think about what a process is trying to achieve and the options for improving it. The analyst might identify that a comprehensive solution formed of many changes is possible, but that this would require an extended time frame. If adopting an agile approach, the analyst will work with the business staff to prioritise the potential changes and define a minimal set that will deliver benefit to the organisation without undue delay.

Failing to consider the whole business system when making changes can result in unexpected emergent properties. For example, automating processes in one area of the business could cause problems for processes in another area. Without looking at the business system holistically, and understanding how the individual parts interrelate, it would be impossible to identify the consequences of a change. Unexpected negative impacts will have the potential to undermine the value that the service could offer to the customer.

Lean thinking

The 'Lean' approach originated from the Toyota Production System. Its focus is on maximising customer value, while minimising waste in order to create better outcomes for the customer with fewer resources. Lean was essentially a process view of the organisation that involved thinking about the business from a cross-functional point of view. This is sometimes called a 'horizontal' view because it represents the set of processes (from different parts of the organisation) that together deliver products or services to customers. This view of the processes is sometimes called a 'value chain'. Such a view contrasts with the 'vertical' view of the organisation, which shows each of the functional areas, such as the customer service department or production facility, operating separately.

The fundamental concept underpinning the Lean approach is that all functions within the business system, or organisation, need to work together to deliver the desired outcome for customers. This desired outcome is usually stated as a value proposition offered by the organisation. Lean thinking focuses on optimising the workflows through the horizontal value stream that exists to deliver the organisation's value proposition. This horizontal view encompasses people, technologies, assets and departments that collectively enable the business to deliver its products (or services) with the greatest level of efficiency. Improving efficiency should enable organisations to reduce expenditure and increase profit margins.

Womack and Jones (2006) defined five key principles that described the Lean concept. These are shown in Figure 3.7 below.

Figure 3.7 Principles of Lean thinking

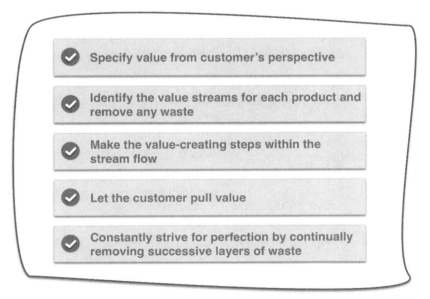

- Specify value from customer's perspective
- Identify the value streams for each product and remove any waste
- Make the value-creating steps within the stream flow
- Let the customer pull value
- Constantly strive for perfection by continually removing successive layers of waste

Ohno (1988) identified seven categories of waste that diminish efficiency in organisations. The seven categories were later extended to include an additional category, the underutilisation of skills, by James Womack and Daniel Jones. These eight categories of waste, are often known as the '8 wastes' and are specific areas where wasted resource and effort may be found in organisations. Therefore, eliminating or reducing the wastes presents opportunities for improving efficiency. The areas of potential waste are summarised in Figure 3.8. They provide an effective and useful checklist of aspects business analysts should consider when working on business improvement projects.

Figure 3.8 The '8 wastes'

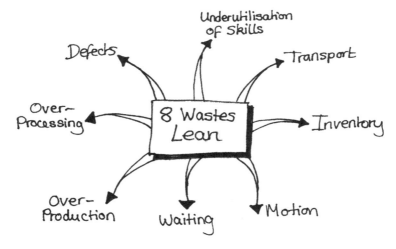

Transport	The unnecessary movement of people, materials or information.
Inventory	The storage of parts, materials and finished products which are not required to meet the current customer requirements.
Motion	The unnecessary additional movements that are taken by staff in order to accommodate problems with the layout of the organisation, defects in the products, overproduction or excess inventory.
Waiting	The time spent waiting unnecessarily for parts, information, instructions or equipment.
Overproduction	Making more of an item than is required or making items too far in advance of when they are needed.
Overprocessing	The additional work performed in order to deal with overproduction, defects or excess inventory.
Defects	Items needing rework or replacement, as they do not meet the product specification or are not satisfactory to customers.
Underutilisation of skills	The underutilisation of the people and their skills, ideas and creativity.

Although originally implemented and used within the manufacturing industry, Lean thinking can apply to other types of organisation where the value streams are concerned with service delivery rather than product manufacturing. Lean is not a technique, tactic or method; it is a way of thinking that is applied when aiming to improve how an organisation operates. Lean thinking aligns with both the philosophy outlined in the Agile Manifesto and with systems thinking, whereby the overall aim is understood and the elements work together to achieve this in the most effective way. While the focus is on streamlining the horizontal, value stream view, any changes to processes will inevitably impact upon other areas as shown in the POPIT™ model. As a result, the adoption of Lean thinking also requires systemic, holistic thinking to ensure that changes to all of the elements that form the business system are considered.

Lean thinking is highly relevant for business analysts. We may be working on process improvement projects with a view to streamlining the work and removing inefficiency, or on projects to develop new or enhanced software that result in corresponding process changes. Either way, our analysis will benefit from understanding the '8 wastes' and how they may be used to improve process efficiency. The adoption of Lean thinking ensures that business analysts focus on establishing the most efficient value stream in order that the organisation's value proposition may be delivered to customers.

Service thinking

Too often we see the phrase 'we deliver value' or 'and this is how value is delivered to customers'. This may be a promotion from an organisation, as in statements such as 'we always deliver value to our customers' or it may be a definition such as 'business analysts understand business needs in order to deliver value to their customers'. However, a service thinking approach causes us to question such statements because 'value' is not for the service delivery organisation to decide, rather it is the recipient who determines whether or not value has been created. In other words, **value is in the eye of the beholder.**

This distinction is at the heart of service thinking, which is based upon the concepts developed in Service Science. Everything delivered by organisations is a 'service', whether tangible goods or intangible services are offered. However, the delivery of service does not mean that value will ensue; sometimes the service delivered does not create or enable value for the intended customer. A good example of this is when devices such as mobile phones provide apps or functionality that are neither desired nor required by the majority of customers.

Service thinking is concerned with the creation and realisation of value and is based upon the fundamental principle that value has to be co-created with customers. So, despite frequent statements about delivering value, organisations cannot *deliver* value as this requires involvement, support and action on the part of the customers. Instead an organisation can propose to offer value by defining a value proposition and ensuring that the capabilities of the organisation are present to deliver what is proposed. Beyond this, collaboration with customers is needed to co-create a valuable service.

Figure 3.9 below summarises the possible outcomes from the delivery of a service. If customers have collaborated and the value proposition meets the expectations, value is likely to result. However, if the customers have not been involved in co-creating value, then the proposition and the expectations may be in conflict and value is unlikely to result. A version of this may also occur when what is proposed is of no interest to the customers and a service is delivered that is ignored as an irrelevance.

Figure 3.9 Organisation versus customer value perception

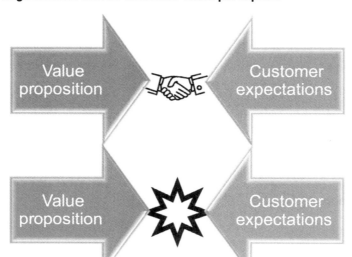

Organisations can offer a value proposition (based on the organisation's capability to create and deliver specific goods or services), but customers have to be involved and have to contribute if there is to be co-creation of value. Traditionally, organisations have held the view of 'value-in-exchange', where an assumption is made that value is delivered in exchange for payment for the service. However, Service Science provides a more contemporary understanding whereby value comes from the use of the service. This concept of 'value-in-use' clarifies that value can only be realised if use is made of a delivered service.

For example, an organisation may believe it has a great product to sell but if it doesn't quite meet the customers' needs or they think it is too expensive, they will not buy the product and no value will be created. Similarly, a customer may purchase a service – such as a training course – but if they do not engage with the service – in this case by ensuring that they learn and apply new skills – then no value will accrue.

So, as stated earlier, from a service thinking perspective, an organisation cannot say that value has been delivered; it is the customer who determines this. The organisation can 'propose' that value will be delivered but if the value proposition and the delivered service do not meet the customers' expectation of value, then value is not realised in the eyes of the customer. To achieve the realisation of value, customers have to provide information and other resources that help to co-create a potentially valuable service and they have to make use of the delivered service in order to ensure that the intended value is realised.

Why is service thinking useful to business analysts, particularly within an agile context? Well, agile thinking focuses on the delivery of solutions that will be valuable for the recipients, but it is not possible to do this if we don't understand where value originates and how it is created.

Service thinking states that value needs to be co-created through collaboration between the service delivery team and the customers. This co-creation of value takes place in two ways:

1. The customer helps the organisation to understand the nature and characteristics required from the service.
2. The customer accesses and uses the delivered service (which could be services or goods) in such a way as to gain the proposed value.

Therefore, it follows that business analysts need to understand how their work can support the co-creation of value within their organisations. The application of the agile philosophy, principles and techniques will contribute to ensuring that analysts understand customer needs and focus on collaborating with them to co-create value. This is particularly relevant given the range of activities conducted by business analysts and the increasing levels of responsibility and authority that business analysts have attained.

CONCLUSION

Business analysts have to be cognisant of the context within which they are working and the goals to be achieved. They have to ensure that the approach taken to the work is relevant and useful; following a standard method blindly will not suffice in many situations. Business analysts should be ensuring that their customer organisations 'do the right things' as well as 'doing the things right' (after Drucker 2003).

Business analysis is concerned with addressing business problems and identifying organisational improvements. These improvements may include changes to various aspects of the business system: the people, processes, organisational governance, information and technology. Agile practices have been used primarily for software development but, if applied in a more holistic way, offer the potential for increasing organisational agility. System, Lean and service thinking can help business analysts to approach their work in a more agile manner, focusing on the delivery of solutions from which business value is realised as early as possible. These approaches provide frameworks, principles and techniques that will help business analysts to apply an agile mindset within an organisational context while pursuing valuable business outcomes.

REFERENCES

Ambler, S.W. and Lines, M. (2012) *Disciplined Agile delivery – a practitioner's guide to Agile software delivery in the enterprise*. New Jersey: IBM Press.

Checkland, P. (1981) *Systems thinking, systems practice*. Chichester: John Wiley & Sons.

Drucker, P.F. (2003) *The essential Drucker*. New York: HarperPB.

Ohno, T. (1988) *The Toyota Production System: beyond large-scale production.* Portland, OR: Productivity Press.

Senge, P. (2006) *The fifth discipline: the art and practice of the learning organization: 2nd edition.* London: Random House Business.

Womack, J.P. and Jones, D.T. (2006) *Lean thinking: banish waste and create wealth in your corporation 2nd edition.* London: Simon & Schuster.

FURTHER READING

Hastings, H. and Saperstein, J. (2014) *Service thinking: the seven principles to discover innovative opportunities.* New York: Business Expert Press.

Paul, D., Cadle, J. and Yeates, D. (2014) *Business analysis: 3rd edition.* Swindon: BCS.

Spohrer, J.C. and Maglio, P.P. (2010) Toward a science of service systems: value and symbols. In Maglio, P.P., Kieliszewski, C.A. and Spohrer, J.C. (eds). *Handbook of Service Science: research and innovations in the service economy.* New York: Springer, 157–94.

4 ADOPTING AN AGILE MINDSET

This chapter covers the following topics:

- relating the agile principles to business analysis;
- collaborative working;
- self-organising teams;
- continuous improvement;
- iterative development and incremental delivery;
- planning for and building in change;
- doing the right thing and the thing right.

INTRODUCTION

The agile philosophy offers an astute way of thinking about business systems, so it makes sense for business analysts to understand what agile means and how it may be applied. The 12 agile principles (described in Chapter 2) reflect some core values that underpin agile software development.

This chapter discusses six core agile values to consider how they apply to business analysis and the development of holistic, business improvement solutions.

RELATING THE AGILE PRINCIPLES TO BUSINESS ANALYSIS

Although the agile principles were written with software development in mind, there is an underlying world view that has a broader application to business change projects. This is supported through the 'Agile Manifesto for business analysts' discussed in Chapter 3. Detailed consideration of the agile principles reveals that they are based upon values such as effective leadership, collaboration and Lean thinking, all of which are relevant to business analysis work.

The application of the agile principles to the business analysis landscape rather than just to software development may be a new concept to some business analysts. However, the adoption of agile thinking can offer significant advantages when used on business change projects, for example where the following situations are present:

- There are opportunities to deliver business benefits at an early stage through addressing straightforward problems.

- The high-level business requirements are understood but the more detailed requirements are unclear and need to evolve.

- There is a high volume, and rapid pace, of change.

The different levels of business analysis were described in Chapter 1 which explored how business analysts may work in a variety of business environments. For example, they may need to understand agile because they are working within a software development team, on a change project where improvements are to be delivered incrementally, or even in an organisation that has adopted agile across its operations. It is clear that the agile principles present several core values that are relevant to business analysis.

The core agile values for business analysts

There are six core values that may be derived from the 12 agile principles and are highly relevant to agile business analysis. These are shown in Figure 4.1 and discussed below.

Figure 4.1 Six core agile values for business analysts

Collaborative Working

Doing the Right Thing and the Thing Right

Self-organising Teams

Planning for and Building in Change

Continuous Improvement

Iterative Development & Incremental Delivery

COLLABORATIVE WORKING

Effective communication and collaboration are essential elements of both agile and business analysis. Collaborative working is the ability of two or more individuals, groups or organisations to work together towards a common goal. At the heart of collaboration is the need to engage with colleagues in order to build trust. Without trust, working relationships become difficult; with trust, an environment for success is fostered. The importance of developing trust is illustrated well by the two quotations below.

> A team is not a group of people who work together. A team is a group of people who trust each other.
>
> (Simon Sinek, n.d.)
>
> When the trust account is high, communication is easy, instant, and effective.
> (Stephen Covey, 2004)

When we work with people, we have an opportunity to build rapport; when we collaborate we have the opportunity to build trust. Establishing trust results in less need for formality. For example, formal documentation doesn't always need to be produced to ensure that work is completed where our experience of working with colleagues tells us that we can trust them to complete the agreed tasks.

Working in direct contact with another person is the primary way to gain trust. This is why collaboration is so important within an agile organisation and why it features so much within agile literature. As a general rule, people don't tend to trust a person they have never met.

Elements of communication

When considering how feelings and attitudes are communicated, Albert Mehrabian (1971) identified three elements of communication and their importance in **liking** and **trusting** the person with whom we are communicating. These three elements, captured in Table 4.1 are:

Table 4.1 The three elements of communication

Words (verbal)	The actual words that are spoken. The literal meaning of the overall message.
Tone of voice (vocal)	How we say the words and the intonation placed on the words that are spoken.
Body language (visual)	This is non-verbal communication that can be facial expression or body and hand gestures.

Mehrabian's studies concluded that these elements were represented by the following percentages, shown here in Figure 4.2.

Figure 4.2 Mehrabian's elements of communication

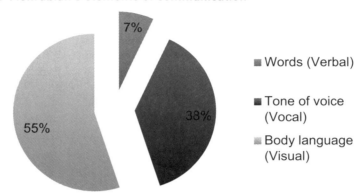

This would suggest that the tone of voice and body language are the most powerful factors concerning feelings or attitudes during the communication process.

Please note that these percentages only apply when somebody is communicating a message about their feelings or attitudes and not just any message. This model does not necessarily apply to other kinds of messages being conveyed.

Mehrabian's model tells us that as much as 93 per cent of the elements of communication may be lost if we are not engaged in face-to-face communication. In today's business world, most communication is carried out through emails or various social media channels. Inevitably this sets up communication barriers, inhibits our ability to interpret messages and causes difficulties for the development of trust within organisations.

Understanding stakeholders

A key aspect of business analysis work involves engaging with the stakeholder community. If an organisation has adopted agile, this helps to ensure greater opportunities for collaboration and communication. Business analysts have a toolkit of techniques for analysing and conveying information, all of which support stakeholder engagement and the achievement of desired business outcomes.

Business analysts understand the importance of analysing stakeholder perspectives. Within the business analysis toolkit we can find techniques such as world view analysis and RACI (see Chapter 7), both of which help us to better understand how to work with stakeholders. Taking the time to understand stakeholders can offer many benefits, such as supporting collaborative working and analysing different perspectives.

Collaboration and organisational culture

A culture of collaboration is not always present within an organisation. It is sometimes the case that employees do not collaborate effectively or value collaboration because they do not see their seniors, or others within the organisation, acting in this way. Instead, they may see their colleagues competing with one another, particularly if there is a focus on recognising individual, rather than team, performance.

Informal collaboration can be encouraged through networking and social events, which can help formal collaboration to develop. The culture of collaboration might not always be seeded within an organisation and those companies with a more formal hierarchical approach may not adjust as well to some of the principles of agile. It is this underlying culture that can often preclude agile from being widely adopted within an organisation, particularly beyond the software development team.

Environmental issues for collaborative working

For many organisations, collaborative working has been critical to the success of agile development. As a result, some office environments have been redesigned to provide a layout more conducive to this style of working. This allows teams to be co-located, either physically or virtually, and often provides an informal workshop-like approach to developing solutions. If the environment is organised into numerous small office spaces rather than open-plan layouts it can result in email exchanges rather than face-to-face communication and can make collaboration more difficult.

Geography can result in teams being physically dispersed, with business analysts in different locations to the customers and the solution development team. This form of business model can be challenging when a collaborative approach is required but can be addressed using technology, for example, video conferencing. Using this technology, individuals can see each other and still obtain some of the verbal, vocal and visual forms of communication that Mehrabian refers to, albeit through a two-dimensional technology screen.

It is useful to consider whether business analysts should sit together or with the development team if they are working on an agile project. The following factors need to be taken into consideration.

- Do the business analysts get help and experience from their practice colleagues?
- Do all business analysts within the practice work on software development projects or is the business analyst service spread wider across the business?
- Is there a chance that the business analyst will become isolated from the practice if they spend all their time with the solution development team?
- Is there a risk that the business analyst may not be fully utilised by the solution development team if they are not part of the development team?
- If the business analyst is embedded within the solution development team, can they become disconnected from the business?

There isn't a definitive right or wrong approach when considering location; it has to be what is right for the business analyst's customers and for the business as a whole. Having early conversations about the business analyst's project responsibilities and accountabilities will help to identify a solution that works for everyone.

SELF-ORGANISING TEAMS

The concept of the self-organising team is a key element of agile software develop-ment. However, the relevance and potential value from self-organising teams can also be considered for any team or group that is working towards a common goal. Business analysts often perceive that they lack authority in situations where they could make a significant contribution to achieving the project goals. The switch from directive govern-ance to team empowerment should enable practising business analysts to work with greater authority.

It is important to distinguish between a group and a team: a **group** comprises two or more individuals who interact with one another, bringing their unique perspectives and experience to achieve a goal or objective.

A **team** is also a group, but with the additional characteristics of a sense of belonging, understanding and awareness of each other's needs and concerns. In *The human touch*, Thomas et al. (2012) describe the additional characteristics of a team as including:

- **Communication:** ease and flexibility of interaction and communication between team members, respecting one another's views and concerns.
- **Cooperation:** individuals are comfortable sharing their feelings and being supported by other team members.
- **Cohesion:** team members work together to agree the goal of the team and appreciate that the goal can only be achieved by working together.

Accepting these definitions, it is clear to see why agile refers to teams rather than groups. From a business analysis perspective, however, much of what is discussed in this section could also apply to groups of individuals who come together for a specific event; for example, an initial workshop to outline a problem or to identify problems with the current business situation.

Micromanagement

Micromanagement involves managing teams in a detailed manner, such that all decision-making is removed from team members. Business analysts may experi-ence project managers instructing them on timing, standards and techniques to be used in order to complete a task. For example, 'you have four weeks to complete the requirements definition for project X by running a workshop and using this template to document each of the requirements'.

This level of instruction can be frustrating for many reasons, but particularly because it implies a lack of faith in the analyst's ability to determine how the work should be done and how long it will take. The immediate effect of such an approach is for the business analyst to feel undervalued and undermined. It may be that the approach and timescale will work, but it is also possible that the analyst could have suggested a more relevant approach and could complete the work quicker. Given that most business analysts are highly skilled, failing to consult them on aspects of business analysis work can only serve to build a sense of frustration. There is also the possibility in this instance that the work takes longer than the allotted timescale, which may add a sense of failure into the unhappy mix of emotions.

To be truly self-organising, the team needs to be empowered to make its own decisions. If the team members cannot make their own decisions, then they cannot be self-organising.

Dr Stephen Covey (2004) commented in the *7 habits of highly effective people*:

> You cannot hold people responsible for results if you supervise their methods. You then become responsible for results and rules replace human judgement, creativity, responsibility. ... Effective leaders set up the conditions of empowerment and then ... get out of people's way, clear their path and become a source of help as requested.

Where a team is micromanaged, its members are not empowered and can feel disenfranchised. This leads to a sense of lack of trust and unhelpful behaviours, causing the team to seek guidance rather than work in a self-organising way. This causes significant difficulty if the team is required to adopt agile and apply the agile principles and techniques.

The best way to empower a team is to let members take responsibility and ownership for their own work, tasks and estimates. The Agile philosophy is that the team should take care of its tasks and the project manager or team manager should take care of the team. This is the essence of a 'self-organising' team. The team decides how long a task takes and how much work can be done to deliver a desired business outcome within the allotted time frame. In an agile environment, the team is trusted to deliver and therefore there is no need for micromanagement. If business analysts are to work successfully in Agile teams, they have to recognise the importance of working within a self-organising team.

In non-agile teams it is usually the project manager who decides how long a task takes.

In agile development, the team – which includes the business owner of the project – takes responsibility for identifying the tasks, and estimating how long they will take. The project manager leads the team by ensuring that no obstacles get in the way of delivering the tasks. In other words, the project manager trusts that the team members know what they are doing and does everything possible to help them achieve success.

Agile teams are also cross-functional, or multi-disciplinary, in so much as the team must contain all the skills necessary to move from a high-level business need through to delivering outcomes that demonstrate value to the business. This includes skills such as business analysis, design, testing and UX (User Experience) design.

The concept behind self-organising teams is empowerment and trust. Without empowerment there is a lack of trust, and without trust there cannot be an agile team. Team members also have to trust and respect each other, recognising the skills they all bring to the work in hand. Where business analysts work as part of an agile team they have to be cognisant of this principle as it applies to the working relationships they have with the other team members and their stakeholders.

Team development

It's not realistic to expect a newly formed team to hit the ground running. It takes time for individuals to get to know each other and to trust one another. A newly formed team will need to move through a series of stages in order to develop the ability to work as an effective, performing team. Bruce Tuckman (1965) developed a four-stage model of group formation that is usually referred to as the 'Tuckman' model. The stages in this model are shown in Figure 4.3.

Figure 4.3 Tuckman's stages of group development

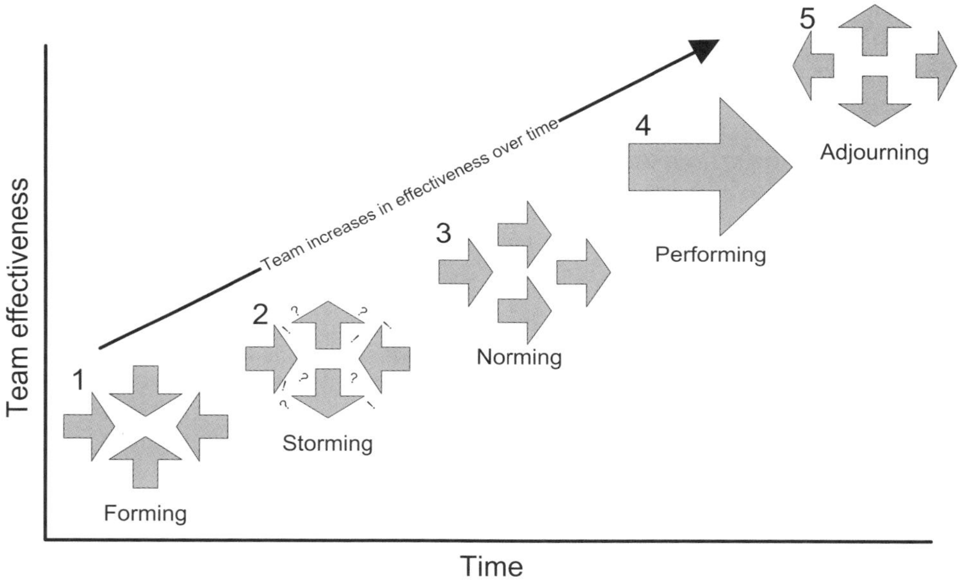

The four stages of group development identified by Tuckman are as follows:

Forming   At this stage, the group has just come together and everyone is very tentative and uncertain about themselves and their relationship to the other group members. They tend to be careful about what they say as they try to get to know each other and establish basic 'ground rules' for their interactions.

Storming   During this stage people start to test the boundaries identified during the forming stage. People often have different working styles and personalities and this can be a source of frustration for other team members. Authority can also be challenged here as team members jockey for positions while their roles are clarified. This can be unsettling as the team have yet to form strong bonds and so individuals may feel isolated.

Norming   This stage occurs once people start to resolve their differences. Team members start to help each other, confide in each other and may even start to socialise outside work. Consensus (about purpose, at least) has been established and the group begins to function reasonably effectively.

Performing Groups that reach this stage really start to perform effectively (think of the most successful sports teams here). Group members know and trust each other and can hand tasks back and forth with confidence. If someone 'drops' something, another team member will step in and pick it up. This is the stage that most teams aspire to and teams at this stage should be left to function.

In a later work, Tuckman and Mary Ann Jensen (1977) identified a fifth stage that groups can encounter:

Adjourning The reasons why the group was formed are no longer valid and it starts to break up. This stage is characterised by disengagement, anxiety about what happens next, positive feelings of past achievement and sadness at parting.

It is important for anyone involved in managing teams to recognise these stages and help the team to develop by working through these stages as quickly as possible. This is why, for example, when faced with a new team and a tight timescale it may be beneficial to organise an off-site, team-development event as this would help the team to move through the first two stages in a neutral environment.

It is not possible to circumvent these stages, for example by mixing a **performing** team with a **norming** team in the hope that this will produce two **performing** teams. In practice, this will often have the opposite effect, as changes to the constitution of a team at any stage will result in them reverting back to the **forming** stage.

Team development can be complicated where organisations have 'virtual' teams. In this situation, team members reside in different locations or even different countries. This is typically the case with outsourced and off-shored development teams and makes it difficult for teams to move through the team formation process. Even if most intra-group communication is by email, telephone and video or audio conferencing, it is worthwhile having team events where people can get to know each other as this will help the virtual team to function more effectively.

CONTINUOUS IMPROVEMENT

Continuous improvement concerns the ongoing effort to improve products, services or processes, with a focus on delivering improvements for the customer. The approach emerged in the 1950s as Japan began its economic reconstruction following the Second World War.

Today, continuous improvement is a fundamental element of frameworks such as Lean manufacturing and Six Sigma. For many years, continuous improvement was seen as having relevance to just manufacturing organisations and their delivery products. However, it became apparent that any business or function that delivered a product or a service could also benefit from adopting a continuous improvement approach to enhance its overall efficiency and quality. This includes software development.

It is worth noting that there is a difference between developing software and manufacturing products:

- Software products are generally built once and improved, adapted or replaced.
- Manufacturing products, once designed and approved, are built many times over.

Even though the manufactured product is improved, and processes updated, the product can continue to be produced. In some cases, the product may be built millions of times over many years (product examples include an Apple iPhone, a digital clock and a car).

Manufacturing organisations strive for uniformity in both the quality of the product and the processes applied to produce it. However, this is not the case with software as each project will be different from any other project. Although there are many similarities between developing software and manufacturing products, applying a strict 'one-size-fits-all' process to software development projects can be the source of many project failures. If we are to apply continuous improvement to software development processes, it is important to recognise the particular features of each project and consider the approach that would be the best fit. While there may be standard methods and techniques that can be used, it is typically the case that some adaptation will be required to ensure that they work within a specific context. Ensuring that there is a focus on adaptation and improvement is a core principle for agile business analysts. One of the ways in which this can be achieved is through using the 'toolkit' approach to the analysis work, whereby the technique or standard that is most relevant is selected.

Kaizen

The American engineer W. Edwards Deming wrote in his book *Out of the crisis* (2000, p. 23):

> Improve constantly and forever the system of production and service: ... there must be continual improvement in test methods and even better understanding of the customer's needs and of the way he uses and misuses a product.

Deming made a significant contribution to Japan's reputation for innovative, high-quality products and had a huge impact on Japan's manufacturing from the 1950s onwards. The developments in Japan resulted in the emergence of *Kaizen*, which is the practice of continuous improvement where everyone, across the whole workforce from chief executive officer (CEO) to cleaner, is involved in making the improvements. *Kaizen* is

Japanese for 'improvement' or 'change for the best' and was first implemented on the Toyota Production System. It influenced Lean and Kanban approaches.

Kaizen is based on the PDCA cycle, also known as the Deming cycle (2000) and shown in Figure 4.4, which stands for:

- **Plan:** establish the objectives and processes (input and output) to deliver the target or goal.
- **Do:** implement the process and collect data to analyse it.
- **Check:** study the results and compare against those expected in the Plan stage.
- **Act:** request corrective actions to put right any differences between the actual results and those planned.

Figure 4.4 *Kaizen* PDCA cycle

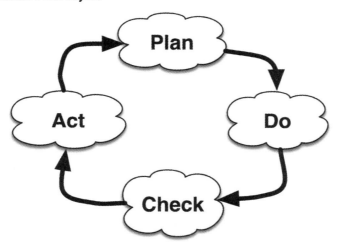

The idea behind *Kaizen* is to include the entire workforce in a culture of continuous improvement. Each person in the company is expected to come up with three to five suggestions for improvement each month. The combined impact of this concept was that hundreds of small improvements could be made each month that would continuously drive the business forward.

Kaizen translates into agile software delivery as follows:

Plan   Within the software delivery process this is done at the start of the time frame, where we plan the goal we want to deliver. We then plan the work required to meet the desired business goal.

Do   Once the tasks have been identified and estimated the agile team start to do the necessary work to complete the iteration goal.

Check   During the iteration, the agile team constantly checks the work they are doing to see whether any adjustments are required. A daily stand-up meeting may be held to check progress and identify any potential problems that need to be resolved.

Act   At the end of the iteration the agile team gets together and discusses what went well and what didn't go so well. Any suggestions are acted upon by making adjustments and changes to improve these aspects for the next iteration. These meetings are often called retrospectives or iteration review meetings and are explored further in Chapter 15.

Business improvement for business analysts

Continuous improvement has its roots in process improvement, which is often the focus of business analysis work. One of the more common frameworks used by business analysts for process improvement or change projects is DMAIC from the Six Sigma process improvement approach. DMAIC contains the following elements.

Define   Define the problem. Understand the problem we are working to resolve, who the customer and stakeholders are, and the benefits that could accrue. Clarify and define the scope.

Measure   Look at the processes to find the potential causes of the problem. Gather data about the problem.

Analyse   Analyse the processes to determine defects and root causes of problems. Gather and analyse additional data as required.

Improve   Improve the process by eliminating defects. Develop potential solutions and test the solutions against agreed criteria.

Control   Control future performance by developing clear standards and procedures for the process.

ITERATIVE DEVELOPMENT AND INCREMENTAL DELIVERY

Agile software development is based on an iterative development and incremental delivery life cycle approach (explained further in Chapter 5). Iterative development refers to how the software is built, whereas incremental delivery refers to the delivery of the software to the business in releases. This can also be used by business analysts and applied to change projects with a broader focus. A holistic view, coupled with systemic thinking, enables business analysts to identify elements of the business system where it is possible to make targeted, incremental changes that have the potential to deliver benefit at an early stage. This approach helps in the smooth introduction of changes and increases stakeholder confidence in the project.

Applying the iterative and incremental approach

Chapter 5 explains how iterative development and incremental delivery are applied during agile software development. Figure 4.5 shows how this iterative development process can be adapted for the business improvement method DMAIC, taken from Six Sigma.

Figure 4.5 Iterative development adapted for process improvement

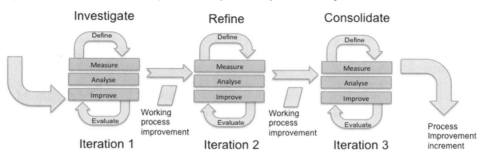

It is possible to release the improvements developed within one iteration. It is also possible to deliver an increment or release that has been developed during multiple iterations. It is possible to have just one major product delivery (which has been developed during many iterations) followed by smaller changes, although this is less likely within an agile environment. In essence, the principles of iterative development and incremental delivery need to be applied in the way that works best for the organisation.

When developing a solution iteratively, the nature of the overall solution evolves as the work progresses. Both during and at the end of an iteration, all working solutions are tested against previously delivered solutions to ensure that they work together. When delivering changes incrementally, it is important to ensure that any additional changes work seamlessly with the earlier 'releases' of change and will deliver the desired outcomes to the business.

A process improvement project provides a good example of how a business analyst might apply iterative development and incremental delivery. In this context, 'development' refers to the design and development of improved processes plus their attendant artefacts.

- **Model the context:** define the scope of the improvement project, possibly using a high-level process map based on the value chain technique. Decide measures/goals to be achieved.

- **Prioritise process areas:** those that would benefit from improvement. The MoSCoW technique is useful for this prioritisation (Chapter 9).

- **Model and analyse:** focus on the highest priority business process; swim lane diagrams would be an effective approach.

- **Identify the tasks:** particularly those that would benefit from improvement and prioritise them.

- **Improve the highest priority tasks:** deploy these into operation when possible. It may or may not make sense to implement each individual process change, as there may be dependent processes that require improvement in order to generate beneficial changes. It will also be necessary to collaborate with the customer during the improvement work and to consider the other POPIT™ elements.

- **Iterate this process:** when new processes are implemented, it is often possible to see where further process improvement possibilities reside. This knowledge then influences which areas of the process are tackled in the next increment or release.

This approach requires collaboration with the customer (another key agile value as discussed earlier), which offers the possibility of discussion and demonstration of ideas as the development work progresses. An incremental delivery approach is likely to minimise disruption during the implementation of process changes, reducing the risk to the continuing performance of the business area.

The first increment

The initial delivery of an IT system or process improvement requires significant analysis as this is going to be the first set of changes that the business customers will experience. When considering what should be delivered in the first increment, it is a good idea to think about the following in order to identify the focus for the project and establish the content of the first release:

- the risks that need to be addressed;
- the assumptions about the project that should be proved or disproved;
- the goals to be achieved;
- dependencies between processes and other projects;
- any timescales that need to be meet;
- the priority of the work in achieving the project goals.

The Minimal Viable Product (MVP) and the Minimal Marketable Product (MMP) are two concepts that are particularly relevant when considering the first increment to be deployed. Prioritisation plays a major part in the discussions about the MVP and MMP. This topic is discussed further in Chapter 9.

MVP: The MVP is the minimum that needs to be done to test, prove or disprove an assumption or risk about the project. For business improvement projects, it may be used to ascertain whether a process improvement is worthwhile or before embarking upon a large improvement programme. The MVP may be an experiment and so may not actually be delivered, as it may not make sense to make the change as it stands. However, it may have been piloted within an area of the business in order to gain necessary information.

MMP: In essence, the MMP is the minimal amount of change or improvement that can be delivered which will produce tangible outcomes that a customer is willing to accept or pay for. Dependencies will have been proven during the iterations and/or MVP, and risks will have been addressed. This work will have been used to ensure that there is value in making the process improvement.

Iterative development combined with incremental delivery is the approach that underpins agile today and it is as valid to business change and improvement projects as it is to the delivery of software.

PLANNING FOR AND BUILDING IN CHANGE

One thing that is almost always guaranteed on any project is that change is inevitable and can happen for many reasons. Some sources of change are illustrated in Figure 4.6.

Figure 4.6 External and internal sources of change

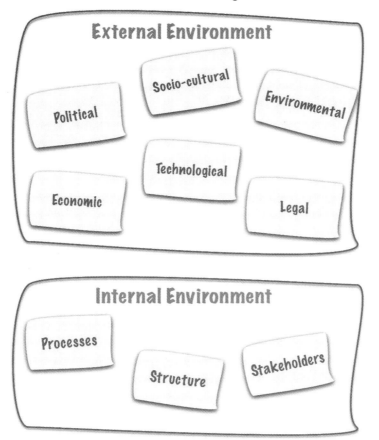

Some requirements are persistent and do not change a lot; data requirements often fit into this category. Other requirements are much more volatile – for example, the details of a user interface – so specifying these requirements in detail at an early stage will undoubtedly waste time and effort. To combat this, agile development attempts to avoid finalising requirements early. Instead, work is planned using high-level requirements and goals that are only protected from change during the iteration within which they are developed. Applying the business analysis technique of establishing a hierarchy of requirements (Chapter 13) and documenting requirements in line with the agile values of **Just Enough, Just in Time**, will reduce the time spent defining the requirements and avoid unnecessary rework. Ongoing customer collaboration and early delivery of increments helps to ensure that the project team are delivering what the customer requires in order to meet the business need.

DOING THE RIGHT THING AND THE THING RIGHT

As agile becomes more widespread within organisations, the void created by a lack of business analysis is becoming more obvious. Agile development teams run the risk of losing sight of the big picture – the holistic view – and failing to understanding the desired outcomes for their organisation. The business outcome or goal is rarely a new IT system; rather it is a beneficial business outcome such as improved efficiency or productivity. One of the key questions business analysts ask is, 'Why?' in order to challenge conventional wisdom and uncover root causes of problems. This is how the actual business needs are uncovered and is in line with Drucker's (2003) principle of delivering 'the right thing' as well as 'the thing right'. These terms are not evident within the 12 agile principles. However, they are important in the business context and for the agile delivery of holistic solutions.

Deliver the right thing

Introducing technology is not always the right solution to solving business problems and yet technology is chosen regularly over alternative options such as business process change or skills development. This is often in the hope that a big investment will bring about big results. While technology is a huge part of businesses today, so are the people working within organisations, the processes they use and the skills they possess.

Delivering the right thing involves making sure that the root cause to a problem is understood and that the solution involves all necessary elements of the POPIT™ model. Therefore, the 'right thing' is likely to be a mix of people, organisation, process, information and technology change. Failing to consider the holistic solution is likely to result in disappointed customers and unrealised benefits.

Deliver the thing right

Agile business analysts can add significant value to their organisations and projects by being aware of the need to tailor their approach as necessary. Although requirements typically evolve during the iterative development process, some requirements may need to be defined in detail at an earlier stage. If it would be beneficial to define a process or rule at an early stage then we should be prepared to do this. If a particular requirement is difficult to understand, perhaps because of the presence of tacit knowledge, then we should consider which techniques would be most relevant to gain the necessary understanding.

It is of paramount importance that the constraints and assets of the business are considered when deciding the development and delivery of the solution. It is possible that the iterative development of the solution may be assisted by adopting a modular business architecture, based on reusable organisational capabilities, components and artefacts.

While incremental delivery enables the early realisation of benefits and the reduction of risk, this may not always be possible within the business context. For example, where a legacy system or processes are to be replaced, it is possible that the solution has to be delivered in one release.

Ultimately, applying any approach – whether agile or not – as a 'cookbook' does not help to ensure the success of a change project. The essence of agility is adaptability and agile business analysts who do this are well placed to ensure that the 'thing' is delivered right.

CONCLUSION

The business analysis toolkit is constantly evolving and business analysts have to subscribe to ongoing personal development. The six core values (Figure 4.1) capture the essence of an agile mindset and should be applied by business analysts when working within an agile environment. Techniques and frameworks such as *Kaizen* and DMAIC are worthy additions to the business analysis toolkit and have the potential to offer benefits to agile business analysts.

REFERENCES

Covey, Dr S. (2004) *7 habits of highly effective people*. London: Simon and Schuster Limited.

Deming, W.E. (2000) *Out of the crisis*. Cambridge, MA: MIT Press.

Drucker, P.F. (2003) *The essential Drucker*. New York: HarperPB.

Mehrabian, A. (1971) *Silent messages: 1st edition*. Belmont, CA: Wadsworth.

Sinek, S. (n.d.) *AZ quotes*. Available from: www.azquotes.com/quote/714917 [7 December 2016].

Thomas, P., Paul, D. and Cadle, J. (2012) *The human touch: personal skills for professional success*. Swindon: BCS.

Tuckman, B.W. (1965) Developmental sequence in small groups. *Psychological Bulletin*, 63 (6): 384–99.

Tuckman, B.W. and Jensen, M.A. (1977) Stages in small group development revisited. *Group and Organisation Studies*, 2: 419–27.

FURTHER READING

Patton, J. (2014) *User story mapping: 1st edition*. Sebastopol, CA: O'Reilly.

Paul, D., Cadle, J. and Yeates, D. (2014) *Business analysis: 3rd edition*. Swindon: BCS.

5 UNDERSTANDING AGILE METHODS AND FRAMEWORKS

This chapter covers the following topics:

- key elements in agile methods;
- popular agile methods and approaches;
- scaled agile approaches.

INTRODUCTION

The majority of business analysts will encounter agile methods while working on change projects, reading online articles or attending training courses and this is likely to utilise, or focus on, a specific method or process. Often, it can feel that there is only one way to 'do agile' and that the techniques, practices and ceremonies of that approach are all there is to know.

Conversely, as explained in Chapter 2, the Agile Manifesto originated as an amalgam of many methods and approaches, took the best parts of them, and derived a set of core values and principles. However, the Agile Manifesto does not specify *how* to apply the values or principles so, since its creation, there have been several attempts to create methods, processes and approaches that fill this gap. And although they vary in many ways, they can all claim to apply agile; it is just that they are agile in different ways.

These methods and approaches may differ in their depth, the scope of the projects they are aimed at and the team roles they describe. They also focus primarily on software development and encourage the elaboration of requirements through discussions between developers and end users. This can make it difficult for business analysts to know where they fit, as very few of the popular approaches specifically mention the need for a business analyst. Despite this, there remains a clear need for business analysis skills in projects today, as this book makes clear. This chapter will briefly describe some popular agile methods and approaches and help business analysts to understand the context within which they may need to work.

KEY ELEMENTS IN AGILE METHODS

There are a number of elements common to all agile approaches. They are described in this book without reference to specific methods. For example, Chapter 11 discusses several techniques that may be used to conduct requirements analysis, whatever the method adopted on a particular project. What makes them agile techniques is the way in which they embody the values in the Agile Manifesto or demonstrate the agile principles. Understanding the core aspects of agile helps when learning new methods and moving from one agile project to another. In practice, very few teams apply a given method in a prescriptive way. Instead, the approach evolves and is continually improved as the method is applied to the development work.

Some of the key elements that are common to agile methods and are of particular relevance to business analysis are described in Table 5.1 below.

Table 5.1 Key elements in agile methods

A list of work to be done	A list of work items must be created for a project and needs to be ordered or arranged in some way. The priorities of the list must be established and it must be kept current as the project progresses. There are several names for this list including backlog, inbox, feature list, requirements list and work items.
	The creation and management of this list, including the elicitation and analysis of the items, plus alignment with expected business benefits, requires good business analysis skills.
Iterative development	Agile methods typically emphasise the need for many regular periods where software is developed and delivered. These periods often follow a regular time frame (for example, every two weeks) and may be known as iterations, sprints or timeboxes. The work of each iteration may be cumulative, where each delivered increment builds on the previous one, adding new functionality or qualities.
	It is important that each iteration focuses on delivering a valuable outcome for the customer; this is an area that requires skilled business analysis.
High levels of customer involvement	In contrast to waterfall approaches, agile methods do not receive or produce comprehensive statements of requirements as a starting point. Instead, they expect the detailed requirements to evolve and change during the development process. To do this, the team needs to have constant and ongoing engagement with the customers.
	Sometimes, development teams can become resistant to change, particularly as the project nears completion. Business analysis is focused on the needs of the customer; it will ensure that the analysis is conducted so that changes are understood and identified quickly.
	There is a wide range of customers and stakeholders; these are discussed in Chapter 7. Balancing the needs of these disparate customers is a fundamental business analysis skill.

(Continued)

Table 5.1 (Continued)

Transparency and sharing progress	Transparency is an important aspect of agile and many teams use physical boards or tables to record progress. The customer needs to be involved in planning and review meetings, and is expected to play a full part in the team. However, this is often difficult in practice, as customers may not be able to give sufficient time at the point it is required. In this situation, it is often the business analyst who can act as a proxy for the customer and provide the required business knowledge.
Regular reviews of progress	At the end of each iteration or phase, meetings are held where progress is reviewed and the team make any necessary changes or even stop working on the project. These meetings are often called retrospectives, but reviewing progress, and reacting to the review outcomes, can also be part of planning meetings. This dedication to continuous improvement should be familiar to business analysts, and many business analysis techniques can help these meetings run smoothly.
A whole team mindset	The team works together and collectively feels responsible for the work. Between them, they have all the skills required to perform the work. Often this means that each team member is expected to have cross-functional skills in addition to their particular specialism. The term 'generalising specialist' has been coined to describe a team member with cross-functional skills. In this context, it is possible that a business analyst may be involved in testing software. However, some activities will require specialist skills, such as those offered by business analysts.

POPULAR AGILE METHODS AND APPROACHES

There are several popular agile methods and frameworks and they are described in outline below; additional reading references are provided at the end of the chapter. Some of the approaches can correctly be described as **methods**, as they specify the details required to implement them. Others are defined in less detail, consisting of guidance and principles rather than complete methods.

Scrum

Scrum is by far the most widely used agile method and, for many people, it is synonymous with agile. It is documented on the www.scrum.org website which is updated frequently and is described in many books.

It was first presented by Jeff Sutherland and Ken Schwaber in 1995 and is based on empirical process control theory or **empiricism**. This asserts that since it is impossible to fully know everything at the start, the team should take an incremental approach, make decisions based on what is known at the time, and build knowledge and experience to make better decisions next time.

Scrum describes three pillars that uphold this approach: Transparency, Inspection and Adaptation. These are sometimes called the Three Pillars of Scrum, and sometimes the Three Pillars of Agile.

- **Transparency:** those responsible for the outcome must have visibility of all the aspects of the process that can affect the outcome. This includes elements such as adopting standard terminology and language, and also means that everyone should be aware of the acceptance criteria and the priority allocated to the work.

- **Inspection:** the work in progress should be inspected in order that it can be improved. This inspection should not impede delivery but needs to be frequent enough to be effective. It should be conducted by skilled inspectors.

- **Adaptation:** when inspection uncovers issues that could lead to the goals not being met, changes must be made to prevent failure. Adjustments should be done as soon as possible.

Scrum is a relatively simple method. It defines four key events, three roles and three artefacts. The activities directly support the pillars of Inspection and Adaptation, and the artefacts support Transparency. There is much that Scrum does not prescribe. For example, it does not dictate how teams should describe requirements or work items. Scrum is a framework or container – it mandates the elements considered to be critical and leaves the rest up to the teams. This is described in the Scrum Guide (Schwaber and Sutherland, 2014) as follows:

> Scrum is free and offered in this Guide. Scrum's roles, artefacts, events and rules are immutable and, although implementing only parts of Scrum is possible, the result is not Scrum. Scrum exists only in its entirety and functions well as a container for other techniques, methodologies and practices.

While many teams implement Scrum in a pure form, there are many variations of it in use. Teams have evolved, adapted and changed Scrum. Many of the other methods described below borrow some elements from Scrum. Some of the Scrum terminology (such as backlog, Scrum and retrospective) are now widely used in agile and usually have the same meaning. Despite being widely used, it is also widely abused and many teams struggle to apply the core principles; typically, the quality of their work suffers as a result.

The sprint

The sprint is at the heart of Scrum. It is a timebox of one month or less, during which the team develop a potentially releasable version of the solution called the **increment**. Sprints have some immutable rules:

- No changes are permitted that can endanger the sprint goal.

- Quality goals cannot decrease.

- Scope may be clarified and re-negotiated (between the development team and the product owner) as more detail emerges about the problem.

- If the sprint goal becomes obsolete or impossible to achieve, the product owner may cancel the sprint.

Sprints can be considered as 'mini-projects', each with a discrete outcome to achieve (the sprint goal), a design and a flexible plan to achieve it. The goals do not have to be IT related, and Scrum can be successfully used for business change or process improvement projects.

Scrum events

The four key events in Scrum sprints are described in Table 5.2 below.

Table 5.2 Four key Scrum events

Sprint planning	Before the sprint begins, the whole team plan what work will be done in the sprint, agree the goal and decide how the work will be done.
	This activity must involve the whole team. Business analysis skills are crucial to ensure that the backlog items being considered are correctly understood by the team, and that non-functional requirements and non-IT aspects of the solution are considered.
Daily Scrum	Each day, the development team holds a short team meeting (less than 15 minutes) called a daily Scrum. This allows the team to **inspect** the work done since the last daily Scrum and forecast the work that could be done before the next one. This may mean the team **adapts** its approach in order to ensure that it will meet the agreed goal.
Sprint review	The sprint review takes place at the end of the sprint and is an opportunity to **inspect** the increment and **adapt** the product backlog if required. This includes taking account of changes such as to the business environment. This meeting is an informal meeting of the development team and stakeholders, and the result is a revised product backlog.
Sprint retrospective	In contrast to the sprint review, the retrospective is strictly limited to the development team and offers the opportunity to **inspect** the work completed by the team and plan what changes the team members wish to make for the next sprint.
	The areas to consider during the retrospective include people, relationships, processes and tools. This focus on people and other non-IT elements of the sprint will be familiar to business analysts and requires business analysis skills. The POPIT™ model and other holistic approaches to solution development may be useful techniques during this work.

It is important that the Scrum events take place and that they are facilitated well. Scrum provides some guidance on the duration of these events during a one-month iteration. Although these timings are a maximum, rather than a target, they provide an indication of the level of importance the authors of Scrum place on them:

- The sprint planning meeting should be no longer than eight hours.
- The sprint review should be no longer than four hours.
- The sprint retrospective should be no longer than three hours.

These events together with the 15-minute daily scrums, amount to 20 hours of elapsed time. This is 12.5 per cent of a sprint that lasts four weeks, with 40 hours of elapsed time per week; a considerable proportion of time. Business analysis skills are extremely helpful in ensuring that teams use this time wisely, both in facilitating the meetings and in providing contributions from a different perspective to that of other team members.

Scrum roles

There are three roles defined within Scrum; they are described in Table 5.3.

Table 5.3 Three Scrum roles

The product owner	The product owner is (or represents) the person (or organisation) that will ultimately benefit from the solution. The holder of this role is solely responsible for decisions about the product backlog, including prioritising the items, ensuring the development team understands what they mean and deciding when they have been completed.
	The skills required for this role closely align with the skills of the business analyst. In some teams, business analysts will help the product owner with their responsibilities. It is possible that in some teams a business analyst will be asked to be the product owner but in doing so, they should assume the responsibilities outlined above.
	If the product owner does not have access to business analysts, then it is important that they, or some of the development team, have or acquire business analysis skills.
The development team	The development team consists of professionals who do the work required to deliver a potentially releasable solution at the end of each increment. They are structured and empowered to organise and manage their own work, which optimises their effectiveness.
	Development teams are cross-functional, and between them they contain all the skills necessary to deliver the work. This requires the team members to be highly competent with regard to some skills and, also, to hold other broader skills at a less specialist level. This aligns with the concept of a T-shaped professional, which is discussed in Chapter 7.
	While business analysis work is required in a Scrum development team, the business analysts (and anyone in any other role) will be called 'developers' and will be expected to do work outside their specialism if it is necessary to complete the increment. This can mean that business analysts joining a Scrum team will be expected to learn new skills.

(Continued)

Table 5.3 (Continued)

The Scrum master	The Scrum master is responsible for ensuring that Scrum is understood and enacted by the team. This role is described as the 'servant-leader' for the team, who provides services to both the development team and the product owner.
	The Scrum master helps the product owner to find ways to manage the backlog, ensuring that the team understand what the product owner is requesting. The role is also concerned with facilitating Scrum events, providing coaching for the development team, helping the team to carry out the work and, most importantly, removing any impediments to the team's progress.

Scrum artefacts

The three artefacts defined within Scrum are described in Table 5.4 below.

Table 5.4 Three Scrum artefacts

Product backlog	The product backlog provides an ordered list of everything that might be needed in the solution. It is the single source of requirements for the project, and the responsibility of the product owner. It exists at the product level, which means that several Scrum teams can operate from a single product backlog.
	The product backlog is never complete and continuously evolves through the lifetime of the project, requiring ongoing attention. It is a living artefact and, as for other requirements artefacts, requires business analysis skills to create it, maintain it and ensure its quality. Chapter 12 considers the backlog in the light of a similar business analysis artefact, the requirements catalogue.
Sprint backlog	A sprint begins with the identification of a subset of the product backlog items; these are the items that must be completed during that sprint in order to achieve the sprint goal. The sprint backlog provides a plan that describes how the goal will be met.
	During the sprint, the sprint backlog will constantly evolve, as more detail emerges about the work to be conducted by the team. As new work emerges, it is added to the backlog, so that it becomes a highly visible, real-time description of the work the team needs to complete.
Increment	This is the sum of all the sprint backlog items completed during the sprint, and the work completed during all of the previous sprints. The increment must be usable by the customer, and meet the criteria that the development team have agreed with the product owner to define that the increment is 'done'.

XP

Many of the participants in the 2001 meeting where agile was conceived were from the XP community, including its founder, Kent Beck. Therefore, it is unsurprising that many core agile ideas derive from XP and are used within other agile approaches.

XP focuses on software development, and describes five basic activities (or 'rules') bound together by five values. These are all focused on building software that delivers customer satisfaction. XP does not specify any particular roles or job titles, instead using the term 'developer' to describe all roles. It requires teams to take collective ownership of the work, focus on the highest value goals first, and adapt how they work depending on the circumstances. As a result, this approach requires multi-disciplined team members.

Despite the need for team members to be multi-skilled and the dominance of software terminology in the method, XP's focus on the customer and embracing of changing requirements requires XP teams to have strong business analysis skills.

The five rules are described in Table 5.5 below, and in further detail at www.extremeprogramming.org. Several of these concepts are covered in further detail in Chapter 15.

Table 5.5 Five rules of XP

Planning	The project is divided into iterations and bound together into a release plan and schedule. User stories describe the functionality to be built for the customer, and the team makes frequent small releases.
Managing	The team is given dedicated open workspace to ensure good communication. There is a focus on a sustainable pace and the team measures the speed of progress in order to be predictable. XP teams move people around to avoid bottlenecks and foster cross-functional training. The day starts with a stand-up meeting.
Designing	XP teams aim for simplicity and measure this using the four subjective qualities: Testable, Understandable, Browsable and Explainable (TUBE).
Coding	The customer must always be available during coding, and there is a strong focus on early and frequent integration. XP teams use techniques such as pair programming and TDD, and apply collective ownership.
Testing	All code must have unit tests and must pass them before it can be released. When bugs are found, new tests are written to catch them earlier next time. Acceptance tests are run often and the results published.

XP has a strong focus on improvement, and describes five essential values that are used to improve a software project: Communication, Simplicity, Feedback, Respect and Courage. XP challenges more traditional development approaches by advocating that teams **'Manage Goals Instead of Activities'** and use user stories to describe goals that are ordered in terms of importance. The team focuses on delivering the most important goal (defined for a user story) first, completing all of the activities necessary to satisfy the customer's acceptance criteria. This part of XP is clearly where a business analyst can add significant value, for example, in identifying user roles and constructing the goal-based user stories. The identification and decomposition of goals are described in Chapter 8.

XP works well where the team comprises between 2 and 12 team members. However, it is hard to scale for larger teams without compromising on the core elements of the approach.

DSDM

DSDM is a vendor independent framework for agile project management and delivery that emerged from the RAD community in order to build quality into the prevailing RAD practices. It is owned by the DSDM Consortium, a non-profit organisation.

The framework has evolved over the years, and the current version (launched in 2014) is called the **DSDM Agile Project Framework**. DSDM incorporates project-focused principles and offers a rich set of roles and responsibilities that make it well suited to agile in a corporate environment. DSDM defines a number of products or deliverables, and teams choose which they require based on the characteristics of each individual project. Tailoring the approach is an important aspect of DSDM, particularly if the project is to align with the agile philosophy to do **Just Enough, Just in Time**.

The DSDM Today (2016) philosophy is that:

> best business value emerges when projects are aligned to clear business goals, deliver frequently and involve the collaboration of motivated and empowered people.

This philosophy is further supported by a set of eight principles, which describe the mindset and behaviours necessary for a DSDM team to succeed. The DSDM principles are:

1. focus on the business need;
2. deliver on time;
3. collaborate;
4. never compromise on quality;
5. build incrementally from firm foundations;
6. develop iteratively;

7. communicate continuously and clearly;
8. demonstrate control.

Unlike other methods (such as Scrum), DSDM describes the entire project life cycle from pre-project through to deployment and post-project. It advocates the use of several core practices, including facilitated workshops, modelling, iterative development, MoSCoW prioritisation and timeboxing. These techniques will be familiar to many business analysts as they are in widespread use, both within traditional and agile environments. Because DSDM is a framework and covers the whole project life cycle, it integrates well with other processes and frameworks such as PRINCE2® and the standards offered by the Project Management Institute (PMI). Teams can also use Scrum, Kanban (see below) or XP in the development phase.

The life cycle phases in DSDM are described in Table 5.6 below.

Table 5.6 DSDM life cycle phases

Pre-project	Ensures that there is a clear business goal for the project.
Feasibility	Establishes whether the proposed project is likely to be technically feasible, and cost effective. This should take just enough effort to decide whether to stop or continue.
Foundations	Establish a fundamental (but not detailed) understanding of the business rationale and potential solution, and how the solution will be developed, delivered and supported.
Evolutionary development	Using iterative development techniques and MoSCoW prioritisation within timeboxed iterations, the solution team create solution increments.
Deployment	A baseline of the evolving solution is moved into an operational environment. This can happen many times as new versions become available.
	This stage consists of three main activities, Assemble, Review and Deploy.
Post-project	The project is formally closed and the team conducts a retrospective on their performance. This phase also checks how well the intended business benefits have been delivered by the solution.

Unsurprisingly for an approach aimed at larger, more complex problems, DSDM describes a much larger set of roles than other agile processes. In total, DSDM describes 13 roles covering project level, solution development and supporting responsibilities; the core roles are described in Table 5.7.

Table 5.7 Roles defined within DSDM

Business sponsor	Responsible for ensuring the delivery of the business case and representing the interests of the business.
Project manager	Responsible for overall management of the project, providing resources, ensuring delivery of the project objectives, and communicating with senior business representatives and the solution development team.
Business visionary	Responsible for providing strategic direction to the project and ensuring that the vision of the business sponsor is interpreted and communicated accurately.
Business analyst	Responsible for supporting the business visionary in fulfilling the business needs determined for the project. Provides analysis and modelling expertise as required. Takes a proactive role in facilitating the communication within the solution development team. This definition is focused on solution development and does not include the pre-project activities described earlier in this chapter.
Technical coordinator	Responsible for ensuring the overall coherence of the technical design adopted on the project.
Business ambassador	Responsible for representing the needs of the business users and providing the communication channels between the project and the business. The business ambassador is a credible representative of the business staff and has knowledge and experience of the business area addressed by the solution.
Team leader	Responsible for facilitating, scheduling and monitoring the work of the solution development team at an iteration level.
Solution developer	Responsible for developing the solution to meet the functional and non-functional requirements.
Solution tester	Responsible for testing the developed solution, including technical and acceptance testing.
Technical advisor	Responsible for providing specialist or specific information about the technical aspects of the solution.
Business advisor	Responsible for providing specialist or specific information about the business needs and working practices.

The roles include a business analyst at both the project level, and in the solution development team. This is intentional, and allows the business analyst to work on behalf of the customer (for example, to develop the business case) or as part of the solution development team (for example, elaborating requirements, modelling or helping the developers understand the requirements).

Unified Process

Although not represented in the group that met in 2001 to conceive agile, the UP was already established at that time and embodies many of the same characteristics of incremental and iterative development. Like DSDM, the UP is aimed more at corporate enterprises, takes a whole life cycle view and describes a large number of roles and artefacts that should be tailored by the team to fit the problem. The most common version is the RUP, which was launched by Rational Software in the late 1990s and is now owned by IBM. Other versions include OpenUP and AgileUP.

The UP defines four phases required to develop the solution, describes workflows that are required throughout the project (including business modelling) and sets out principles that should be followed by the project team. As with DSDM, the UP can easily be misused by teams that forget the first (and only) mandatory step: **Tailor the Process**.

The four phases of the UP are described in Table 5.8 below; each phase consists of one or more iterations.

Table 5.8 Four phases of the UP

Inception	Establish the business case for the system and define the system scope. Identify at a high level how the system interacts with users and describe all the high-level use cases. Provide more detail for significant use cases.
	Gain agreement with stakeholders on project scope and cost/schedule estimates.
Elaboration	Establish a sound architectural foundation and eliminate the highest risks to the project. Gain a 'mile-wide and inch-deep' view of the system. This can include developing prototypes.
Construction	Develop all remaining features incrementally. Reach 'Initial Operating Capability' with a usable version of the solution produced in each iteration.
Transition	Deploy the solution to the user community.

The RUP is a specific, and popular, implementation of the UP. RUP advocates a set of overarching principles known as the six best practices:

1. develop software iteratively;
2. manage requirements;
3. use component-based architectures;
4. visually model software;
5. verify software quality;
6. control changes to software.

The UP methods place high importance on requirements and on business modelling, and business analysis skills are essential for this work. Since the various artefacts are developed incrementally – or elaborated – throughout the project, business analysis work is required at all phases at the level of detail needed to address the risk of each phase.

Kanban

Kanban is not strictly an agile method, as it describes how to optimise the services delivering the knowledge work, rather than the delivery of the work itself. This distinction is an important one, and explains why Kanban is often used alongside other methods. It describes an approach to incremental and evolutionary process and systems change. It focuses on delivery flow, and on managing and optimising Work in Progress (WIP, also sometimes called Work in Process) to offer teams more flexible planning options, faster output and a means of continuously improving performance.

Kanban is derived from the Lean manufacturing approach and has been popularised for software and business change projects by David J. Anderson. Kanban is based on six core practices:

1. visualise;
2. limit WIP;
3. manage flow;
4. make process policies explicit;
5. implement feedback loops;
6. improve collaboratively, evolve experimentally (using models and the scientific method).

The first of these practices – visualise – is often done using a board or table. The steps required to implement a requirement are set out as columns as shown in Figure 5.1. Work to be done is written on a card (a Kanban) and begins on the left, in the 'Inbox'. As requirements are worked on, the team moves the card to the appropriate column.

Figure 5.1 Example of a Kanban board

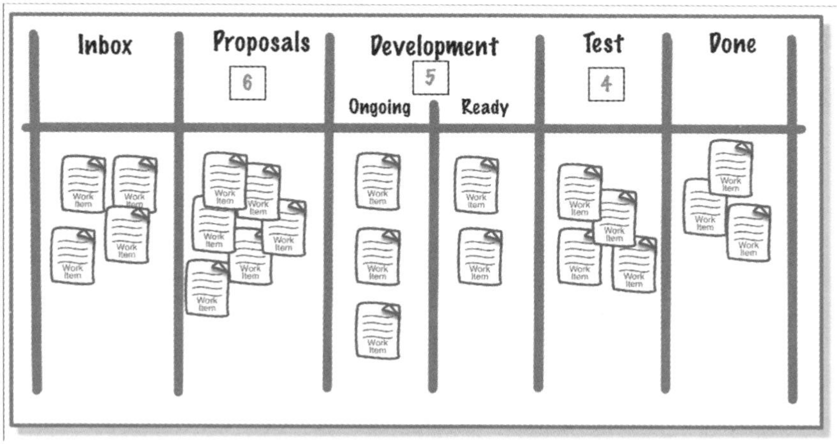

This is just one of six practices, but it is common for teams to carry out just this one practice and think that they are applying Kanban. However, to get value from this approach, each column must have a maximum WIP limit that dictates how many requirements can be in progress. The team then focuses on choosing work that enables flow, and creates space for more work to be pulled in.

Bottlenecks become obvious when using Kanban and the team is motivated to find ways to remove them. For example, if only one person is able to do the testing, they could quickly find that work cannot be moved into the 'Test' column because it is already full and this will prevent the commencement of other work in the pipeline. To unblock this, the other team members may need to learn how to do the testing work and provide additional staff resources for the test activity.

Business analysis is not specifically mentioned in Kanban but since the focus for the team is improving flow, all team members should be able to work across several columns. Some of the most important business analysis work involves ensuring that the work in the Inbox column is correctly described.

Kanban can be used with other agile approaches, such as Scrum or XP, and some of the Kanban principles (especially the use of an agile board) are part of other methods. In contrast with many other agile approaches, Kanban does not use timeboxing; instead, releases are made when there are sufficient Kanbans (or cards) in the 'Done' column.

Lean software development

Lean software development is a method that was derived from the manufacturing principles in the Toyota Production System. The approach focuses on the elimination of waste (*muda* in Japanese) and considers wasteful any effort that does not result directly in the provision of value for the end customer. The seminal reference text is *Lean software development* by Mary and Tom Poppendieck (2003). There are seven key Lean practices that are translated into software development principles. The Poppendiecks present an 'agile toolkit' of 22 tools that are mapped onto the principles shown in Table 5.9.

Table 5.9 Agile toolkit of Lean software development

Lean principle	Lean software tool
Eliminate waste	1. Seeing waste
	2. Value stream mapping
Amplify learning	3. Feedback
	4. Iterations
	5. Synchronisation
	6. Set-based development
Decide as late as possible	7. Options thinking
	8. The last responsible moment
	9. Making decisions

(Continued)

Table 5.9 (Continued)

Lean principle	Lean software tool
Deliver as fast as possible	10. Pull systems
	11. Queuing theory
	12. Cost of delay
Empower the team	13. Self-determination
	14. Motivation
	15. Leadership
	16. Expertise
Build integrity in	17. Perceived integrity
	18. Conceptual integrity
	19. Refactoring
	20. Testing
See the whole	21. Measurements
	22. Contracts

The approach focuses more on improving the process than developing a solution. Many of the tools identified within the toolkit benefit from the application of good business analysis skills. Lean software development can also be combined with other agile approaches.

Lean Startup

Lean Startup provides an approach to creating and managing startup organisations using some of the Lean and agile principles. It is not intended to be used exclusively for new startup companies; it is also used for the development of new products (or new versions of products) within existing enterprises. As a result, business analysis skills to engage with customers are essential. Lean Startup also recommends the use of analysis techniques such as the '5-Ws' (Why, What, Who, When and Where) and prototyping, which form part of the business analysis toolkit.

SCALED AGILE APPROACHES

When agile approaches began in the early 2000s, they were applied, in the main, to small, relatively simple problems that were resolved by small teams; within this context, they worked extremely well. As the agile movement has grown and become more prevalent, organisations are trying to achieve the benefits of agile for larger and more complex problems, with larger and more diverse teams.

As the history in Chapter 2 explains, this is not how agile began so it should be no surprise that some common approaches and methods do not work well when faced with large and complex problems. This has led to numerous attempts to find ways to scale agile approaches so that they can work across larger and more complex projects and programmes, whilst still retaining the benefits of small, autonomous teams with highly collaborative work practices.

Some of these attempts to scale agile have become popular, but there are still many bespoke, company specific methods that business analysts may come across. This is because many companies who were relatively early adopters of agile quickly came up against difficulties, as the problems they were trying to solve were not the kinds of problems that agile was initially intended for. So, they tried to solve problems themselves, perhaps with the aid of external agile coaches or experts, and developed proprietary solutions that suited their problem spaces. This has been happening for years and some of these bespoke variants have coalesced into generic approaches that are now gaining popularity.

Organisations deciding to adopt agile practices today are comparatively lucky. Not only are the classic agile methods well understood but there are also several new frameworks and methods to select that are designed for more complex or extensive problems.

Disciplined Agile 2.0

Scott Ambler has been helping companies apply agile principles to complex enterprise problems for many years, and in that time has published several books and methods. His latest framework is developed with Mark Lines and is called Disciplined Agile 2.0 (DA 2.0); it is an evolution of their disciplined agile delivery approach. It restates the Agile Manifesto from a strategic perspective, focusing more on solutions and stakeholders than software and customers; it also adds some principles around enterprise reuse and the importance of the enterprise ecosystem.

DA 2.0 is a process decision framework that is scalable both at a tactical (team) level and a strategic level. It is a people-first, learning-oriented hybrid agile approach with a risk-value life cycle and is highly goal driven. It extends Scrum with proven techniques from a wide range of other agile approaches and methods, including the UP and agile modelling. It thinks beyond construction and considers the end-to-end development life cycle, including roadmaps, enterprise architecture, IT governance and DevOps; all from a highly agile mindset. It encourages teams to understand their environment properly and use that knowledge to select the right elements for their approach. In this way it is highly flexible.

Although it does not specify a business analyst role, DA 2.0 relies heavily on sound business analysis skills in the team, particularly for the identification and specification of stories/work items, and in the agile modelling practices.

SAFe

Den Leffingwell's Scaled Agile Framework (SAFe) is based on a number of Lean and agile principles and provides a way to apply them to enterprise software development where there may be many teams, perhaps geographically distributed, building highly complex, integrated systems.

SAFe applies a portfolio approach which ensures alignment with the enterprise strategy. The portfolio backlog is used to drive out programmes of work, each defined through a programme backlog. Each programme may then have several teams which operate as 'normal' Scrum teams with their own team backlog. Integration and delivery are managed through programme increments and iteration goals. One of the key concepts used in SAFe, is the agile release train, which is formed of all the development teams and is focused on a common mission to which all the teams contribute.

There is no business analyst role specified, but there are many elements of SAFe where business analysis skills are needed. For example, when identifying artefacts such as the epics described at the SAFe portfolio level or ensuring that goals are defined that align to business needs. Furthermore, SAFe recommends the Weighted Shortest Job First (WSJF) prioritisation approach (see Chapter 9), which requires the ability to understand and analyse business priorities.

Nexus and LeSS

The Nexus Framework is a means of scaling Scrum such that multiple Scrum teams are able to work together, using a central product backlog and working jointly on the increments for release.

Large Scale Scrum (LeSS) is a framework for scaling Scrum to large product developments. While there are several development teams, they focus on the whole product rather than just the work they produce individually. LeSS uses one instance of the product backlog and there is one product owner across all of the teams. The teams work together in one sprint to deliver a collectively developed product release.

CONCLUSION

Although there are many ways to develop solutions using agile methods, Scrum is the dominant approach, either as a method in its own right or as part of a larger, scaled framework. The software heritage of agile is very obvious within the most popular methods, and, in the main, this has resulted in the lack of recognition of business analysis. DSDM alone identifies the business analyst role as a means of providing a link between the project level and the solution development team. However, the agile values of high customer interaction, achieving business goals and delivering business benefit, are inherent in all of the agile methods and it is important to recognise that the achievement of these values requires business analysis skills.

Whichever agile method is to be adopted, business analysis will be required prior to the initiation of a software development project in order to ensure that the business needs are understood and met. If the project is concerned solely with the development of software, it is probable that business analysis skills will be needed to explore usage and work practice needs, including the often-complex business rules. However, it is likely that a software product alone will not deliver the changes needed by the business and a holistic solution will be required if the business needs are to be met. This will encompass elements such as processes, job roles, organisational structures and people competencies; these elements are natural territories for the business analyst. However, business analysis work in these areas would benefit from the adoption of the agile principles and some of the practices advocated by the methods and frameworks described in this chapter and in this book.

REFERENCES

Poppendieck, M. and Poppendieck, P. (2003) *Lean software development: a toolkit.* Boston, MA: Addison Wesley.

Schwaber, K. and Sutherland, J. (2014) The Scrum Guide™

The Definitive Guide to Scrum:

The Rules of the Game. Available at: www.scrumguides.org/docs/scrumguide/v1/scrum-guide-us.pdf (18 January 2016).

FURTHER READING

Ambler, S., Lines, M. and Vizdos, M. J. (2012) *Disciplined Agile delivery: a practitioner's guide to Agile software in the enterprise.* Upper Saddle River, NJ: IBM Press.

Ambler, S., Nalbone, J. and Vizdos, M. J. (2005) *The enterprise Unified Process: extending the Rational Unified Process.* Upper Saddle River, NJ: Pearson Education Inc.

Anderson, J. and Carmichael, A. (2016) *Essential Kanban: the guide.* Washington, DC: LeanKanban University Press.

Beck, K. (1999) *Extreme programming explained: embrace change.* Boston, MA: Addison Wesley.

Cadle, J. (ed.) (2014) *Developing information systems.* Swindon: BCS.

Cohn, M. (2009) *Succeeding with Agile: software development using Scrum.* Boston, MA: Addison Wesley.

DSDM Today. Available from: www.Agilebusiness.org/content/philosophy-and-fundamentals [7 December 2016].

DSDM Consortium (2008) *DSDM Atern: the handbook.* Available from: www.agilebusiness.org/resources/dsdm-handbooks/dsdm-atern-handbook-2008 (18 January 2017).

Kennaley, M. (2010) *SDLC 3.0: beyond a tacit understanding of Agile: towards the next generation of software engineering.* Fourth Medium Press.

Kruchten, P. (2003) *The Rational Unified Process: an introduction, 3rd edition.* Boston, MA: Addison Wesley.

Larman, C. and Vodde, B. (2016) *Large-scale Scrum: more with less*. Boston, MA: Addison Wesley.

Martin, J. (1991) *Rapid application development introduction*. USA: Macmillan.

Measey, P. (ed.) (2015) *Agile foundations, principles, practices and frameworks*. Swindon: BCS.

Monden, Y. (1998) *Toyota Production System, an integrated approach to just-in-time*, 4th edition. Boca Raton, FL: Productivity Press.

Poppendieck, M. and Poppendieck, P. (2009) *Leading Lean software development: results are not the point*. Boston, MA: Pearson Education Inc.

Schwaber, K. (2004) *Agile project management with Scrum*. Washington, DC: Microsoft Press.

Schwaber, K. (2007) *The enterprise and Scrum*. Washington, DC: Microsoft Press.

Sutherland, J. (2014) *Scrum: the art of doing twice the work in half the time*. New York: Random House Publishers.

USEFUL WEBSITES

www.ambysoft.com/unifiedprocess/agileUP.html

www.disciplinedagiledelivery.com

www.dsdm.org

www.dsdm.org/resources/dsdm-handbooks/the-dsdm-agile-project-framework-2014-onwards

http://epf.eclipse.org/wikis/openup/

www.extremeprogramming.org

www.ibm.com/developerworks/rational/library/content/03July/1000/1251/1251_bestpractices_TP026B.pdf

www.leankanban.com

https://less.works

www.scaledagileframework.com

www.scrum.org/Resources/The-Nexus-Guide

www.scrumguides.org/scrum-guide.html

6 MODELLING THE BUSINESS CONTEXT

This chapter covers the following topics:

- organisational agility;
- using modelling techniques;
- modelling at a business level.

INTRODUCTION

This chapter looks at agile through an organisational lens. As discussed in Chapter 5, the agile methods and frameworks have a software development basis and tradition, and this can lead to two misconceptions:

1. Agile is solely concerned with software development.
2. Agile has no relevance to the delivery of business changes that do not involve software.

However, if you talk to business analysts about the work that they do, fundamental principles such as the need to engage and collaborate with customers, the focus on trying to deliver 'quick wins' and the importance of aligning with business goals come to the fore. Consequently, if we look underneath the roles and activities defined in the agile approaches, we find a lot that aligns with the business analysis world view. Change is a good example. We are constantly reacting to, or even predicting, changes in the business environment – both internal and external. Business analysts know that we need to be alert to these changes and that it is possible to embed adaptability in the new processes, structure and capabilities we recommend. We can add to this: our focus is on understanding the root causes of problems rather than merely addressing symptoms. As stated in Chapter 1, business analysis should be the most agile of the IS disciplines because business analysts help to identify the most relevant solutions, confirm business alignment at every step and make sure that any changes are beneficial for the business.

This chapter explores some of the techniques that contribute to the success of business change projects, the role of the business analyst in conducting this work and the ways in which agile can help to ensure successful outcomes for organisations.

ORGANISATIONAL AGILITY

Organisational agility is evident where a business is able to adapt and respond quickly to internal or external pressures. However, achieving this can be extremely difficult and requires effective analysis at strategic, tactical and operational levels. Business analysis contributes to achieving organisational agility by ensuring that requests for change, or required features, are not accepted at face value; they have to align with the MOST (described in Table 6.1) of the organisation and the critical success factors (CSFs) and key performance indicators (KPIs) that are used to provide direction and evaluate performance.

It is important that business analysts understand the organisational viewpoint, including the business domain, the strategic vision, the tactical goals and the organisational work practices. This contextual understanding helps in the analysis of problems, the recognition of constraints and the identification of relevant options for change. Further, understanding the business context increases awareness of external factors that might impact the organisation. These changes can originate from many sources. Technology changes are often highly visible, but we also need to be aware of more subtle changes such as increasing customer expectations and demographic variations. Competitive actions may also require the organisation to change the way it promotes, sells and packages products and services in order to maintain, or extend, market position.

The tactics required to respond to external factors often need to be considered carefully, taking into account the prevailing business architecture, in particular the organisational capabilities that are available to support or enable change. A capability-based approach can aid agility by providing a basis for reuse and modularisation. For example, if a new product is identified, existing capability may by applied or adapted for the development of the product, removing the need for 'reinventing the wheel'; also, where the business architecture encompasses self-standing components, such as outsourced payment processing, it may be possible to apply this component as part of the new product offering.

Business analysts can support organisational agility by understanding the following:

- the strategic context within which the organisation operates;
- the business architecture blueprint for the organisation;
- the techniques and models that help in the investigation, analysis and definition of business changes;
- the systems, Lean and service thinking approaches (discussed in Chapter 3) that help to ensure a focus on customer needs and efficiency of delivery.

Understanding the business strategy

The business mission and strategy are developed from matching the internal capabilities with the external environment within which the business is operating. Business analysts rarely take responsibility for business environment analysis but may provide information and insights, for example, with regard to opportunities offered by technological changes. More frequently, business analysts help to define the tactical and operational solutions that enable the achievement of the desired business mission, strategy and objectives.

The techniques shown in Table 6.1 are used when undertaking a strategic analysis.

Table 6.1 Strategic analysis techniques

Name of technique	Description
PESTLE analysis	Investigation and analysis of the Political, Economic, Socio-technical, Technological, Legal and Environmental factors within the business environment that is external to an organisation. These factors may provide opportunities for business development or may threaten the success, or even continuation, of an organisation.
Porter's 5-forces	Investigation and analysis of the forces within a designated business domain that may impact upon an organisation. The 5-forces are Strength of competitors, Power of buyers, Power of suppliers, Potential for new entrants and Availability of substitute products. Again, these factors may provide opportunities or may threaten the existence of an organisation.
MOST analysis	The defined direction for an organisation based upon four elements: Mission, Objectives, Strategy and Tactics. The analysis considers the clarity, coherence and communication of the MOST in order to identify where an organisation has strengths and weaknesses.
Resource audit	An examination of five key areas of resource and the level of capability they may provide the organisation when addressing factors in the external environment. There are three tangible areas: Physical, Financial and Human Resources. There are two intangible areas: Reputation/goodwill and Use of internal knowledge and information.
SWOT analysis	A summary of the strengths and weaknesses (internal factors) and opportunities and threats (external factors) that have the potential to impact upon the organisation

The internal and external business environments do not remain static and, therefore, the organisation has to review them on a regular basis to ensure that a significant opportunity or threat is not missed. This also provides a means of reviewing internal strengths and weaknesses in order to identify where additional investment is required to build the required organisational capabilities. Therefore, strategy review is an iterative process, as shown in Figure 6.1 below. The MOST is defined to provide direction for the organisation, setting out the desired outcomes and the means of achieving them. However, this only persists as long as it continues to align with the forces evident within the business environment. Where there are changes, whether internal or external, these are summarised in a SWOT analysis and this is used to review and revise the MOST.

Figure 6.1 The iterative nature of business environment and strategy analysis

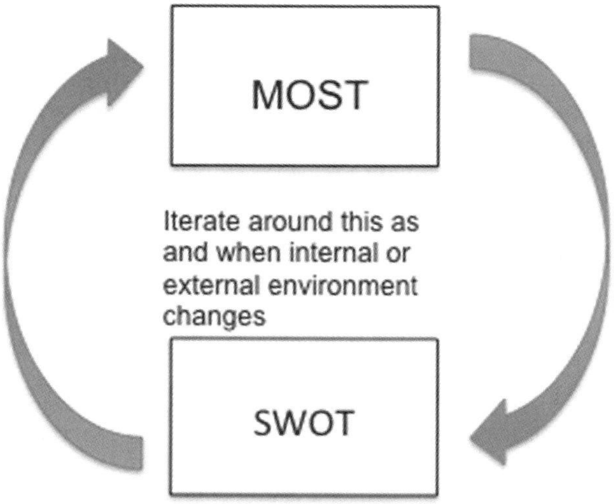

Business analysis is concerned with the definition of the tactics and operational working practices that are required to execute the strategy. These tactics and working practices will need to align with, and may be enabled by, the business architecture as discussed earlier. Business analysts have highlighted the need for early analysis of change initiatives for many years. They have been keenly aware of the dangers of pursuing projects where a considered evaluation of drivers, objectives and options has not been undertaken. This work can avoid unnecessary investment – and wasted funds – and ensure that the most relevant solution is selected. Applying business analysis at this early stage supports strategy execution and organisational agility and helps to ensure that only work that benefits the organisation is embarked upon.

Understanding the business architecture

An agile business analyst should help to ensure that there is alignment with the organisation's strategic context and business architecture. Two of the key artefacts used in business architecture are particularly relevant to the work of an agile business analyst. These artefacts represent the value streams and the business capabilities of the organisation.

Value stream	The value stream provides an overarching view of the key activities required to work together in order for the value proposition to be delivered to a particular customer group.
Business capability map	The business capability map sets out the areas of capability that the organisation needs to possess in order to be able to conduct the work of the value stream activities.

81

Value streams and capabilities provide business analysts with a contextual view for their work on change projects and may support or drive new initiatives. For example, where a required capability is identified but is not available within the organisation, a change project may be initiated to develop the capability. Given that a capability is a repository of the skills, information, work practices, technology and communication channels that are required to deliver an aspect of organisational performance, this project would need to consider changes to multiple elements of the business system so will require a holistic view. An agile mindset and approach will help to ensure that the project goals are prioritised and, where possible, there is early delivery of the changes required to develop the capability.

Understanding the business system

Business analysts take a holistic view of the organisation and the business systems that operate within it. This view is essential if an agile software development project is to deliver business benefits and important factors are not overlooked. The POPIT™ model (see Chapter 3) is one of the key business analysis techniques used to take a holistic view of a business system. POPIT™ provides a framework for analysing problems inherent in a business situation and for identifying the impact of potential solutions. The use of the POPIT™ model in this context will support organisational agility by helping to identify where reuse is possible and where there are gaps that will need to be addressed.

USING MODELLING TECHNIQUES

Models provide a diagrammatical representation of a particular view of a situation and help analysts to understand a complex problem or describe a real-life subject or system. Modelling is a proven and well-accepted technique that has been used within business and engineering for many years. Models are simplifications of reality, built so that we can better understand the problem we are addressing. Different models provide different perspectives on the problem and can be used at different levels within a business. For example, one model may provide a strategic view of the business while another may be a visualisation of a user interface for an IT system.

Benefits of modelling

Modelling offers two main advantages: first, the act of modelling provides an effective basis for discussion and collaboration; second, the resultant model provides an effective medium for communication of information. Models may be used at different levels of abstraction to represent different aspects of the business, which can also aid the communication process.

Exploring this further, we can identify several benefits of using models:

- to aid communication amongst stakeholders;
- to provide a basis for rigorous analysis;
- to provide a standardised approach to analysis and documentation;
- to reduce ambiguity;
- to enable opportunities for reuse;

- to provide a means of decomposing different levels in a hierarchy;
- to understand or reduce risks.

Models are used in many disciplines. For example, business analysts build models to explore the business problems that need to be addressed; engineers build models to test design possibilities; and architects use models to provide a physical representation of an enterprise, technical infrastructure or building.

Many models provide a basis for discussion and collaboration because they remove the need for pages and pages of text, and offer a clear representation of a particular view of a business system. For example, a business process model has a limited notation set that enables business analysts to depict how the work is conducted in an accessible way. Similarly, a data model may be used to provide a diagrammatic representation of data requirements and will cause business analysts to question aspects such as information needs, business rules and deletion strategies.

Deciding the modelling approach

It is helpful to use models irrespective of the approach to be used on the project. In an agile environment, models may be created that are hand-drawn rather than produced using software tools. The informality of this approach helps engender collaboration and agreement between analysts and other stakeholders. Figure 6.2 shows a hand-drawn, high-level business model for a training company booking system. This figure demonstrates the use of a rich picture to represent a business situation.

Figure 6.2 Informal model of a business situation

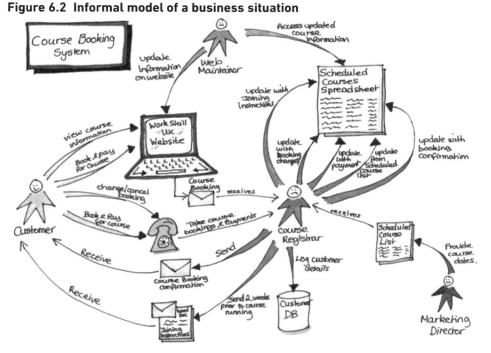

The majority of formal modelling techniques show just one aspect of a situation, such as a process or data view. However, this model provides a holistic view, showing the processes, people, documents and IT systems involved in the business system. Ultimately, it is important to use models advisedly, taking into consideration the following:

- Who is the model for?
- What does it need to represent?
- Who is going to use it, why and when?
- Does it need to be kept and updated or is it only required for temporary use (a throwaway model)?

These questions help analysts to decide whether an informal or formal model would be preferable and the type of model, or models, that would provide the most useful representation of the situation. For example, where a model needs to be used throughout the duration of the project, it is a good idea to ensure that it is created such that it can be accessed and updated easily. A model requiring only short-term use may be drawn informally and then discarded. Another factor to consider is that models are likely to change over time, particularly those concerned with display and processing, and ensuring that models are up to date can be very time consuming. Some key principles for using models when conducting agile business analysis are as follows:

- **Envisioning:** using models during the Inception or pre-project phase, to collaborate with stakeholders in order to understand the vision and focus for a project.
- **Engaging stakeholders:** using models to encourage collaboration and gain additional insights and buy-in.
- **Just good enough:** ensuring that models are sufficient for the work in hand, no more and no less.
- **Prioritisation:** using models to understand priorities and goals, and as a basis for decomposition.
- **Iterative modelling:** elaborating models only when needed by the project.
- **Just in time modelling:** producing or elaborating models when they are required in order to avoid them becoming out of date and, as a consequence, having to waste time on unnecessary maintenance and revision.

The Functional Model Map

In the BCS publication *Developing information systems – practical guidance for IT professionals* (Cadle 2014), Julian Cox uses a Functional Model Map (FMM) to explore different levels of abstraction across a change project. The FMM is shown in Figure 6.3 below and identifies the focus of the modelling tasks, from the summary level business system requirements through to low-level technical design and realisation.

The FMM shows three perspectives (applied from Cockburn (2000)) to be modelled as described in Table 6.2 below.

Figure 6.3 The FMM

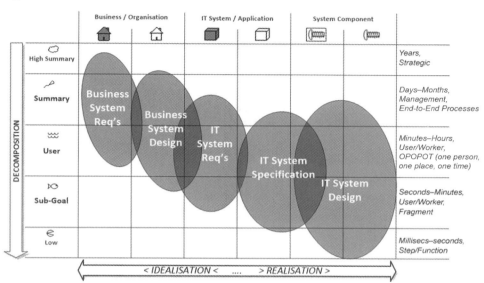

Table 6.2 Three perspectives of the FMM

Business/organisation	The business or organisational system and the value it is proposing to its customers. This includes its manual and IT elements as well as value streams.
IT system/application	The software application.
Component	An architectural element required as a building block of the system.

For each perspective, the modelling may adopt a black or white box approach, as follows:

- **Black box:** a view of a system or element where we are concerned with the exterior view rather than the inner workings. A context diagram is a good example of a black box view.

- **White box:** a view of a system or element where we wish to represent the internal working. A use case diagram is a good example of a white box view.

The FMM moves across the three perspectives at increasing levels of granularity. Cox has used Alistair Cockburn's (2000) icons to represent the different levels and goals. The goals will be different at an organisational level from a system level and understanding this will help the analyst to recognise where a particular model is relevant and the level of definition and detail required.

Cockburn expresses these goals as shown in Table 6.3 below.

Table 6.3 Cockburn's levels of goal

 High level summary (cloud).

 Summary goal (kite level): for example, a goal for an end to end business process.

 User goal (sea level): equivalent to a task performed by a single person/application.

 Sub-goal (fish level): not a goal in its own right – only decomposed if it is to be reused within several other user goals.

 Low (clam level): lines of code – not suitable for modelling.

At each level, and in each area, different models can be applied. Not all boxes need to have a model, as in some situations it may be decided that models will not serve any useful purpose. The value of the FMM is that it provides a helpful vehicle for agreeing on the overall approach; in particular, where and why models need to be produced to meet a particular business problem or serve as instruments for collaboration with a particular stakeholder or stakeholder group.

We have simplified this model to make it easier to understand from the business model-ling perspective. The adapted model is shown in Figure 6.4 and is called the **Simplified FMM.**

MODELLING AT A BUSINESS LEVEL

There are many techniques that can be used to model the business situation, each of which offers particular insights and viewpoints. The following techniques are often useful when modelling a business system at Cockburn's three highest levels of abstrac-tion shown in the FMM above:

- **summary level, cloud:** business process map (based on a value stream or value chain); business activity model;
- **summary level, kite:** business process model; business use case diagram; business epic; context diagram;
- **user level:** system use case diagram and description; user story; persona.

Figure 6.4 The Simplified FMM

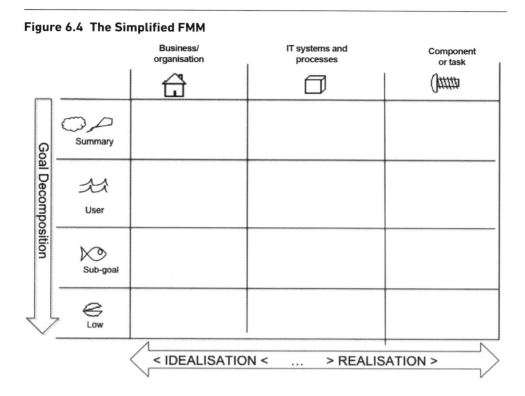

These techniques have much to offer business analysts when working within an agile environment. The summary-level diagrams provide a contextual view for the business changes proposed and help the identification of options and impact analysis. They can also support prioritisation and the identification of business goals. Once a project is underway and there are teams working on the detail of the changes to be delivered (which is likely to encompass several of the POPIT™ elements), these models help to provide a cross-programme view, which is essential for an incremental delivery approach as it highlights links and dependencies.

The summary-level techniques are described below; the user-level techniques are discussed in Chapters 11 and 12.

Business process map

A business process map provides a high-level view of the process areas that need to work collectively in order to deliver a particular service to a customer. Porter's (1985) value chain, particularly the primary activities, can be helpful in creating this diagram as it provides a framework for thinking about the different processes. The primary activities of the value chain for a training service are reflected in Figure 6.5 below.

Figure 6.5 Value chain for training service

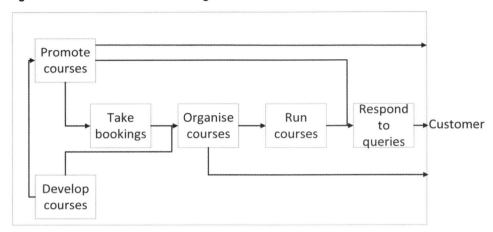

The generic primary activities are mapped to the value chain in Figure 6.5 as follows:

- **inbound logistics:** develop courses; take bookings;
- **operations:** organise courses;
- **outbound logistics:** run courses;
- **marketing and sales:** promote courses;
- **service:** respond to queries.

This diagram can be very useful during feasibility or pre-project analysis, as it provides a context for thinking about process and system improvements and helps to determine where there are inefficient and ineffective areas of process.

An alternative approach is the value stream diagram proposed by Womack and Jones (2003). This provides a view of the steps required to produce a product or deliver a service. The value stream may be created at different levels of abstraction, depending upon the particular situation. It is also possible to model different 'streams', such as the physical product development or the information flow. The focus of the value stream is on identifying where value is added in the process and highlighting where there is waste (in line with the '8 wastes' of Lean as defined in Chapter 3).

Business activity models

A business activity model (BAM) provides a conceptual view of a business system as perceived by a stakeholder or group of stakeholders. It is an informal diagram that shows the key areas of activity for a business system and helps in the identification of gaps or inefficiencies. Five types of activity are modelled: planning, enabling, doing, monitoring and controlling. The BAM shown in Figure 6.6 provides a conceptual overview of a business system where the perspective focuses on the delivery of training courses.

Figure 6.6 BAM of a training business system

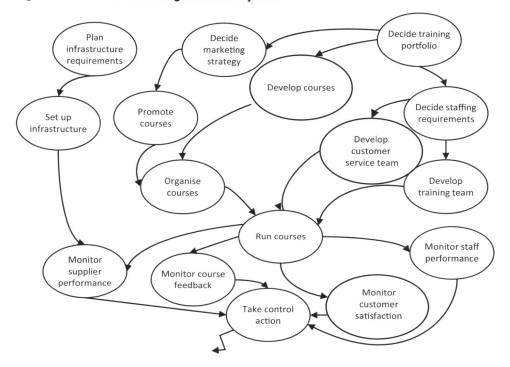

Underlying this model are also performance measures such as CSFs and KPIs, which are decided within the planning activities (such as 'Plan infrastructure requirements' and 'Decide marketing strategy') and reviewed within the monitoring activities (such as 'Monitor course feedback'). The enabling activities (such as 'Promote courses' and 'Develop courses') ensure that the resources required to operate the business system are in place. The doing activities ('Organise courses' and 'Run courses') represent the primary task of the business system.

Business process models

A business process model, often known as a swim lane diagram, shows the response of an organisation to a business event in terms of the actors and the tasks they conduct. The triggering event is also shown on the diagram, as is the final output or outcome. Two key variants are the 'as is' model, which represents an existing process and the 'to be' model of the redesigned process. This technique is particularly useful in identifying clearly where there are bottlenecks and duplication.

A business process model related to the process map above is shown in Figure 6.7.

This business process model provides the response to the business event 'Training service request received', which is part of the Develop courses activity on the business

Figure 6.7 Business process model for bespoke course development

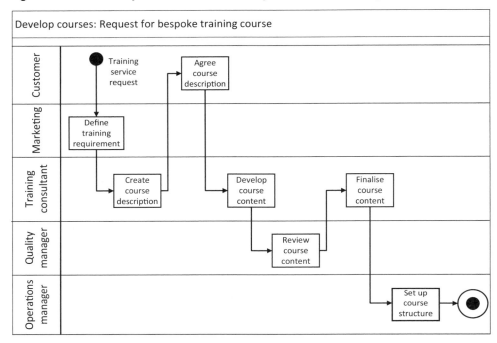

process map. Understanding the events encapsulated within the process map, and identifying which ones are particularly relevant and the associated level of priority, enables the business analyst to explore where there are inefficiencies or wastes and where changes are needed. Where process changes are to be made, the 'to be' business process model also sets out the design of the process and the context for the more detailed developments necessary for its deployment.

Business use case models

A business use case diagram represents the work of the business system within the context of its business environment. The elements represented are **who** interacts with the business system, such as partners, suppliers and customers, and **what** should be done as a result of those interactions. A business use case diagram can be used to model an entire organisation, but it is more typical to model a business system that conducts part of the work of the organisation. The business use case diagram does not distinguish between manual or automated interactions or identify whether they are carried out by people or by IT systems – or by a combination of both. Its focus is on representing features that make up the business system, leaving consideration of 'how' they are achieved to be discussed and analysed separately. Business use case diagrams are highly effective when conducting the initial analysis of a business system; they provide a clear standard for representing the following aspects:

Boundary	The boundary of the system of interest. This could be the organisation itself, or it could be a business system within the organisation. This clarifies what is in scope and what is out of scope for a change project.
Business actors	The actors that wish to interact with the business system. Actors require the business features to be offered and the business goals to be achieved. They may be user roles or other systems.
Business use case	Each business use case will be of interest to at least one business actor and will be triggered by a business event. A business use case represents a business feature with a corresponding goal that is to be achieved by the business. This will attract a level of priority within a change project, depending upon the relative importance of the business goal. Priorities may vary amongst the business use cases for a particular system under consideration.

A business use case diagram provides an overview of the required features of a business system. A more specific view is obtained by decomposing elements of the diagram, such as the actors and business use cases. This will require the decomposition of the business goals and the corresponding priorities. Goal decomposition is discussed in Chapter 8 and prioritisation is covered in Chapter 9. The goal for each business use case should support the achievement of the organisation's CSFs and KPIs. A goal can be achieved in many ways, such as by introducing new business processes, a revised organisational structure or enhanced IT systems – or by a combination of these changes.

A business use case diagram may provide the basis for deriving a system use case. For example, it is possible that an aspect (or sub-goal) within a business use case may be delivered by an IT system. In this case, a system use case representing the feature required to achieve the sub-goal may be derived. A business use case diagram is at a high level of abstraction and reflects general business requirements (see Chapter 10), therefore it does not represent detailed functional requirements. Techniques for investigating and analysing these requirements are discussed in Chapters 11 and 12.

When working within an agile environment, a business use case diagram may be used both during the pre-project analysis phase and when taking a change programme view. The minimal notation set is easily accessible and helps to provide an effective basis for collaborating with stakeholders when agreeing the scope and the business features to be addressed. Therefore, it is the starting point from which further work may be agreed and prioritised.

Business use case diagrams are drawn using the standard UML notation. An extended version of this notation, which builds upon the UML standard, is available to support modelling use cases at a business level. This version distinguishes business from system use case diagrams by placing a diagonal line across the business actor and business use case icons. This notation is shown in Figure 6.8 below.

The actors who are external to the business system are represented in a business use case diagram. A business use case may be explored in further detail by analysing the scenarios leading to the achievement of the decomposed goals. An alternative approach

Figure 6.8 Business use case model

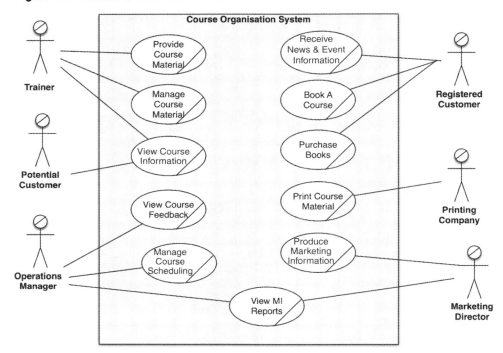

is to use business process models (swim lane diagrams) to analyse the work required to achieve the business use case goal.

Business epics

A business epic is based upon the user story technique (see Chapter 12) and provides a business level of abstraction. Business epics can be used to understand business goals and features from an actor's perspective. To this end the business epic, much like the business use case, sets out a feature the business system needs to offer at an overview level. A set of business epics for the 'Course Organisation System' is shown in Figure 6.9.

Each business epic is likely to encompass a broad area of functionality, so will require decomposition in order to ascertain how the overall goal might be achieved and whether the business epic is feasible. The example shown in Figure 6.10 is of a business epic and reflects the high level of abstraction and the need to explore the requirement in further detail. The template used in Figure 6.10 would provide a basis for capturing key information about a business epic. The business justification, impact and affected areas help to determine the overall priority of the business epic.

Figure 6.9 Example of business epics

As a... Registered Customer
I want to... Book a course
I want to... purchase books
I want to... receive news and event info
As a ...Potential Customer
I want to... view course information
As a... Trainer
I want to... manage course material
I want to... produce course material
As a ... Marketing Director
I want to... produce marketing material
I want to... view MI reports
As an... Ops Manager
I want to... view MI reports
I want to... manage course scheduling
I want to view course feedback
As a ...Printing Company
I want to... print course materials

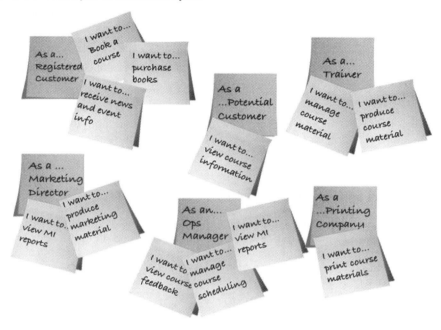

Figure 6.10 Template for a business epic card

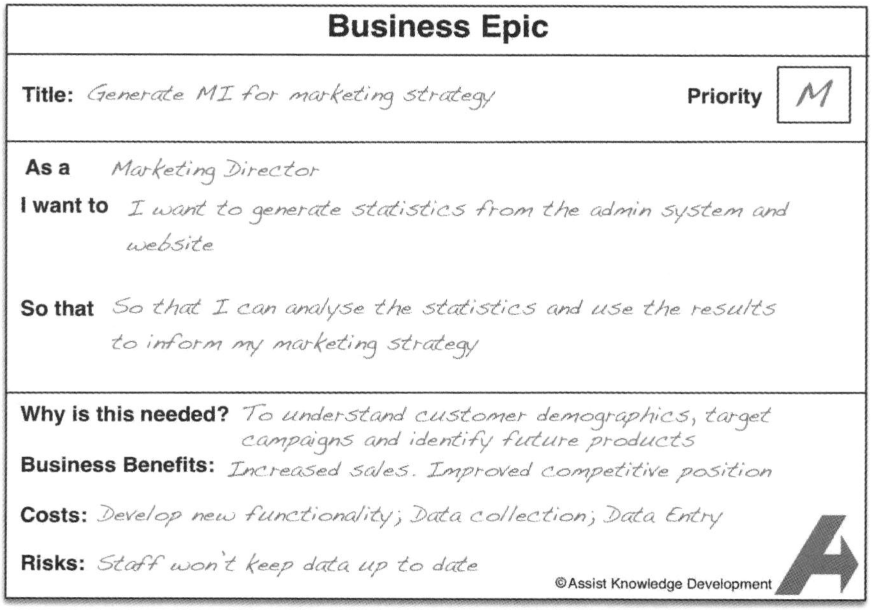

Business Epic
Title: Generate MI for marketing strategy
Priority M
As a Marketing Director
I want to I want to generate statistics from the admin system and website
So that So that I can analyse the statistics and use the results to inform my marketing strategy
Why is this needed? To understand customer demographics, target campaigns and identify future products
Business Benefits: Increased sales. Improved competitive position
Costs: Develop new functionality; Data collection; Data Entry
Risks: Staff won't keep data up to date
©Assist Knowledge Development

Combining business use cases and business epics

When developing business epics, it is useful to map them to an overview picture to provide context and a visualisation of the suite of business epics. Without careful management, business epics can become disassociated from the wider context. It is possible to avoid this by recording them on a white board or by creating an organised set using sticky notes and a board or flip chart. Another approach is to map the business use case diagram to the business epics, as this marries the holistic view with the specific actor requirements and business goals.

In practice, business use case diagrams and business epics are both useful techniques that can easily sit alongside one another. They address different perspectives of the business system and when used together help to provide a coherent view that is accessible to the business users.

Modelling in an agile context

Why is it important to use different models to demonstrate the various system perspectives and levels when using agile? As mentioned earlier, modelling provides a visual means of representing ideas and requirements, so it encourages collaboration and improves communication. Models can also be used in both a formal and informal way: formal, if they are needed to document an aspect of the change project that needs to be recorded – a good example of this is 'to be' business process models, which typically provide recorded designs for a process; informal, if they are needed for communication and exploration purposes – a BAM is a good example of a technique that is typically used in this way. Whichever models are used, they help the analyst to clarify the desired outcomes, support prioritisation and better understand the problem to be addressed.

It is important that agile business analysts recognise the need to avoid over-engineering models. There can be a temptation to analyse aspects that are not relevant to the work in hand, resulting in models that are extensive and include unnecessary detail. When applying the tenets of agile business analysis, we need to focus on **'just enough'** modelling, ensuring that we support the needs of the project at the time and no more. With this approach in mind, there is the potential for modelling to be highly effective in an agile project context.

CONCLUSION

Models provide an excellent means of understanding the organisational context, gaining insights into business needs, facilitating a common understanding and collaborating with stakeholders. They can be helpful when making decisions about the prioritisation of the features to be delivered by the business system.

It is possible to create models at several levels of abstraction, including a 'cloud' level and a system interaction level. However, they have to be used when relevant or the time spent creating them will be wasted. Agile business analysts should have a range of modelling techniques in their professional toolkit that they are able to deploy when the situation demands.

REFERENCES

Cadle, J. (ed.) (2014) *Developing information systems – practical guidance for IT professionals.* Swindon: BCS.

Cockburn, A. (2000) *Writing effective use cases: the Agile software development series.* Boston, MA: Addison Wesley.

Porter, M.E. (1985) *Competitive advantage: creating and sustaining superior performance.* New York: Free Press.

Womack, J.P. and Jones, D.T. (2003) *Lean thinking.* London: Simon and Schuster.

FURTHER READING

Ambler, S. (2002) *Agile modeling: effective practices for eXtreme programming and the Unified Process.* New York: John Wiley & Sons.

Ambler, S. and Lines, M. (2012) *Disciplined Agile delivery: a practitioner's guide to Agile software in the enterprise.* Upper Saddle River, NJ: IBM Press.

Cadle, J., Paul, D. and Turner, P. (2014) *Business analysis techniques.* Swindon: BCS.

Checkland, P. (1981) *Systems thinking, systems practice.* Chichester: John Wiley & Sons.

Harmon, P. (2014) *Business process change: a manager's guide to improving, redesigning and automating processes.* Burlington, MA: Morgan Kaufmann.

OMG (n.d.) UML Resource Page. Object Modelling Group. Available from: www.uml.org/ [7 December 2016].

Paul, D., Cadle, J. and Yeates, D. (2014) *Business analysis: 3rd edition.* Swindon: BCS.

7 WORKING WITH STAKEHOLDERS AND ROLES

This chapter covers the following topics:

- the nature of stakeholders;
- the multi-skilled team: the T-shaped professional; the generalising specialist;
- customer categories;
- stakeholder engagement;
- stakeholder categories, roles and perspectives.

INTRODUCTION

Effective business analysis requires ongoing engagement with stakeholders across a range of roles and disciplines. This requirement is likely to apply irrespective of the characteristics of the project and the approach to be taken to the work. However, the adoption of agile places particular demands upon both analysts and stakeholders because of the collaborative and iterative approach to the development and delivery of solutions. In this chapter we discuss the different categories of stakeholders and explore the engagement between the business analyst, stakeholders and customers. In addition, we introduce the concept of the T-shaped professional.

THE NATURE OF STAKEHOLDERS

Working with key stakeholders such as customers and understanding the roles they play is always an important aspect of any change project. These stakeholders are likely to be directly affected by new ways of working and will often have a detailed understanding of existing work practices and inherent problems. There are also stakeholders who may not be directly affected by any business changes but are involved in developing the changes or have to be consulted about them. These stakeholders often hold roles with responsibility for areas such as project governance or enterprise architecture, and may have different perspectives that will impact upon the project. Whichever the case, any business analyst working in an agile environment needs to be aware of the different groups of stakeholders and how they should be engaged with. There are three key groups to consider.

- The customers who will need to work closely with the project team to collaborate on the development of the solution. These stakeholders will need to understand the agile philosophy and principles and the agile work practices to be adopted, providing the required support to customers is likely to fall within the remit of the business analyst role. There are several categories of customer that are explored in detail later in this chapter.

- The stakeholders who are not the direct recipients of the solution but need to be consulted or informed about various elements. Again, there may be a need to support these stakeholders, particularly if they have not worked within an agile environment·previously.

- The stakeholders who will form part of the project team. Business analysts will work closely and collaboratively with these project colleagues.

Collaborative working

The *Oxford English Dictionary* defines the term 'collaborate' as: 'work jointly on an activity or project'. Collaborative working is a fundamental principle of the agile philosophy. However, in an agile work environment collaboration is not just about working jointly with stakeholders, it is about working towards a common goal, negotiating the conflicts that inevitably arise and achieving consensus. Constant, ongoing collaboration is to be expected as a means of ensuring that business needs are understood and incremental solutions are delivered early. Business analysts need to recognise that this approach changes the dynamic of working relationships and places additional responsibilities on analysts, project team members and other stakeholders. For example, when using a traditional linear approach it would usually be the case that customers would be invited to a workshop or an appointment would be made for an interview; when using agile, customers may need to work within the project team rather than just providing their input on request.

The business analysis skill set includes a range of interpersonal skills, such as communication facilitation and rapport building, which are invaluable for collaborating with stakeholders. Further, the holistic nature of the work encourages business analysts to have a broad skill set that includes an understanding of business and the business domain, each of which will aid the collaboration process. These skills enable business analysts to work well with stakeholders and communicate with both the business and technical representatives. While this is important for the success of any change project, it is essential on an agile project where documentation is minimised and effective communication is imperative.

Working with stakeholders

Communication and business skills are even more important where stakeholders are geographically dispersed. Many organisations operate across different countries and cultures, and, therefore, their business analysts need to be able to communicate within environments where there are constraints caused by different languages, time zones and technology. Such constraints require careful consideration and planning if they are to be managed within an agile context.

A common error is to consider a stakeholder as someone who can be slotted neatly into a job title or role and let this determine the engagement and communication approach. This overlooks the critical point that each stakeholder is an individual with their own ideas, constraints, priorities and needs. So, when working with stakeholders, business analysts need to apply an analytical approach and consider the following:

- Do we need to work with this stakeholder as an individual or as part of a group?
- How closely do we need to work with this stakeholder?
- What level of information does this stakeholder need or can this stakeholder provide?
- What perspective does this stakeholder have on this project?

Consideration of these points will help to ensure that there will be effective working relationships with stakeholders of varying levels of seniority and with differing communication needs. The last point about understanding perspectives is particularly important. This often relates to the role and responsibilities of the stakeholder. For example, if someone is responsible for the regulatory compliance of the solution, this is where they will focus their efforts and feel the priorities lie. The range of stakeholder roles and responsibilities is described later in this chapter.

On projects using more traditional approaches, obtaining access to stakeholders is often an area of difficulty. Agile projects place responsibilities on both the organisation and the stakeholders, including requiring significant access to those working within the project team. It is also the case that the stakeholders will need to have an appreciation of the agile philosophy and the impact this will have on the working practices undertaken by projects. Successful application of agile may require business analysts to provide guidance, or even training, in the adoption of an agile mindset and approach.

Business analysis on agile projects

The types of business problems being solved by agile project teams today are not significantly different to the types of business problems that have been solved by teams using more traditional approaches. Since those teams rely heavily on sound business analysis skills to achieve success, it should be evident that agile teams also need these skills. This is especially true when agile approaches are being applied to complex, novel or high-risk change projects or projects with large amounts of user interaction.

One problem facing business analysts (and an important reason for this book) is that the value of business analysis is not as widely recognised as it should be, and many agile training courses, books, blogs and methods appear to ignore business analysis. Dig a little deeper, however, and it becomes clear that this is not always the case. Scrum is by far the most common agile method, and the Scrum Alliance (2016) guide states:

> Scrum recognizes no sub-teams in the development team, regardless of particular domains that need to be addressed like testing or business analysis.

What this means is that business analysis needs to be addressed, but this doesn't mean there must be a dedicated business analyst on the team. This is true of many published methods – just because there isn't a dedicated role for a business analyst does not mean that business analysis skills are not needed.

In some circumstances, it may be possible for the development team to assume responsibility for business analysis, as may be the case with other specialist work. So, business analysts may be able to support areas of testing and testing specialists may be able to help with some analysis. However, there are risks associated with this approach that may result in conflicts and a failure to explore the business needs in sufficient detail. Also, the individuals performing these roles may not have the time or expertise required to understand the root causes of problems or to explore the rationale for requirements, resulting in time spent on ill-conceived ideas.

While agile recommends the formation of self-organising, multi-skilled project teams, this needs to be done with care. Where roles attempt to encompass specialisms such as business analysis and assume that specialist expertise is never required, they can become single points of failure and cause difficulties in the longer term. The concept of the T-shaped professional, discussed in the next section, can help to clarify the need for IS professionals to have both generic and specialist skills, including the interpersonal skills required to work effectively with stakeholders.

Given the importance agile attaches to strong and constant customer engagement, and a **Just Enough, Just in Time** approach to the project deliverables (including the requirements definition and acceptance criteria), the skills of a business analyst are critical for successful agile projects.

THE MULTI-SKILLED TEAM

The concept of the self-organising team was introduced in Chapter 4. Achieving a team that can self-organise, however, requires team members to be multi-skilled and we explore the multi-skilled team further here.

The T-shaped professional

Service Science theory underpins the service thinking approach (discussed in Chapter 3) and has popularised a concept known as the T-shaped professional. This term refers to professionals who have a suite of generic skills that supplement and enhance the specific skills required of their particular profession. The definition of a T-shaped professional from the *Handbook of Service Science* (Spohrer and Maglio, 2010) is as follows.

> Those who are deep problem solvers with expert thinking skills in their home discipline but also have complex communication skills to interact with specialists from a wide range of disciplines and functional areas.

An example of a T-shaped professional profile for a business analyst is shown in Figure 7.1 below.

Figure 7.1 The T-shaped BA professional

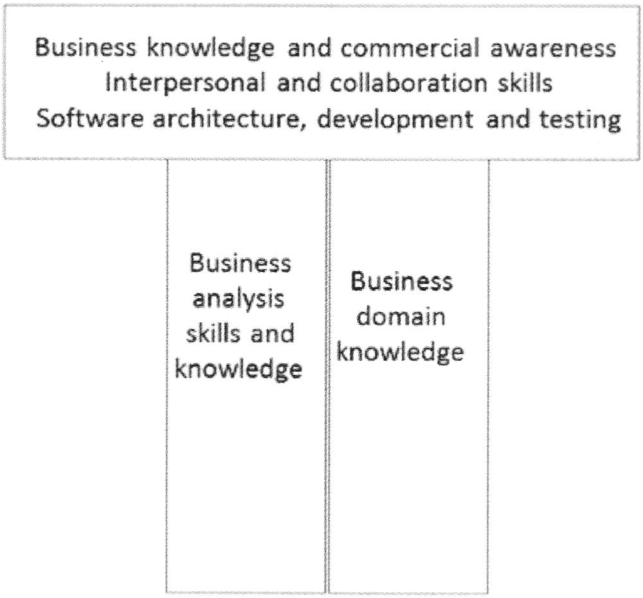

Business knowledge and commercial awareness
Interpersonal and collaboration skills
Software architecture, development and testing

Business analysis skills and knowledge

Business domain knowledge

Source: Spohrer and Maglio (2010)

The vertical and horizontal components of this model focus on the following aspects:

- The vertical depth, or specialism, is a combination of skill and experience of the broad range of business analysis practices and techniques coupled with the experience of applying them in one or more business contexts or sectors.

- The horizontal breadth is the understanding of, and ability to contribute to, specialist tasks in other disciplines coupled with cross-disciplinary interpersonal skills and generic business knowledge.

The horizontal skills

Business analysts require competence in three key areas – business, personal and technical skills – if they are to be T-shaped professionals and contribute effectively across a range of change projects. They require generalist business skills and knowledge in order to be able to communicate effectively with stakeholders from different external and internal constituencies; this includes a broad commercial awareness. They also need strong interpersonal skills to ensure that they engage with stakeholders and members of the project team. Effective collaboration requires this mix of professional and interpersonal skills.

A good understanding of the business change and solution development processes, including more technical domains such as data management, application architecture and software testing, is also necessary, for business analysts to contribute effectively when working in cross-functional agile teams.

The vertical skills

Whereas the generalist skills above are held by many IS professionals, business analysts also need to possess the specialist skills that enable them to investigate ideas and problems, and identify and help to evaluate potential solutions.

Business analysis is a specialist discipline, so business analysts need to develop and maintain an extensive professional toolkit containing many analytical techniques and frameworks. In addition to the analytical skills, business analysts also need to have an in-depth understanding of the business domain within which they work. This includes knowledge of the terminology, concepts and particular concerns of the business domain. For example, business analysts may require knowledge of relevant governance structures, or legal and regulatory matters.

Specifically for an agile business analyst, the core skills also need to include the understanding of, and the ability to apply, the agile principles and values across business analysis activities. When working on an agile project, business analysts need to have generic and specific agile skills as follows:

- **Generic:** an understanding of the agile development process and the range of techniques that may be adopted when developing software using an agile approach.
- **Specific:** expertise in applying agile techniques such as user stories, prioritisation, prototyping, user roles and personas.

The T-shaped professional concept is highly relevant to today's business world where collaborative working helps to break down traditional barriers and apply a cross-functional view of the organisation. This has been assisted by the use of thinking frameworks such as service thinking (Chapter 3). An agile mindset, coupled with a T-shaped toolkit, will help business analysts to work successfully on agile change projects and, ultimately, support organisational agility.

The generalising specialist

The concept of an agile team formed of 'generalizing specialists' was developed by Scott Ambler and Mark Lines (2012); and has many similarities to the T-shaped professional concept. The definition, below – provided by Ambler and Lines – states that a generalising specialist is someone who has multiple skills.

1. Has one or more technical specialties (e.g. Java programming, Project Management, Database Administration, etc.).
2. Has at least a general knowledge of software development.
3. Has at least a general knowledge of the business domain in which they work.
4. Actively seeks to gain new skills in both their existing specialties as well as in other areas, including both technical and domain areas. (http://agilemodeling.com/essays/generalizingSpecialists.htm#Definition)

Ambler and Lines (2012) suggest that an agile development team should be formed of multi-skilled professionals. Team members should possess a cross-functional understanding of the entire solution development process, enabling them to work successfully with colleagues across the different specialist domains. They should also have at least one, but possibly more, specialist area of competence. While the detailed investigation and analysis work will be, in the main, the responsibility of the business analysts, there may be occasions when other team members are required to conduct business analysis; for example, when working alongside the business users to develop some software functionality or define business rules. There may also be business analysts working within the agile team who can perform other tasks such as supporting testing activity.

This approach helps to remove the strict role delineations that are often found during solution development and can diminish the occurrence of hand-offs and delays. Hand-offs may occur when a requirements expert hands over the completed requirements to the developer for coding, or the developer hands over the code to the tester for testing and so forth. This approach can result in a 'silo' mentality, whereby individuals focus on their part of the process and work towards their own personal targets; or work on low priority tasks in their own specialism despite other, high priority tasks in another specialism being incomplete. Unfortunately, this can also mean that accountability for the finished product inevitably gets lost while the team is working towards delivery. The formation of agile teams from generalising specialists is a means of overcoming this issue and enabling greater collaboration.

Adopting this approach enables agile development teams to provide the skills and experience required to develop the solution in a collaborative way. While each team member will not have a full range of the required skills, and is likely to specialise in a specific area, it does mean that they will have a sufficient grasp of other disciplines. This will improve communication, ensure that the team is better able to complete the high priority work, and enable everyone to make contributions during the development of the solution.

The business analyst in a multi-skilled team

Business analysts are well placed to work in a generalised environment because of the breadth of the role and the range of skills and knowledge they are expected to possess. When working within a relatively small project team, it is often the case that a business analyst is expected to take on an additional area of responsibility such as project management or business acceptance testing. Some business analysts may be required to review code or database structures. Similarly, other types of specialist may attend business analysis training and undertake some business analysis tasks, perhaps under the supervision or guidance of a more experienced analyst.

Figure 7.2 shows how the two concepts of the T-shaped professional and the generalising specialist may be combined to define the skill requirements of some specialists. These examples identify the types of skills and experience three different T-shaped professionals in an agile development team may need to have.

Many business analysts began their careers working in technical disciplines; this has enabled them to develop into T-shaped BA professionals. Where this is the case,

Figure 7.2 Example of different types of T-shaped professionals in a development team

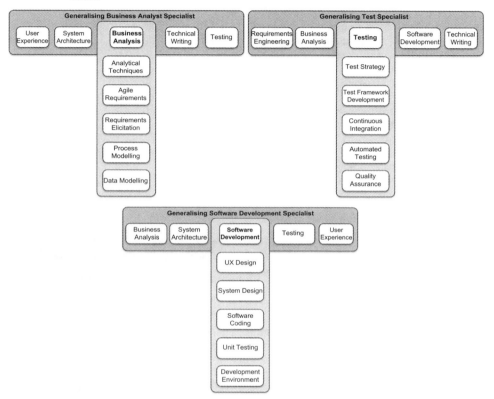

individual business analysts may have the ability to support the work of other disciplines, thereby contributing to the agility of both the development team and the organisation.

CUSTOMER CATEGORIES

It is often the case that the term 'customer' is used to refer to anyone who is the recipient or beneficiary of a new product or service. However, grouping customers together in this way risks overlooking different perspectives and priorities. As a result, it is important that we do not categorise customers as one group but understand the range of different customer roles, each of which has the potential to hold different perspectives and have varying business requirements. Agile techniques such as user stories and personas (see Chapter 11) help us to consider a situation from the viewpoint of a given role. Where this is a customer role, understanding the customer categories can provide insights into the different needs that are likely to exist.

Within an agile development environment, business analysts may work with many different types of customer and need to appreciate where their requirements might differ.

Although some customers, such as business managers, may be relatively straightforward to identify, it is possible to overlook others. For example, project stakeholders such as solution developers or technical architects should be perceived as customers because they consume some of the artefacts delivered from the business analysis work, and can have specific needs that the project should meet (for example, training). Also, the term 'end user' may cover a range of different types of business customer, each of which might have differing needs to be met.

Throughout a project, we need to look at the standard roles and consider where a customer/supplier relationship exists and where we need to take into account different categories of customer, each with the potential to have a different perspective on the situation or project.

Figure 7.3 sets out six possible types of business customer, all of whom may be perceived as 'end users' depending upon the project context.

Figure 7.3 Types of business customer

The characteristics of each customer category are described below.

Employees	The people who work for the organisation and will use the new processes and systems.
Managers	The management team who set the business objectives and determine the strategy and tactics for the organisation; there may be several levels of manager.
Owners	The owners of the organisation. In a commercial organisation, the owners will expect to receive dividends from the profits; in a non-profit organisation, the owners may be trustees; in a government organisation, the owners may be politicians or senior government executives.
Partners	The intermediary customers such as partner or reseller organisations who sell (and often deliver) the organisation's services and products to the consumer.

Purchasers The customer who orders the products or services and ensures that payment is made, but does not 'consume' the purchased items. This may be a stakeholder working in a procurement capacity.

Consumers The 'end customer' who receives or consumes the services and products.

Anyone working as an agile business analyst should recognise the different categories of customer. This is for two reasons:

1. The perspectives will vary widely between each of the categories. For example, an intermediary may be concerned with the level of commission or discount payable for a particular product or service; a consumer may be more concerned with the quality of the delivered product or service.

2. These high-level categories help the business analyst to identify different 'customer' user roles when analysing the features to be delivered. The set of user roles can then be used in the development of user stories and personas. If we do not know that there may be several different categories of customer, we may just focus on the end-user or consumer role and miss other important user roles and their business requirements.

Understanding the different types of customer and their varying priorities and perspectives will help us to recognise where there may be issues relating to the realisation of value for customers. Customer expectations exist whenever an organisation sells a service or product. While organisations often say that they deliver value, in reality value cannot be delivered – it can only be offered by an organisation. Hence the term 'value proposition' – the organisation proposes a service or product that is intended to offer value. Any actual value has to be realised by the customer engaging with the service or product. For example, an organisation can purchase a software package that offers extensive functionality but if the employees do not use the package, then no value will be realised.

Given that it is customers who obtain value from a delivered product or service, they need to determine whether or not something of value has been delivered. However, where a project is concerned with several different categories of customer it is important to recognise that the nature of 'value' may also differ. As discussed in Chapter 3, an organisation has to identify and deliver a value proposition to their customers but it is not necessarily the case that organisational and customer perceptions of value are aligned; there is the potential for value misalignment, as represented in Figure 7.4. Understanding different customer categories and their different perspectives on what constitutes 'value', will help to ensure that customer and organisation value expectations are aligned.

When working on a change project, business analysts should be concerned with investigating the value expectations of different customers in order to identify where problems may arise through misalignment. Techniques such as use cases, user stories and personas, particularly when considered at a business level, can help with analysing customers and their value expectations. Failure to do this may result in dissatisfied customers and may risk the success of the change project.

Figure 7.4 Organisation versus customer value perceptions

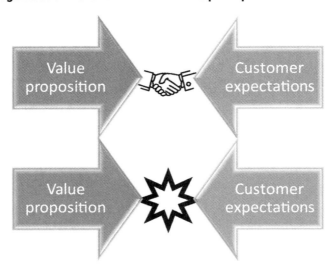

STAKEHOLDER ENGAGEMENT

Stakeholder engagement requires the identification, analysis and management of anyone involved in the project or affected by the outcomes. It also requires effective communication and rapport building to establish working relationships and, importantly, ensure they persist. Stakeholder engagement is a key area of business analysis work and is essential if there is to be collaboration on an agile project. Therefore, agile business analysts are often closely involved in engaging with stakeholders and facilitating collaborative working relationships.

There are four aspects that are necessary to support effective stakeholder engagement. 'Identify, analyse, communicate, review'. These aspects are described below.

Identify

It is important to identify who needs to be involved, their level of involvement and when they will be involved. Different stakeholders will need to be included at different times and this needs to be thought through carefully before embarking on attempts to collaborate with the stakeholders. One way of identifying stakeholders is to use a framework such as the stakeholder wheel shown in Figure 7.5.

Another means of identifying stakeholders is to break down some of these groups into four categories: external stakeholders, business/governance stakeholders, architectural stakeholders and project team stakeholders. The types of stakeholder roles within these four categories are described in detail later in this chapter.

Figure 7.5 Stakeholder wheel

Analyse

Once stakeholders have been identified, some thought must be given about how the engagement with the stakeholders needs to work. It is not possible to collaborate with every individual stakeholder, as there will usually be far too many of them with an interest in the project. An analysis of the individual stakeholders both at an individual (typically, for more senior stakeholders) and group level needs to be carried out at this point. An understanding of the perspectives held by the stakeholders, particularly the more influential stakeholders within the business and the roles that they are going to play in the project, is vital for the successful development of the solution. Techniques such as the power/interest grid, RACI and world view analysis (described below) are invaluable for thinking about different stakeholders and their perspectives. Analysis of personas and extreme characters (see Chapter 11) can also provide useful insights, particularly regarding customer stakeholders.

**Power/
interest grid**

This matrix (shown in Figure 7.6) provides a means of considering the level of power wielded by a stakeholder or stakeholder group and the level of interest in the project that these stakeholders have. This helps to determine how communication and engagement with the stakeholders will be conducted.

Figure 7.6 Power/interest grid

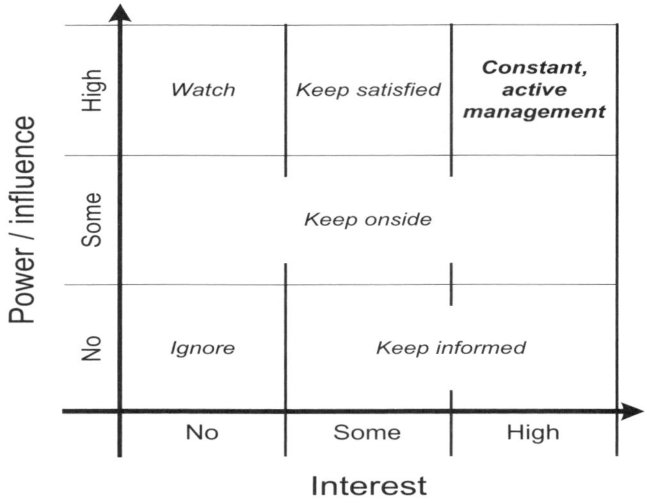

RACI/RASCI

A RACI chart (which is sometimes extended to RASCI) provides a summary of the stakeholders and the way in which they will engage with the project. The choices are:

R: responsible
A: accountable
C: consulted
S: supportive (if included)
I: informed

Again, this provides a means of understanding the stakeholders and their responsibilities, and helps to decide how we should engage with them.

**World view
analysis**

We often talk about 'perspectives' that people hold on situations or systems. World view analysis attempts to view the system under investigation from the position of an individual or group. It seeks to understand why people hold certain views or priorities by analysing their values and beliefs. A frequent – and often highly publicised – example of world view analysis occurs with regard to politicians, whereby their comments or statements are analysed and conclusions drawn about why they are taking up a particular position. However, this can also be done with stakeholders. Understanding why an individual or group holds a particular view, or has expressed certain thoughts, can be invaluable in helping to engage with stakeholders.

Communicate

Once we have some understanding about the stakeholders, it is important to think about how we will communicate and collaborate with them, and their level and frequency of involvement within the project. The power/interest grid, RACI chart and world view analysis help when considering this.

Examples of the different styles and frequency of stakeholder engagement are:

a. Engagement with the project sponsor, or the business owner for the change project. This is highly important given the responsibilities of this role. Therefore, the communication will need to be regular and specific. Rapport is likely to be extremely important in this relationship so we should make efforts to build a good working relationship with the sponsor and to maintain this over the longer term. We should also make an effort to communicate in a responsive manner, ensuring that any information required is provided when it is needed.

b. Engagement with the business staff who will be working within the project team will be ongoing during the project. This will require the development of highly collaborative working relationships, which will involve in-depth discussions about the requirements to be incorporated in the solution.

c. Engagement with external suppliers will depend upon the nature of the change project and the timing of the communication. For example, a software package supplier may be heavily involved in the project and a highly collaborative communication approach required, if there is to be extensive customisation of the package. Alternatively, a supplier of consultancy resource may only be involved at specific points during the project and communication may be minimal.

Review

Throughout any project, it is important to appreciate that stakeholder engagement is ongoing. Rapport can be built but also needs to be maintained if working relationships are to endure. It is all too easy to break rapport, for example, by ceasing communication with a stakeholder because they are no longer important to the project. Changes in views also need to be borne in mind throughout a change project. Perspectives can alter over time and a stakeholder who has perceived a requirement to be of low priority can suddenly adopt a completely different position and expect delivery of the required feature to be imminent. As a result, we need to revisit the analysis of the stakeholders regularly and consider whether positions or perspectives have changed.

When working with stakeholders on an agile project, there will be some who sit within the project team and others who represent areas external to the project. Everyone within the team will need to work closely and collaboratively with each other, including the business analysts. Where these stakeholders are customers, their views are likely to be at the forefront of the project work, so frequent, focused communication will be required.

There will be other stakeholders who are not working within the project team but still need to be on the communication radar because they have concerns and interests that the project needs to take into account. It is also the case that these concerns and interests can change as the project progresses. For example, someone who was not very engaged with the project at the outset may become more interested as the work progresses and delivery moves closer; this increasing engagement with the project is likely to result in a need for more frequent and active communication.

One final thought about stakeholder engagement. We often talk about collaboration and rapport but can find it difficult to sustain this approach, particularly when there are time pressures. The best maxim is to treat stakeholders as you would want to be treated yourself. We often talk about understanding the 'voice of the customer' or standing in the customers' shoes, and it is extremely helpful to think about how the situation looks from their perspective. Failing to do this can result in assumptions being made, stakeholders being overlooked, rapport breaking and general difficulties arising for the project.

STAKEHOLDER CATEGORIES, ROLES AND PERSPECTIVES

Working on business change projects often means that business analysts are involved with a wide range of stakeholders, both internal and external to the organisation. The stakeholder wheel in Figure 7.5 identified some of the key stakeholder categories that we might investigate. However, as we have already seen, within the customer category there are many different perspectives to uncover. The 'employee' and 'owner' categories will contain a range of stakeholders and roles that are relevant to a change project. Understanding these different categories is important if we are to ensure that we don't overlook any perspectives and are clear about the priorities for the change project.

Within an agile project, there may be fewer defined job roles and, as discussed earlier, there may be team members who have a range of skills and the ability to adopt a number of roles. However, it is still important to be aware of the different stakeholder roles and their areas of interest. Engaging carefully with stakeholders is highly relevant to agile business analysis, as it helps clarify what needs to be delivered, the business constraints to be complied with, and how the project aligns with other projects and the enterprise architecture. It should also help us to distinguish between 'wish list' thinking and requirements that really can address business issues and opportunities.

Understanding roles

It helps to think about the four different constituencies represented by stakeholders: the business/project governance, the architectural domains, the external environment and the development team. Within each of these constituencies there will be numerous roles that are adopted by the stakeholders. The term 'role' is often used on agile (and other types of) development projects and it is useful to understand what is meant by this and how the roles can change, depending upon the nature of the project.

A role can be thought of as a hat that a stakeholder takes on − however, they don't always wear just one hat. You often hear people saying 'I am wearing a number of hats at this meeting' and by this they mean that they are playing, or representing, a number of different roles, with each role looking at the situation from a particular angle or viewpoint. For example, many stakeholders may have an 'end-user' role for a new IT system but some may also be subject-matter experts (SMEs), and one of them may have the project sponsor role for the project. The term 'end user' might also cover a number of roles, each of which has different characteristics and requires the delivery of different features. For example, in a payroll system, all of the employed stakeholders will have the 'employee' role, but some will also have the 'line manager' role (and authorise salary increases) and there may also be a payroll manager role, responsible for authorising all of the payments.

It is important to understand the nature of roles if we are to work successfully with stakeholders. Roles and individual stakeholders have a many-to-many relationship, as shown in Figure 7.7 below.

Figure 7.7 The relationship between stakeholders and roles

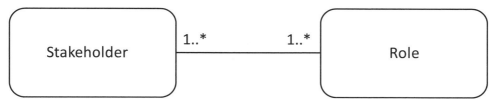

This means that each stakeholder may take on one or more roles and each role may be covered by one or more stakeholders. However, this doesn't mean that all of the job titles will be represented. For example, in a Scrum agile development team, each participant – other than the Scrum master – is called a developer and there are no specialist job titles. However, the need for different roles still exists because there is specialist work to be carried out. Recognising these roles, their responsibilities and the skills required is essential if the work is to be carried out successfully. Similarly, we need to be aware of the different roles and responsibilities that are external to the project team but still impact upon the project activities.

The roles typically found within the four stakeholder constituencies are discussed below.

The business/governance perspective

Each change project has business representatives who are responsible for various aspects of the business involvement. These stakeholders provide the business viewpoint and governance. The most important roles are shown in Figure 7.8 and discussed below.

Figure 7.8 Business/governance roles on change projects

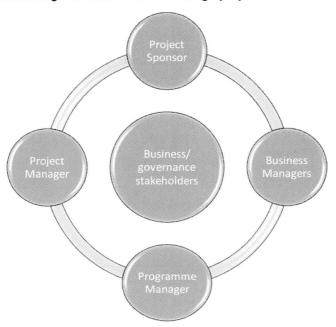

Project sponsor

This is the most senior governance role for the change project. The project sponsor acts as the business representative who champions the project within the business and is ultimately accountable for its success. The project sponsor has to ensure that sufficient funds and other resources are available to the project and will accept (or reject) the deliverables. As the person who commissioned the project, the project sponsor is the owner of the business case and has responsibility for the delivery of the business benefits.

There should be one project sponsor who is in post for the duration of the project, providing a clear escalation route for problems and issues and setting the strategic direction.

Business managers

Business managers typically manage the staff who will use a new system and carry out new processes and procedures. However, they may be users of the system themselves in some situations. They are often owners of requirements, even if the sources were more junior staff. As a result, in addition to providing information regarding the requirements, they will have to be consulted to find out the underlying rationale. This is particularly important where there are conflicts or a lack of clarity around the requirements. For example, where two of the end users have requested opposing functional requirements or where there is uncertainty surrounding non-functional requirements.

Programme manager	Programmes comprise a series of inter-dependent change projects that, together, contribute to the achievement of business objectives. Each project may focus on a different element of the programme, for example the software development, the process changes or possibly a different workflow area. The programme manager is responsible for managing the programme, in particular the dependencies between the projects, and ensuring that the work on the projects is aligned so that the programme is delivered successfully.
Project manager	Responsible for ensuring that the project is delivered according to the defined terms of reference. These include the project objectives and the time, cost and quality constraints. The project manager also manages the agile process adopted for the project.

The architectural domains perspective

Each change project needs to align with the enterprise architecture and the sub-domains such as business, applications, data and infrastructure architecture. The stakeholders working in these areas ensure that this alignment is in place. Business analysts may have to work closely with these stakeholders, in particular the business, solution and data architects. Most projects, particularly those that have an IT or technology component, will have a number of architectural stakeholders that must be considered.

These stakeholders will often have perspectives and responsibilities that extend beyond the scope of the change project and it is important that their views are properly considered. This may mean that they provide requirements (functional and non-functional), acceptance criteria or undertake a formal approval role. It may be that the project doesn't need to include their requirements until a later stage which could require some sensitive stakeholder management.

Architectural stakeholders will often have longer term interests and be concerned with trying to ensure that projects are future proof and can enable future developments. This can cause some conflict with agile project teams where early delivery of business benefit is important and longer term constraints can seem unnecessary. In such situations, the business analyst may be required to negotiate a path through some difficult issues by applying their stakeholder management skills. The approach to stakeholder engagement described earlier, whereby stakeholder views and responsibilities are analysed, can be very helpful when conducting this work (Figure 7.9).

Figure 7.9 Architectural domain roles on change projects

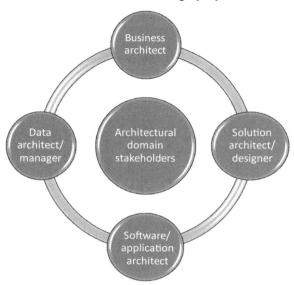

Business architect

The Object Management Group's Business Architecture Specialist Interest Group (BAsig)[1] defines business architecture as follows:

> A blueprint of the enterprise that provides a common understanding of the organization and is used to align strategic objectives and tactical demands.

The business architect role is focused on ensuring a solution aligns with the business architecture blueprints for the organisation, so that the strategic objectives and tactical demands are met. The blueprint provides a representation of the structure and behaviour of a business system and covers the business capabilities, value-adding processes and the actors who conduct the work. The capabilities and processes are aligned with the business goals and business services they support, and the applications and data needed to realise them.

Solution architect/ designer

The solution architect or designer is responsible for creating the design artefacts that set out the blueprint for the whole solution including business and infrastructure layers. These artefacts need to align the services provided by the solution components to the business architecture in line with the standards governed by the enterprise architecture.

Software/ application architect

Where the solution involves considerable reuse and integration with existing software components and sub-systems, a software or application architect may be involved to ensure that existing services and standards are maintained.

Data architect/ manager	The data architect or manager is responsible for the governance and coordination of the definition, structure, storage and movement of data that supports the information requirements of a business, especially data maintained by the software applications. Their focus should be on aspects like data quality, consistency and security.

The external perspective

Some stakeholders are not only external to the project team but to the entire organisation. Consequently, it is difficult to collaborate with some of these stakeholders and the information they offer may need to be obtained through various communication channels. For example:

- In some industries it is not possible to communicate directly with end consumers as this has to be done through intermediaries.

- Governmental and regulatory organisations may provide information primarily through written communications.

- Competitor information may need to be obtained through market or business research.

It is important not to overlook these stakeholders as they can be extremely important to the success of the project and business analysts are often responsible for analysing the information these stakeholders provide. Some of the key external stakeholder roles are shown in Figure 7.10 and discussed below.

Figure 7.10 External stakeholder roles on change projects

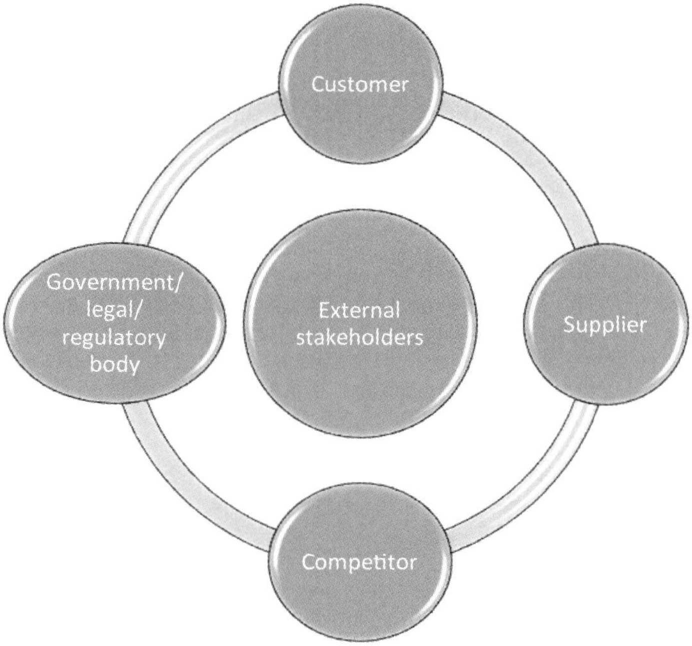

Customer	This is the end customer role, typically the person paying, or representing an organisation that is paying for the product or service delivered. Customers are a complex set of stakeholders, as discussed earlier.
Supplier	The supplier provides products or services to the project or organisation. These stakeholders may be significant particularly if they are providing outsourced services or off-the-shelf software products. Where the supplier is providing bespoke products, they may themselves be operating agile delivery models, so the business analyst may be a stakeholder of the supplier team.
Competitor	Competitor organisations may not seem to be obvious stakeholders. However, a change project may need to take into account competitor strategies and actions, or may need to consider how the project may affect competitors. In some cases it is essential to think about potential responses from competitors and, in some situations, it may be desirable to collaborate with a competitor. New information about a competitor's product could affect the project goal or change key drivers in the business case. This could require the project team to change course or, in extreme cases, to shut down.
Government/ legal/ regulatory bodies	These organisations are the sources for rules and regulations with which the organisation needs to comply; new or changed regulations are often the reasons for initiating change projects. No matter how embedded the agile philosophy is within an organisation, compliance with such regulations is usually mandatory and this may impact upon the approach to be adopted on projects.

The project team perspective

The project team is responsible for ensuring the requirements are elaborated and developed into product increments. Business analysts typically work within the project team, facilitating communication, analysing requirements and clarifying the business rules. They also ensure that there is alignment with business objectives and needs. While some agile approaches, such as Scrum, do not define individual job roles, it is important to recognise the skill areas of certain stakeholder roles that need to be represented within the project team. These roles are shown in Figure 7.11 and discussed below.

Domain expert	The domain expert (also known as the SME) is a business person who has significant knowledge and understanding of the business domain. This knowledge is necessarily more extensive than that of the end user and often derives from having taken a senior role within the organisation or having experience across the particular industry. An example may be an individual with extensive experience and knowledge of retail business operations or taxation law. The domain expert is able to provide information about

Figure 7.11 Stakeholder roles within the development team

the area of business that the solution will be deployed within and is able to clarify business requirements.

This role provides input to an agile project by providing information about the broader business domain, the particular business situation and any issues that can arise.

The domain expert may be an employee of the company or may be an external consultant. The advantages of having an external consultant fill this role are that the consultant will be able to:

- provide an objective view;
- identify where local practice is not necessarily best practice;
- bring ideas from other organisations operating within the business domain;
- distinguish between requirements based on business need rather than tradition or assumption.

Where an external consultant is performing the domain expert role issues may arise due to a lack of understanding of the organisation and the politics, power bases and culture that exist.

Customer/ end user	The end-user role represents the business staff who will use a new system or work with a new product. Within an agile project, there should be representatives of the customer community working within the project team. This may be one person or could be a team of people, depending upon the size of the customer community to be represented and the complexity of the work. The end users within the project team must be empowered to make decisions on behalf of the user community.
Team leader	The team leader is responsible for ensuring that the project team is operating in a collective and collaborative manner, and is meeting its objectives successfully. This role reports progress and issues to the project manager.
Solution developer	The solution developer interprets business requirements and translates them into a deployable solution that meets the functional and non-functional requirements. The work of the developer usually entails building software components and unit (program/ component) testing their work. Where the focus is on the development of the entire solution, covering processes and organisational aspects, the role may have a broader remit, possibly encompassing aspects of business analysis. In some organisations there may be a product developer role that is responsible for developing the products to be offered by the organisation. Whichever is the case, developers need to work closely with the business analyst in order to ensure that the business requirements are understood and the desired product or service is delivered.
	In agile systems development, the solution developer role may also encompass the role of the solution architect/designer.
Solution tester	The solution tester role is responsible for defining test cases and test scenarios that will be used to identify whether or not the solution meets the requirements. There may be different levels or types of tests such as integration testing and system testing (where an IT system has been developed as part of the solution). Business acceptance testing may also be required to ensure that the solution meets the business needs.

It is worth reiterating that agile teams may not designate specific roles. However, that does not mean that the work for which those roles are responsible is not carried out. It is part of the agile philosophy that project teams are multi-skilled and have the responsibility for the different areas of work required to develop the solution. Therefore, individuals may be called upon to support or conduct work across a range of areas. For example, if there are testing tasks to complete, a team member with a 'developer' job title may perform a 'tester' role for the duration of the testing tasks. In some cases, the whole agile team may be responsible for defining test cases and test scenarios.

CONCLUSION

Stakeholder engagement and management is vital within any project. However, this is particularly the case when using agile, given the emphasis on effective collaboration. Business change projects tend to require the involvement of a wide range of stakeholders from different constituencies; some may be internal to the project team, others may be from within the organisation but external to the project, while others may be external to the entire organisation. While business analysts should have the ability to facilitate communication and collaboration through effective stakeholder engagement, the nature of this engagement will differ depending upon the role and the level of collaboration required. To work effectively in an agile environment, business analysts need to adopt the 'mindset' encapsulated in the agile philosophy and principles. They also need to support stakeholders to adapt their working practices to the needs of agile projects.

Business analysts are concerned primarily with ensuring that business needs are met and value is realised for the customer. Although many agile approaches identify the need to focus on end-user customers, in reality the business customer landscape is much more complex and encompasses many different customer roles.

While some agile methods do not require the involvement of a business analyst, change projects will always need business analysis. This is indisputably the case for projects using agile, where stakeholder collaboration is key to project success.

NOTE

1 When originally established by the OMG in December 2007 it was known as the Business Architecture Working Group (BAWG).

REFERENCES

Ambler, S.W. and Lines, M. (2012) *Disciplined Agile delivery*. Upper Saddle River, NJ IBM Press.

Scrum Alliance (2016) Scrum alliance home page. Scrum Alliance. Available from: www.scrumalliance.org/ [20 December 2016].

FURTHER READING

Ambler, S. (2003) *Agile database techniques*. New York: John Wiley & Sons.

Maglio, P.P., Kieliszewski, C.A. and Spohrer, J.C. (2010) *Handbook of Service Science. Service Science: research and innovations in the service economy*. New York: Springer.

Paul, D., Cadle, J. and Yeates, D. (2014) *Business analysis: 3rd edition*. Swindon: BCS.

Spohrer J.C. and Maglio P.P. (2010) Toward a science of service systems: value and symbols. In Maglio, Paul P., Kieliszewski, Cheryl A. and Spohrer, James C. (eds). *Handbook of Service Science. Service Science: research and innovations in the service economy*, Part 2. New York: Springer.

8   DECOMPOSING GOALS

This chapter covers the following topics:

- the relevance of goal-based analysis;
- goal and functional decomposition;
- understanding goal levels;
- using goals to achieve business agility;
- using goals to define iterations and releases.

INTRODUCTION

Agile business analysts need to apply goal decomposition to ensure that the focus of an agile change project is on the delivery of business goals. The ability to understand business goals and then separate them into things that can be logically achieved by the business is necessary for any business to thrive. Achieving this, however, can be problematic as large goals often get divided into functional areas of the business and the original goal can become confused or lost. In this chapter, we discuss how to break down goals so that smaller goals can be achieved earlier, without losing sight of the bigger goal. Decomposing goals in this way is critical to the success of agile change projects because the success of change can only be determined by the value received by the customer. The only way of achieving earlier success is therefore by understanding and delivering smaller goals.

THE RELEVANCE OF GOAL-BASED ANALYSIS

Goal-based analysis is a logical mechanism for breaking down and orgnising business goals. All organisations have goals but we tend to call them business objectives or strategic outcomes. In simple terms, a goal is something that the organisation or business wants to achieve, such as 'increase sales by 5 per cent within the next 12 months'. We analyse goals because it helps us to keep the focus on what the business is trying to achieve strategically. Goal-based analysis has been discussed in the context of requirements for some time. The easiest way to understand a goal-based structure is to look at a high-level business process for an organisation.

Figure 8.1 Organisational chart showing a high-level business process

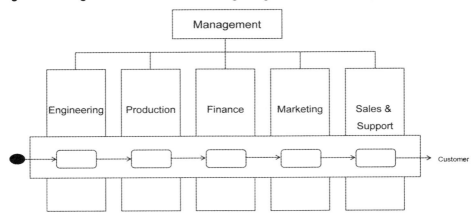

It is clear to see that the organisation is split into functional areas represented by the vertical boxes shown in Figure 8.1. While all of the functional areas are valuable, they need to operate and work together to achieve any outcomes for the business. If each functional area were given the individual goal to 'increase the size of their function by 5 per cent within the next 12 months', this may not result in the organisation achieving the overall goal of 'increasing sales by 5 per cent within the next 12 months'. Each function cannot deliver an overall business outcome on its own.

The business process, which runs horizontally, shows how an end-to-end business process utilises all of the functional areas of the business required to deliver a defined outcome. So, if the goal of this business is to increase sales by 5 per cent, it is the functional areas conducting their parts of the business process that will achieve this goal. In this example, the business process represents the work to achieve this high-level goal. At an enterprise level, these processes are often called value streams and represent the value that the business offers through delivering its products or services. This is discussed in more detail in Chapter 6.

Decomposition is the process of breaking down complex entities into smaller parts. Breaking things down in this way helps us to analyse the individual components, as they become easier to understand. Business analysts are well versed in decomposition and things that are commonly decomposed include:

- requirements: overview to detailed requirements;
- processes: organisation to business process to task and to step level;
- work breakdown structures: elicit, analyse, document, validate requirements;
- goals: strategic goals, business goals, project goals.

It is important to maintain a view of the higher-level goal when we are decomposing this into lower levels. This helps to ensure that we have actually achieved the overall goal.

GOAL AND FUNCTIONAL DECOMPOSITION

It is human nature to want to break a problem down into its constituent areas, such as process steps or functionality, to make it easier to conceive and understand. Each process step or functional area is only an element of a decomposed goal and the goal cannot be achieved until all steps or functionality have been delivered. This makes it harder to deliver value earlier, as the smaller goals are divided amongst the process steps or functional areas of a business. When decomposing goals we need to maintain the focus on the following:

- breaking down the goal into smaller goals;
- keeping sight of the value expectation of the customer;
- ensuring that a process is not decomposed.

When we decompose a process or function it is called functional decomposition. Functional decomposition is useful if you want to understand how to do something and it assumes that 'what is being done' and 'why it is done' are understood. Given this, it is also assumed that there is a high-level context that is unlikely to change. Each decomposed element of a function will be performed according to defined steps and business rules, which functional decomposition allows us to focus on investigating and understanding. When a function is decomposed, the sub-function does not focus on the achievement of a business goal but on completing a piece of work that contributes to the overall work of the function.

Goal decomposition

Let's consider an example scenario.

Ben and Jasmine have aspirations to run their own profitable business. The business they have chosen is a café. Opening and running a profitable café is their ultimate goal.

If we assume that the ultimate goal is correct, and won't change, and that opening a café is the only goal they are focusing on, we could decompose the goal into the functions shown in Figure 8.2.

Figure 8.2 Functional decomposition of the goal, 'Open a café'

Figure 8.2 shows the results of functional decomposition. While this is not an exhaustive list of functions it provides some key functions that Ben and Jasmine will need to carry out.

Although Ben and Jasmine have aspirations to open and run a profitable café, they have neither run their own business before nor worked in a café. Therefore, there are things they need to learn. They are concerned about the location of the café and are not sure it has enough passing trade. Also, they know what drinks and food they like to eat in a café, and how much they are willing to pay, but they are not sure who their customers will be and whether their customers will want to eat and drink the same things that they do. As a result, they are unsure whether their ultimate goal is achievable. To address this issue, they have decided to try out some ideas before committing too much money, time and resources to a business that might not be successful.

The functions identified in Figure 8.2 are focused on achieving the original goal, which would require them to give up their day jobs and invest all their time and money into setting up a café that may never be profitable.

This seems too risky to Ben and Jasmine, so they have sought advice. They have been advised to start smaller, to test the market and to incrementally grow their business. This way, if it doesn't work they haven't invested all their time and money and, if things don't work out first time, they can learn lessons from the experience and adapt their approach. To do this they have decided to identify smaller goals that can help to lead them to their ultimate goal.

Their goal of 'Opening a profitable café' has been decomposed into smaller goals as shown in Figure 8.3.

Figure 8.3 Goal decomposition of the goal, 'Open a café'

Now they can focus on achieving just one goal, such as 'serve hot drinks'. This can be further decomposed as shown in Figure 8.4.

Figure 8.4 Decomposed goals for the 'Serve hot drinks' goal

Decomposing goals in this way allows choices to be made about which goal, or goals, to do first. Each goal contributes to achieving the higher-level goal. For example, **'serve tea with a tea bag'** or **'serve filter coffee'** are both ways of serving hot drinks. This demonstrates how a high-level goal can be decomposed into smaller or mini goals, each of which will offer potential value to the customer. In each of these cases, customers will be served a hot drink.

Using a goal decomposition approach, it is straightforward to prioritise the decomposed goals and provide a means of delivering the product in one initial increment and subsequent increments. In this scenario, we may want to serve three types of hot drink from the outset or alternatively we may want to focus solely on serving good quality coffee, leaving the other options to be added later. The initial investment and effort to be made is dependent on the goal(s) agreed and how well they are achieved initially. It could be that a stand serving tea with tea bags and instant coffee, using hot water from flasks, is all that is required in the first increment. This will provide essential management information such as whether there will be enough passing trade, if customers are requesting 'good' coffee, the variety of drinks customers request and whether it is worth investing further in the business. Prioritising the decomposed goals is an effective means of setting up an enterprise that is adaptable to customer needs and can develop as the business grows. Techniques to prioritise goals are described in Chapter 9.

When decomposing goals, the following considerations should be borne in mind:

- What value will the actor, or customer, get from this goal?
- Is this goal delivering a partial service or product to the customer?
- Why do we, or the customer, want to achieve the goal? For what purpose?
- Each goal must offer value in its own right.

Functional decomposition

Functional decomposition is a way of breaking down the function or process into small pieces, or chunks, to make it easier to conceive. However, the whole process can only work if all the steps or parts are completed. This means that each task or step does not achieve any goals, and this is only done by combining the functions across the entire process. For example, in Figure 8.2, 'obtain equipment to make drinks' is an essential part of making a hot drink, but on its own does not offer any value to the end customer. Only when it is combined with the other functions/tasks will the value of serving a hot drink, such as serving instant coffee, emerge. Also, once there is a clear decomposed goal, the entire sub-function may not be necessary; in this example, a goal of serving tea and instant coffee would require far less equipment than providing a range of specialist filter coffees. Applying a functional decomposition approach can result in increments being developed that do not offer the possibility of deployment, as they do not achieve anything tangible for customers. Therefore, it can preclude agile teams from working effectively, as there is limited focus on achieving relevant goals.

Within organisations there are always limitations on the funds and time available. This inevitably results in there being more work to be done than is possible within these limitations. This is why projects and businesses need to focus on delivering the highest priority aspects first. It may turn out that once we have achieved the initial goals, priorities change and we decide to not try to achieve any more. Alternatively, it could be that achieving the initial goals has been so successful that additional funding is made available for further work. If we had decomposed the ultimate goal of opening and running a profitable café on a functional basis at the outset, we may have a lot of equipment but still be trying to set up and open a café. Decomposing goals provides a route to begin work and to move forward and therefore helps in the achievement of both the ultimate and intermediate goals.

UNDERSTANDING GOAL LEVELS

Understanding the range of goal levels is important. In his book, *Writing effective use cases*, Alistair Cockburn (2001) introduced 'goal levels' as a way of reflecting the different levels at which functional requirements may be expressed. These elements were discussed in Chapter 6. Figure 8.5 describes Cockburn's levels within the context of understanding goal levels. For simplification, the clam level has been omitted.

When decomposing goals, ensure that the goals stay above the surface and remain visible (i.e. sea level or above). Fish-level goals add no value to the customer. They are essentially sub-tasks that need to be done in order to achieve the goal. Figure 8.6 shows how the, 'Open a café' scenario can be broken down through the different Cockburn goal levels.

Figure 8.5 Cockburn's levels of goals

(cloud icon)	Cloud (High summary level)	These are business goals. Often reflected in strategic business objectives, they are the goals that drive the business towards the required direction.
(kite icon)	Kite (Summary level)	These are goals that are achieved through end-to-end processes within the business system. They may take hours, days or even weeks to complete.
(sea icon)	Sea (User goal level)	These are the goals that are generally achieved by one person. Together they contribute to the delivery of the end-to-end process goals, which, in turn, contribute towards meeting the business objectives.
(fish icon)	Fish (Sub-goal level)	These are not goals. They are sub-goals and are achieved by discrete tasks. Sub-goals, such as 'buy instant coffee granules', offer no value in their own right. They are only carried out so that the user goal, in this case 'serve instant coffee', can be achieved.

Figure 8.6 Examples of different goal levels

USING GOALS TO ACHIEVE BUSINESS AGILITY

Goal decomposition is extremely helpful when an enterprise is deciding what to do in order to offer value to customers. As discussed earlier, it helps to identify where an organisation should focus its efforts and at what point. However, it is also important to ensure that the decomposed goals are achieved in a way that aligns with the business architecture for the organisation. The business architecture provides a blueprint which defines aspects such as the value streams and capabilities of the organisation, and how these capabilities may be achieved. The POPIT™ model is a useful way of viewing the elements required to build the capabilities within the business architecture.

One approach that may be applied is called 'modular business architecture', whereby the business goals are realised through individual 'components' or 'modules'. These components should be self-standing so that they are tightly cohesive (the component has all the functionality to provide the service) and loosely coupled (the component interacts with other self-standing components in order to form desired configurations). These may be software components that communicate via standard interfaces that send and receive messages and data. Alternatively, they may be business components that interact with the rest of the business through interfaces. A typical example of a modular component used by many businesses is the payment management capability offered by organisations such as Worldpay and PayPal. These components offer the delivery of a business goal – enabling customers to make payments securely – and are self-standing. They may also be used as part of several value streams within an organisation, providing a basis for standardisation and reuse.

Organisations can outsource the achievement of goals – such as customer payment – or can build internal business modules that deliver specific goals. These modules can be deployed where necessary across the entire organisation. This is particularly useful when embarking upon business change or business improvement projects. Goal decomposition enables organisations to consider which capabilities are needed to achieve a sub-goal and identify where a modular business architecture can provide a basis for organisational agility.

USING GOALS TO DEFINE ITERATIONS AND RELEASES

Goals are not only useful to break down strategic business objectives or build a modular business architecture, they also help to define the iterations and releases for business change projects. If we understand the goals and sub-goals, we can prioritise them such that the goals to be achieved first are developed and released at an early stage. This may involve working on a particular business use case or epic as described in Chapter 6; these may require the decomposition of business goals (possibly at cloud or kite level), each of which may be delivered by various combinations of the POPIT™ elements. Within software development projects, 'user stories' (Chapter 12) define the goals to be achieved and form the basis for deciding the content of an iteration or release. For most software development projects, the sea-level goal is the goal that is agreed at the start of iteration. Each user story defines a goal that should deliver an outcome for the customer or business and should be small enough that it can be completed within an iteration. Iterations are discussed in more detail in Chapter 15.

CONCLUSION

Goal decomposition is a valuable technique that aids the adoption of agile and offers business agility to organisations. It helps projects to deliver working solutions in increments and offer beneficial business outcomes at an early stage. The goal decomposition approach is highly relevant to business analysts, as it ensures a focus on business outcomes. The contrast with functional decomposition highlights how completing a functional task, such as providing part of an IT system, does not necessarily contribute to the achievement of business goals. When decomposing goals, it is important to remember two things:

1. Decompose the goal itself, not the steps needed to achieve the goal
2. Stay at goal level, above the sea where it is visible and not at a sub-goal level.

Agile business analysts need to apply goal decomposition to ensure that the focus of an agile change project is on the delivery of business goals. They should also support the customers in identifying the required business outcomes and the decomposed goals that will contribute to their achievement. Ultimately, business analysts should be concerned that the changes made improve the working lives of their customers and the work conducted within each iteration. The changes deployed in each release and the overall results from the change project should be focused on achieving this.

Goal decomposition is important to the success of delivering small incremental business outcomes that enable business agility. If we fail to decompose the business goals we may run the risk of trying to deliver something too big, or too risky, which can consume more time and money than we have. Breaking down goals and only achieving small goals allows learning to take place and provides time to adapt on the basis of this learning.

It is important that agile business analysts focus on delivering outcomes that are of value to the business. After all, if the goal is to drink a cup of tea and all we have is a cup and a tea bag with no milk or hot water, it would be impossible to claim that the goal has been achieved and something valuable has been accomplished.

REFERENCE

Cockburn, A. (2001) *Writing effective use cases*. Boston, MA: Addison Wesley.

FURTHER READING

Paul, D., Cadle, J. and Yeates, D. (2014) *Business analysis: 3rd edition*. Swindon: BCS.

Cadle, J. (ed.) (2014) *Developing information systems*. Swindon: BCS

9 PRIORITISING THE WORK

This chapter covers the following topics:

- the importance of prioritisation;
- prioritising requirements;
- applying prioritisation;
- prioritisation decomposition;
- prioritisation issues.

INTRODUCTION

All businesses introduce changes. Small changes happen frequently as part of day-to-day business as usual. Major changes are more likely to be the subject of a change project. A change might be made to the way in which a task is conducted or might involve the development of a new product. However, whether small or major, process or product, organisations need to prioritise their changes. This may be an obvious statement, but too often prioritisation gets overlooked, particularly when we are in pursuit of higher-level goals. To be truly agile in business and on projects, we have to prioritise – otherwise we risk delivering late, if at all.

Business analysts need to understand and facilitate prioritisation to ensure that businesses are focusing on achieving the most important goals first. After all, there is always more work to be done than there is time and money for. Prioritisation is key to getting this balance right. This chapter discusses the importance of prioritisation to business analysts and agile change projects, and the different techniques that can be applied. Additionally, the significance of particular prioritisation levels are discussed, together with the issues that can ensue if prioritisation is not carried out effectively.

THE IMPORTANCE OF PRIORITISATION

All businesses recognise the need for prioritisation. What is less obvious is how we go about prioritising, and how understanding prioritisation is more than just identifying that one change is more important than another change. Prioritisation can tell us which changes we need urgently, which ones could be delayed and which we might think about never introducing. Prioritisation can also tell us which changes should not be considered, but can be 'parked' for consideration at a later date. Sometimes, prioritisation can indicate which changes are really just vague ideas that we probably don't need at all.

Given these different categories, prioritisation can tell us where to invest money and when to work on a new initiative. It can also be very helpful in preventing 'headless chicken' syndrome, where people rush around trying to do every task that has arrived in their in-tray. If we understand prioritisation we can be really focused, recognising the key goals we need to achieve and the elements that can be paused, delayed or dropped.

Business today often seems like a frantic rush to get too much done in too little time. In the software development world, prioritisation has become second nature. As soon as we start defining requirements or developing the backlog of user stories, we know that entries have to be prioritised. We also know that business customers will request changes or new features that may not actually be required, or not by everyone anyway, or might not even be feasible. So, we use prioritisation techniques to make sense of the battery of ideas, features, goals and enhancements that regularly head in our direction.

However, in the business world prioritisation is less formalised and techniques not as well developed. So, as business analysts, we need to ensure that the importance of prioritisation, and the relevant techniques for prioritising, are used beyond the software development arena. Using an effective prioritisation technique is essential if an organisation is to adopt the agile philosophy and principles and gain any benefit from them. This will enable the organisation to focus the effort where the most benefit will accrue. It will ensure that skills are directed where they are most needed. And, perhaps most importantly, it will deliver the business goals that are really critical to the organisation's success. The agile business analyst should be able to support and, where necessary, direct, the prioritisation effort, in order to help organisations spend investment funds wisely and deploy other resources effectively.

PRIORITISING REQUIREMENTS

Prioritisation is the responsibility of the business stakeholders. However, whichever technique is used, prioritisation involves a degree of subjective decision-making so the stakeholders usually need some guidance and support when prioritising. Business analysts are typically the most appropriate people to offer this support because they have an understanding of the business domain and, therefore, are well positioned to challenge and question the allocated priority levels. They also understand how to analyse the impact of implementing, or not implementing, different proposals and requirements. For this reason, business analysts should be knowledgeable about the prioritisation techniques that may be applied and the contexts within which they work best. This section looks at the techniques that are used during change projects; they apply to software or product development and can also be used to prioritise business or process changes.

Prioritisation techniques

A standard for prioritising can be as simple as levels 1, 2 or 3, with level 1 being the highest priority and level 3 being the lowest. A prioritisation technique using this approach might define the levels as follows:

- **level 1:** most important; must be delivered;
- **level 2:** highly desirable; must be a good reason for non-delivery;
- **level 3:** a nice extra but can be left out of the final change or product delivered.

Variants of this approach can also be used, for example:

- level A, level B, level C (with A being highest priority);
- essential, desirable, nice to have (categories);
- high, medium, low.

All of these prioritisation approaches are straightforward to understand and can be easy to use as long as the differences between each of the levels can be clarified. They help us to identify where to focus our efforts first and with greatest volume. The Kano approach is another technique that uses a similar basis for categorisation, applying three categories:

- **Dissatisfiers:** a requirement that must be included in the delivered product if it is to be considered successful.
- **Satisfiers:** a requirement specified as needed by customers; the delivery of satisfiers will increase customer satisfaction with the delivered product.
- **Delighters:** a requirement that hasn't been specifically requested or is not expected by the stakeholders but will increase customer satisfaction significantly if it is included in the delivered product.

Use of the Kano approach causes analysts to ask questions such as:

- Would you consider this product to be successful if this requirement was not delivered?
- Would you expect this requirement to be included in the product?

Other techniques are more analytical and can be complex to implement. For example:

- **$100 Allocation:** when using this technique, stakeholders distribute a fictional amount (in this example $100) among the requirements in order to determine which are the most important. They can agree the amount allocated as a group or do this individually and then divide the total allocated to each requirement by the number of stakeholders to give a priority amount. This is used to determine the priority ranking of the requirement.
- **Analytical Hierarchy Prioritisation (AHP):** this approach considers pairs of requirements and, for each pair, asks which is the most important and to what degree (such as 'A and B are of equal importance' or 'A is extremely important when compared to B'). Allocating a value to each paired comparison and applying a mathematical formula to all of the defined values results in a priority, which provides a numerical rank for each requirement.

- **WSJF:** this approach is recommended in the SAFe, but can be used in any situation that calls for an ordered list of work. It uses the principles of Relative Mass Estimation (see Chapter 14) and uses the cost of delay to allocate a weighting to a job or item of work. WSJF splits the cost of delay into three separate elements, and measures them independently to get a more accurate result. It also requires the jobs to be sized, perhaps by using a unit of time such as story points, in order to know which jobs will deliver their value quickest. The premise here is that the smallest, highest-value jobs should be completed first and is referred to as the overall cost of delay.

The overall cost of delay is calculated by considering three separate factors for each job in the list. The jobs are compared with each other so that each one has a score relative to the other jobs for that factor. Each factor is considered independently so that they do not affect one another. The example below uses the three factors recommended in the SAFe approach:

- **User business value:** this is a measure of the value that the business will realise once this requirement is delivered.

- **Time criticality:** How time critical is this job? Is there a deadline for delivery or does the value reduce over time?

- **Risk reduction/opportunity enablement:** Does this job allow other jobs to start or finish or does completing this job reduce the risk to other jobs or to the overall project?

Each of the factors is considered independently, using an agreed scoring mechanism. Typically, several people are involved in applying the following process:

- Identify which requirement the team thinks has the **lowest** value for the factor being considered. Place this against the number 1. Each job is then compared to the lowest-value job and placed against one of the scores depending on its relative position. For instance, if it is about the same 'cost' then place it against 1. If it is five times as much, place it against 5. This is repeated for all of the jobs and the scores for this factor are recorded.

- This process is repeated for the other two factors and the three scores for each job are added up to create the **Total Cost of Delay**. This is divided by the job size to create the final score, as shown in Figure 9.1.

Figure 9.1 Calculation for WSJF

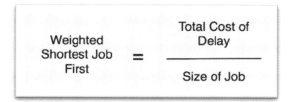

133

The scores for all jobs are then used to create an ordered list. The low scores represent the smallest jobs that deliver the highest value and should be done first.

Prioritisation and timing

While it is essential to know the level of importance of a requirement if we are using an agile approach, there is a problem with many techniques in that they offer a level of priority but this is not linked to time criticality – for example, do we need this feature yesterday, straightaway, can we wait a few months or do we think about it next year. Some techniques also offer categories that are not sufficiently granular and are open to interpretation.

A technique that is popular amongst agile practitioners is the MSCW framework or MoSCoW, as it is typically known. This technique, coupled with the iterative development and incremental delivery of features, is extremely powerful and has much to offer the agile organisation and business analysts.

The agile ethos of on-time, on-budget delivery often means that some of the features originally envisaged for inclusion in a product may have to be left out initially. This is a fundamental principle of the agile philosophy and one that is highly relevant to all types of new initiative, whether involving an IT system, process redesign or product development. It is extremely unusual to be able to incorporate everything that has been requested, as sufficient time and budget are rarely available; to manage this we need to ensure two things:

1. the most important and business critical requirements are delivered first;
2. it is only non-critical requirements that are omitted.

What an agile approach ensures is that we consider the first 'release' to be just that – the first release. We know that there will be refinements and additions coming along afterwards. This is highly liberating, as it means that we don't have to nail down every last item before providing something to the stakeholders who need it. However, effective prioritisation ensures that what is delivered is sufficient and doesn't mean a product that is unusable – who would want a car without wheels? No one! However, a car only available in a basic model might suit many people.

The other advantage of an agile approach is that it enables us to develop solutions iteratively. This means that we can develop some elements of the IT system or business product during a focused time period (known as an iteration) and then enhance or extend these via further iterations until we achieve something that we are ready to release to the stakeholder community. An initial version of a system or product might be released as a result of just one iteration; alternatively, several iterations may be needed to develop the first release of the product or system.

MoSCoW

The key to ensuring that the most important features and goals are delivered first is to clearly prioritise them, and the MoSCoW framework provides an excellent basis for doing this.

The MoSCoW approach has become a de facto standard prioritisation system for requirements, especially on projects that are developed and delivered in an iterative and incremental way. MoSCoW helps to clarify different priorities by using the following prioritisation categories:

- **Must have:** these are the requirements, features or goals that are fundamental to the success of the product to be delivered, whether a new business system (solution), working software or any other item offered by an organisation. This could be a new insurance product or training course. Whatever the product to be delivered, the 'must have' features form the minimum set of requirements. Without them, the delivered product – whether system or business – would fail to meet the business objectives. In short, these are the top priority and without them, we may as well deliver nothing at all.

- **Should have:** these are important requirements that need to be included but may be deferred, in the short term, to a subsequent product increment or release. However, it is important to recognise that the delay in implementing these requirements must be short, as the system will not be complete without them and therefore the project will be deemed as a failure if these are not met. They are mandatory requirements, but may be deferred temporarily where the project has time constraints.

- **Could have:** these are the requirements that can be quite easily left out of the current increment to be delivered. In fact, if there are budget and/or time constraints these requirements may eventually be dropped altogether.

- **Want to have, but won't have this time:** these are the optional requirements that should wait for a later phase/increment of the development. These requirements are specifically excluded from the plans for the current feature set to be delivered. It may be the case that these requirements are implemented in a later release of the system or product, but it is also possible that they are never implemented. It might be that the requirements become absolutely mandatory at a later point in time. Whatever the category, these requirements are recorded but deferred for the time being and must not be considered for inclusion in the current release. The reasons for deferring requirements are various:

  - they relate to an overall business strategy but are recognised as being part of a second or later phase for the strategy implementation;
  - they are not needed at this point, for example, they relate to a forthcoming legal or policy change;
  - they are possible enhancements to the product or system that would increase the complexity if implemented at this stage.

Figure 9.2 shows a representation of a list of requirements, work items or features that have been prioritised using the MoSCoW technique.

The MoSCoW rules provide the basis on which decisions are made about which features a product or solution development team will concentrate on at various points:

Figure 9.2 Prioritised list of requirements or work items using MoSCoW

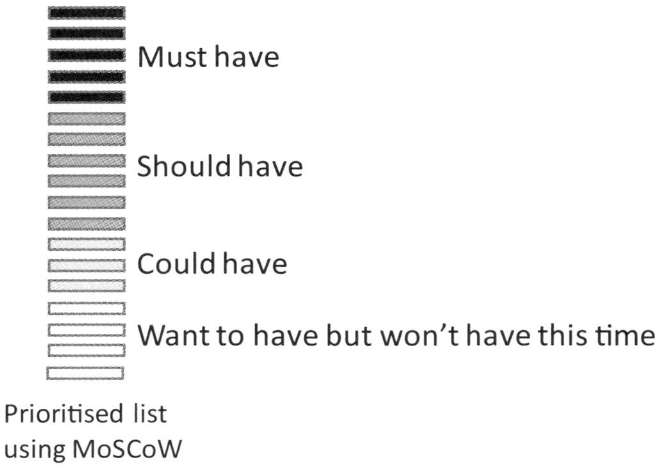

Must have

Should have

Could have

Want to have but won't have this time

Prioritised list
using MoSCoW

- during a timebox or iteration (for an increment of the product);
- within an increment that is to be released to the stakeholders;
- across the lifetime of the entire project.

The four MoSCoW categories are relevant where several increments are to be delivered and this is the case whether an agile development approach is used or not. However, where a project is using a linear approach, such as a standard 'waterfall' life cycle, which will involve one delivery of the solution, MoSCoW is not as appropriate as other techniques. In this situation it is preferable to use a framework with levels of priority that do not imply timing.

While MoSCoW has been used extensively in software development, it is an excellent prioritisation technique for any set of required features or changes. For example, the development of a new insurance product might involve a set of prioritised features that are introduced as follows:

- an initial set of features are introduced, possibly to appeal to a particular customer demographic, when the product is launched;
- other features are introduced to appeal to a different group of customers a short while afterwards;
- some features are included with one of the first two releases if it is not too time consuming to do so and they offer additional value;
- some features are deferred until the product has been in operation for a while and there is sufficient time to evaluate the level of importance of each feature.

Table 9.1 provides a list of the more popular prioritisation techniques available and provides advantages and disadvantages for each.

Table 9.1 Prioritisation techniques

Technique	Advantages	Disadvantages
Priority levels, e.g. 1, 2, 3; mandatory, desirable, nice-to-have	Easy to understand	Highly subjective Categories can be unclear No timing element
Kano technique: disatisfiers, satisfiers, delighters	Easy to understand Clear categories Outcome focus	Subjective No timing element
$100 allocation	Easy to understand Compares requirements	Highly subjective No timing element
AHP	Complex to understand Systematic comparison of requirements	Limited subjectivity Time consuming No timing element
WSJF	Complex to understand Systematic evaluation of requirements Timing addressed	Limited subjectivity Time consuming
MoSCoW	Straightforward to understand Timing addressed	Limited subjectivity Less rigorous than AHP and WSJF

APPLYING PRIORITISATION

A well-formed prioritisation approach such as MoSCoW is invaluable when planning a release, and the development iterations required to achieve this, as it provides a means of both identifying the essential features to include and building in contingency. Using software development as an example, we might identify a batch of requirements or backlog entries that are to be worked upon during an iteration, and these might have the following priorities:

- **The 'must have' items:** it is essential that these are delivered within the designated iteration (which means within the pre-defined time frame constraint).

- **The 'should have' items:** these need to be delivered as part of the system but can be deferred if necessary, although only in the short term.

- **The 'could have' items:** these can be included if time allows but they are not essential features.

So, how does using a prioritisation technique such as MoSCoW help during the application of agile business analysis to support the project? First, it enables the team to be aware of the immediate needs where non-delivery is not an option. Second, it allows the allocation of features that are essential and will be advantageous to the project if they are delivered during this iteration but, if delays or problems occur, could be deferred.

Third, it provides a means of considering the additional, 'wish list' features so that they could be included if there is time and effort available. Where these are small additions to higher priority features, including them can require little additional work (although they can succeed in gaining additional appreciation from the stakeholders). Sometimes, the work to include the higher priority items takes less time than anticipated so the 'could have' items ensure that there is no wasted effort during the iterations; other times, progress is slower than predicted and these items can be dropped without need to discuss with stakeholders or worry about the impact on the overall product. Provided there is agreement amongst the business and technical members, the team has the authority to reduce the scope and remove 'should have' or 'could have' requirements from the work of the iteration. This does not apply where a change of priority is proposed with regard to a 'must have' requirement; this has to be referred to the business sponsor, and possibly a wider group of business stakeholders.

Figure 9.3 shows a release schedule with the potential priorities included.

Figure 9.3 Release schedule showing MoSCoW priorities

Release 1	Release 2	Release 3	Release 4
Priorities: Must have Should have (if time) Could have (if time)	Priorities: Must have (were 'S') Could have (if time)	Priorities: Must have (were 'W') Should have (were 'W'; if time) Could have (if time)	Priorities: Must have (were 'W') Should have (were 'W'; if time) Could have (if time)

When deciding which 'should have' or 'could have' requirements are to be dropped from the work of an iteration, it is useful to review against the following criteria:

• Do the requirements relate closely to the 'must have' requirements? It makes sense to include requirements that extend the 'must have' requirements and remove those that have little connection to them.

• What is the potential business benefit that would accrue from delivering the requirements? If selecting which 'should have' or 'could have' requirements to include or remove, it is important to consider where the greatest benefit to the organisation would be derived.

Effective prioritisation helps to ensure that time and effort is not wasted during an iteration and provides a means of embedding contingency. As a result, the agile business analyst needs to be aware of the potential impact and application of prioritisation during iterations and the benefits this can deliver when managing the requirements document or backlog.

PRIORITISATION DECOMPOSITION

Requirements are identified at various levels of detail from a high-level strategic viewpoint through to a more detailed, deployable level. Therefore, it follows that high-level requirements can often be decomposed into lower-level requirements. For example, a general business requirement might state the need to reflect the corporate marketing policy in every aspect of a business change. This might be decomposed into lower level, non-functional requirements that are concerned with usability and navigation, and functional requirements concerning information provision and format.

It is also the case that the overall goal to be achieved by a requirement may be decomposed and there may be different priorities assigned to each decomposed requirement or goal. Goal decomposition is discussed in Chapter 8. An example decomposition with differing priorities is shown in Figure 9.4.

Figure 9.4 Decomposed requirements/goals with priority levels

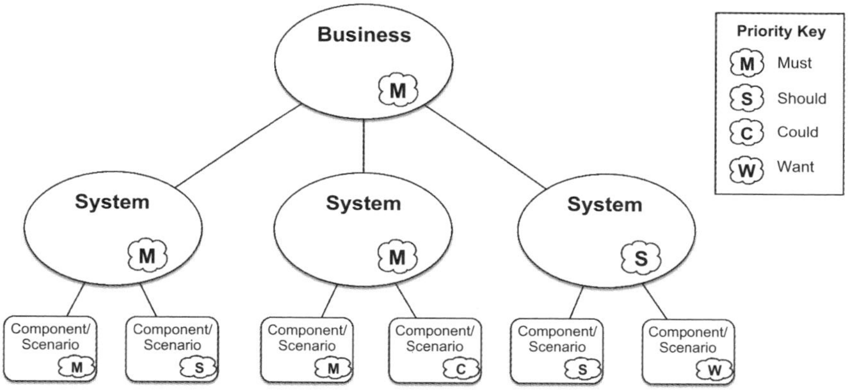

An example might be as follows:

- A general business requirement regarding information security is prioritised as a 'must have'.

- A non-functional requirement setting out the need for access permissions to be allocated to a defined user role is prioritised as a 'should have'.

- Another non-functional requirement setting out the need for encrypted data to be transferred to another system is prioritised as a 'want to have but won't have this time'.

PRIORITISATION ISSUES

Prioritisation is not a straightforward process. It requires a great deal of thought and needs to be firmly embedded within the business context, with a focus on understanding what the business needs are and where the most business value might be derived. As a result, there are some issues that are regularly encountered during the prioritisation process.

Everything is a must

The major problem encountered with prioritisation is that while we know what to do once the requirements have been allocated a level of priority, the process to do this can be difficult and require a great deal of thought. The customer has to have an understanding of the prioritisation approach and the relevance of each of the priority levels. The business analyst is well placed to support and facilitate the prioritisation process, helping the customer to understand the value or impact of a requirement and the dependencies between them, and therefore helping to decide on the relative priority of each.

The starting point is to consider the business value that will accrue from the delivery of a requirement or achievement of a defined goal and, correspondingly, the degree of importance it would be allocated by the customer. However, this often results in the majority of requirements being in the 'high', 'mandatory' or 'must have' category; this is typically the initial position taken by the business managers and staff when they are asked for the level of prioritisation to be allocated to requirements. Unfortunately, it is extremely unlikely that there is sufficient budget or time to meet all of the requirements in one fell swoop; this is rarely achievable. However, it is also the case that if this were true, the flexibility derived from a prioritisation technique such as MoSCoW is completely lost. Without lower priority requirements, there is no opportunity to focus on early delivery of a more limited solution that includes only the key requirements. Equally, the possibility of reducing the scope of the solution, possibly in order to bring the project back onto time and budget, is removed.

Therefore, it is important to prioritise requirements and understand which ones fall within the minimum set for the initial product delivered, and which can be deferred or left out altogether. Given that human nature tends to favour the highest level of priority, the following steps can be useful in sorting the absolutely vital requirements from those of lesser importance:

- Discussing the factors that might prevent or delay delivery of the requirement is vital. These include the costs likely to be incurred, the complexity and the corresponding level of effort required to define or develop, and the risk of non-delivery (which may relate to the technical risk associated with the requirement). It is often the case that once the level of difficulty likely to be involved with the delivery of a requirement is considered, the decision regarding the priority becomes more focused.

- Prioritise requirements from the lowest priority to the highest. The natural tendency is to work through the priority levels in the order set out by the framework, so:

  - level 1, followed by level 2, followed by level 3, and so on;
  - 'must haves', followed by 'should haves', followed by 'could haves', followed by 'want to have but not yet' requirements.

  However, a more rigorous approach is to set the priority for each requirement as 'nice to have' or 'want to have but won't have this time' and then require a good justification to move the requirement into a higher level of priority.

- An alternative approach that can be very helpful is to begin by asking which features could be deferred or which goals may not be met for a given period. An extension of this is to assume that they can all be deferred unless a clear argument can be made for this not to be the case. This then leaves a set of requirements that need to be included, or at least considered for inclusion, straightaway. The next step is to discuss which features could be left out if necessary, as they are not essential. One way of determining how essential a feature is involves asking who will be responsible for providing the detailed information (particularly if this is a relatively complex feature), as this helps to focus the mind of the source or owner of the requirement on whether or not it is actually as important as first thought. The final step is to ask which of the remaining essential requirements can be left out until a second release of the product.

- The ranking approaches – $100, AHP and WSJF – can provide a more rigorous approach when prioritising and as they use comparison between items, can help to clarify which requirements really are 'essential' for inclusion in the current iteration.

These step-by-step approaches are very helpful when conducting agile business analysis. They enable us to focus the discussion by asking questions that consider prioritisation from a different angle. Rather than asking, 'What level of priority or importance should be allocated?', we begin by asking 'Which of these requirements can be deferred for a while?'; or 'Which of these requirements might be left out altogether?'; or even, 'Which of these items is more important than the others?' and then progress through the lower priority levels towards the essential features. Suggested questions to ask during the prioritisation process are shown in Figure 9.5 below.

Figure 9.5 Questions used during prioritisation

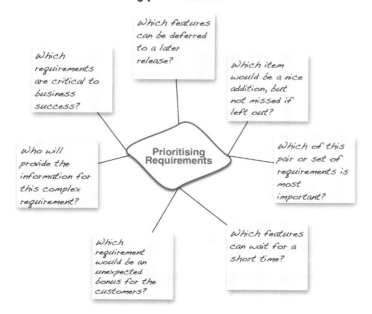

141

Too early or too late prioritisation

Prioritisation is often conducted at an unnecessarily late stage. Sometimes, we wait until we have fully understood the business requirements, and obtained significant detail on them, but in this situation we may have wasted time investigating and defining requirements that will later be removed or deferred. To combat this, it is beneficial to prioritise early and concentrate on the aspects of highest importance first. If a high-level business requirement is not of top priority, there is little to be gained from investigating the detail at an early stage; this can be deferred until the specific area is being considered for delivery.

Therefore, it is a more effective use of time, and is more in line with the agile philosophy, to prioritise the high-level business requirements or business use cases at an early stage, and then use these priorities as a basis for identifying where the early work needs to be done. This will help to identify the key business goals that need to be tackled first and the less urgent goals that can wait until a later stage. All of this is the pre-project work that is essential to defining a solution backlog and yet is often omitted from agile methods.

Working in this way will help the agile business analyst to adopt a levelled approach to the initial analysis and help the project team focus on where early value can be obtained. Prioritising at a business level and decomposing only those items of high priority, ensures that time is not wasted detailing requirements that are not to be a high priority, which would delay the delivery of the working solution. After all, it is the delivery of the working solution that is the measure of success and builds trust with the customer.

There is often an assumption made that all of the requirements identified initially should be defined to the same level of detail, but this is the antithesis of the agile philosophy. It is more efficient, and focuses effort on the more important areas, if the following approach is adopted:

- The high-level business requirements are investigated and defined. A business use case diagram is extremely beneficial in performing this work.

- The high-level business goals to be achieved by the business use cases are defined.

- The business requirements/use cases are prioritised.

- The 'must have' business requirements are investigated in further detail. The goals are decomposed and the priorities allocated at the decomposed level.

- The 'should have' business requirements may be investigated in further detail and the priorities decomposed if this is felt to be beneficial. For example, they are 'should have' requirements that may be delivered as part of the first release.

- The other requirements are left at an overview level of definition until it would be beneficial to investigate them in more detail.

This approach would result in higher priority requirements being defined in greater detail than others, and this focuses the effort where it is likely to derive the greatest benefit for the organisation. An additional benefit to this is that trust in the relationship with stakeholders is developed as they see that the work is progressing and that they are likely to receive some of their requirements early through the delivery of the working solution. This principle applies whether we are working on business improvement, product development or software development projects.

New requirements often emerge as existing requirements are defined in more detail and as the project progresses. These requirements need to be prioritised, typically using the MoSCoW framework, as they arise in order to establish when they need to be considered in detail.

Changes to priorities

As solutions develop, it is inevitable that there will be changes to requirements and goals. This is to be expected on an agile project and, as a result, it is also expected that the work will be prioritised and re-prioritised on an ongoing basis as the project progresses. This is highly productive and helps to ensure that:

- There is a focus on what is most important at any point in time.
- A sense of trust is developed between the project team and the customers.
- The most important features are delivered first.
- The need to manage change to the requirements, particularly those of a lower priority, is reduced.

Re-prioritisation should be limited to the period between iterations rather than occurring during an iteration, and if possible should be concerned with planning for the next release or increment. If we are using MoSCoW, once the initial set of 'must have' requirements (plus possibly some 'should have' and 'could have' requirements) has been delivered, the planning for the next increment should begin with a re-prioritisation of the requirements catalogue or backlog. At this point, it is likely that any 'should have' requirements will be allocated a 'must have' priority level. However, it is also important to review the requirements in the other priority categories:

- The 'could have' requirements may have increased in importance due to changes to the organisation, or external forces within the business environment or a new goal being set.
- The 'want to have but not yet' requirements may now need to be considered for early delivery. This could result in them being re-prioritised such that they are now categorised as 'must have' or 'should have'. It is also possible that once they are investigated in detail, they are recognised as 'could have' priorities or that they lead to decomposed requirements that are at different levels of priority.

All in all, it is possible for the priorities to change significantly as a result of re-prioritisation, bringing new requirements to the fore in order that they may be included in the next release of the product or system.

CONCLUSION

Prioritisation is a fundamental activity for scheduling the work of agile projects. It is also an important area for business analysts, as it enables clarity of understanding about where to focus immediate efforts and provides an excellent basis to support the customers in achieving their business goals. Without prioritisation, there may be a temptation to do too much at once and make hasty decisions. Resources may be spread too thinly and not used effectively. Ultimately, this can lead to a diminished clarity of purpose that may result in a failure to deliver anything of value.

Business analysts who have adopted the agile philosophy and mindset recognise the importance of facilitating the focused, early prioritisation of requirements and goals, and understanding the need for decomposition and prioritisation at different levels of definition. This enables them to work on delivering the features that achieve the most important goals as soon as possible. Using this approach, agile business analysis can ensure that there is improved support for organisations through the early delivery of solutions, which will help customers realise the business benefits as quickly as possible.

FURTHER READING

Agile Business Consortium (2016) The DSDM Agile Project Framework (2014 onwards). Agile Business Consortium. Available from: www.dsdm.org/resources/dsdm-handbooks/the-dsdm-Agile-project-framework-2014-onwards [20 December 2016].

Paul, D., Cadle, J. and Yeates, D. (2014) *Business analysis: 3rd edition*. Swindon: BCS.

Pohl, K. and Rupp, C. (2011) *Requirements engineering fundamentals*. San Rafael, CA: Rocky Nook.

Saaty, T. (1994) The analytic hierarchy process. *Interfaces*, 24 (6): 19–43.

Scaled Agile Inc. (2010–2016) WSJF (Weighted Shortest Job First) Abstract. Available from: http://scaledAgileframework.com/wsjf/ [20 December 2016].

Scaled Agile Inc. (2014–2016) SAFe 4.0 for Lean Software and System Engineering. Available from: www.scaledAgileframework.com/ [20 December 2016].

10 DECIDING THE REQUIREMENTS APPROACH

This chapter covers the following topics:

- the requirements engineering framework;
- planning the requirements approach;
- issues with requirements engineering;
- agile requirements elicitation;
- requirements elicitation techniques;
- the role of business analysis in elicitation.

INTRODUCTION

Understanding the customers' requirements is a major area of business analysis activity, which requires careful consideration at the outset of a change project. This involves determining how the requirements are to be elicited, and the extent to which they will be defined. While detailed requirements are expected to evolve during agile software development, this is also the case for the other areas of the solution, for example, the requirements that are to be met by business process changes. However, there remains a need for a clear definition of the high-level requirements that provide the context for the change project.

This chapter considers a means of determining the requirements approach and how the requirements engineering framework may be adapted and applied within an agile project.

THE REQUIREMENTS ENGINEERING FRAMEWORK

Requirements engineering is a framework for obtaining, defining and managing good quality requirements. There are some fundamental stages of requirements engineering that need to be understood and utilised within any project and these stages are defined in the requirements engineering framework shown in Figure 10.1. Deciding the approach to requirements engineering will vary, depending on several factors that may include the project scope, complexity of the project, budget and resources available and expected business outcomes. A framework, such as that provided in Figure 10.1, is only a starting point as all projects are different and it should not be assumed that one requirements engineering approach will be suitable for all.

Figure 10.1 Requirements engineering framework

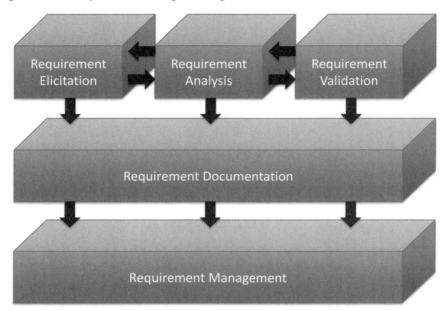

Looking at each stage within the requirements engineering framework allows us to explore their use and validity within an agile approach as follows:

Elicitation   The requirement is identified through collaboration with stakeholders. In the early stages of a change project, the elicitation activity may have a wide scope, typically by focusing on higher-level business requirements, and limited detail. As the project progresses, the requirements elicitation work may take a more detailed approach, concentrating on a narrower scope. Elicitation is an iterative and enduring activity that takes place throughout a project.

Analysis   Requirements are analysed to determine whether they are relevant, realistic, ambiguous in any way, can be tested, contribute to business goals, or overlap or conflict with other requirements. The priority level for each requirement is agreed with the appropriate stakeholders. Modelling requirements can assist the analysis activity. For example, a system use case diagram provides a means of understanding the outline scope of the required system and the actors who are interested in the system features. This helps put the requirements in context, ensuring that a fragmented picture is avoided and supporting both iterative development and incremental delivery. It also provides a summary visualisation of the functional requirements and avoids the need for lengthy textual descriptions. Other models may also be used to help in the analysis of areas such as data, interface and processing requirements.

Validation Requirements are validated by review, typically using visual techniques such as prototypes and models; these may take the form of physical or automated prototypes or diagrams. In the early stages of a project, requirements validation may focus on agreeing an outline scope and a set of initial, business requirements that provide a basis for further elaboration. When using agile, a requirement is not validated until it is 'in use' and may be demonstrated within a working solution provided by new or improved processes or software.

Documentation Requirements need to be documented to clarify what it is that the business wants the solution to provide. However, the amount of detail in the documentation depends on factors such as the levels of complexity and priority. Further, the detail of the requirement description is likely to increase as the time for implementing the requirement draws near. The level of requirements documentation needs to be decided by the project team and should be minimised such that it is '**just enough**' to enable the project team to plan, design and develop working solutions.

It is important to distinguish between requirements documentation and system design documentation. Accurate system design documentation is concerned with the way in which the requirements are delivered, so should reflect the working software rather than the requirements.

Management Once documented, requirements must be managed. A '**just enough**' approach to documenting requirements minimises the amount of management. Managing requirements includes agreeing such things as where agreed requirements will be stored, how the link between solution requirements and the business objectives and project goals is ensured, and how they should be organised.

Traceability of requirements is an important area that needs particular consideration when working on an agile project. The extent to which traceability is required should be considered before putting in place any mechanisms to enable traceability. It is also the case that the potential for ensuring traceability will be affected by the documentation approach selected. For example, if it is decided to document the general requirements in a list and to use a model such as a use case diagram to document the scope of the system requirements, it may be sufficient to adopt the following approach (also see Figure 13.1):

- **Vertical traceability:** for each use case, define which general requirement is supported.
- **Horizontal traceability:** for each general requirement and use case, document who raised each requirement and the status (such as when it will be delivered).

Consideration should also be given to the extent to which changes to the requirements should be recorded. It is the nature of general requirements, which are focused on stating policy constraints and identifying business objectives, that they remain relatively static. However, at a solution level, where the requirement descriptions comprise detailed definitions, this is rarely the case. Where it is felt that a requirement needs to be documented in specific detail, it will be necessary to ensure that the documentation is maintained in line with any changes made. However, in an agile environment it is typically the case that solution requirements are described as outline features and the detail is elaborated during the development of the solution. In this case, the changes that need to be recorded and linked to the documentation are those that affect the outline descriptions. Otherwise, the view may be taken that the exploration of detail involves exploring various options and that the requirement does not change but has evolved as greater understanding is achieved.

Requirements slices

The application of the requirements engineering framework is determined by the solution development approach adopted. A linear approach would require each stage to be undertaken in depth to ensure that a comprehensive requirements document is produced. An agile approach necessitates iterative development and incremental delivery and may result in revisiting each stage many times as the requirements evolve and are further understood, decomposed and prioritised. It is still important that each of the stages is undertaken when using agile, but the extent to which this is done, the techniques applied and the required outcomes, will differ.

One way of considering this is to think of applying the requirements engineering framework in 'horizontal slices' as shown in Figure 10.2. At an initial stage, such as a feasibility or pre-project analysis, the focus may be on eliciting and defining the general requirements, with less emphasis on the solution requirements. This reflects that there is little point in elaborating all the solution requirements in considerable depth at an early stage, as it is likely that the details will be subject to change. The next 'slice' may then be concerned with a subset of the initial requirements so that the relevant solution requirements are elaborated to the level required for further development. This can continue through several slices in line with the number of increments required to deliver the entire solution.

It is likely to be the case that more effort is expended initially on elicitation, with less spent on the other stages. Similarly, more analysis may be carried out in a later iteration once the scope and context is understood. Initial collaborations with stakeholders typically result in the elicitation of requirements, which are then recorded in outline only. During the next iteration, a subset of the elicited requirements will need to be analysed and this may require a detailed analysis of the selected set, depending upon the characteristics of each requirement. For example, where a set of requirements is concerned with delivering features that contain complex calculations, an analysis of the business rules at an early stage will be beneficial to the project.

Figure 10.2 Slices of requirements engineering applied iteratively

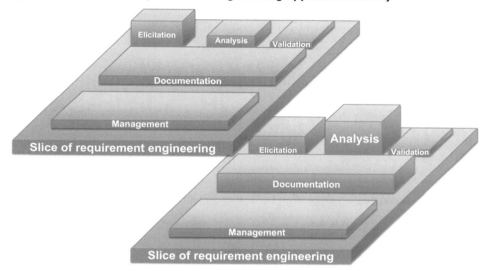

During each of the 'slices' the approach to documenting requirements may differ, with some requiring more detail than others. Similarly, the extent to which validation and management of the requirements is needed will need to be determined. This is discussed below.

In contrast, a project following a more linear approach may spend more time in each stage sequentially and therefore the slices will be much deeper and there will be fewer of them, with maybe only two or three slices per project whereas an agile project may have far more horizontal slices.

PLANNING THE REQUIREMENTS APPROACH

It is prudent to plan the requirements engineering work so that all participants are agreed on an approach that will meet their needs. There are three aspects to consider: the level of detail of the requirements documentation, the types of documentation to be created and the timing of its production. To do this, the purpose of the requirements artefacts needs to be considered; there is little benefit to be gained from producing models or other documents that no one is likely to use or understand. When documentation should be produced will relate directly to the selection of the requirements for development. Until this point, there is little benefit to be gained from documenting the requirements in any detail.

When planning requirements, it is useful to consider the following questions:

- Are the scope of the solution and business goals well understood?
- Are there business or technical constraints that need to be considered?
- Are the different POPIT™ elements for the proposed solution understood?
- Who will use the requirements and/or models?
- What format should be used for the requirements or models to meet the project needs?
- Do the requirements or models need to be kept up to date?
- How long do the requirements or models need to be retained?

A useful tool to help with the planning of requirements is the simplified FMM introduced in Chapter 6. Figure 10.3 sets out a planned approach to the requirements artefacts and shows how the simplified FMM can be used to develop the requirements approach.

Figure 10.3 A suggested FMM plan for the requirements approach

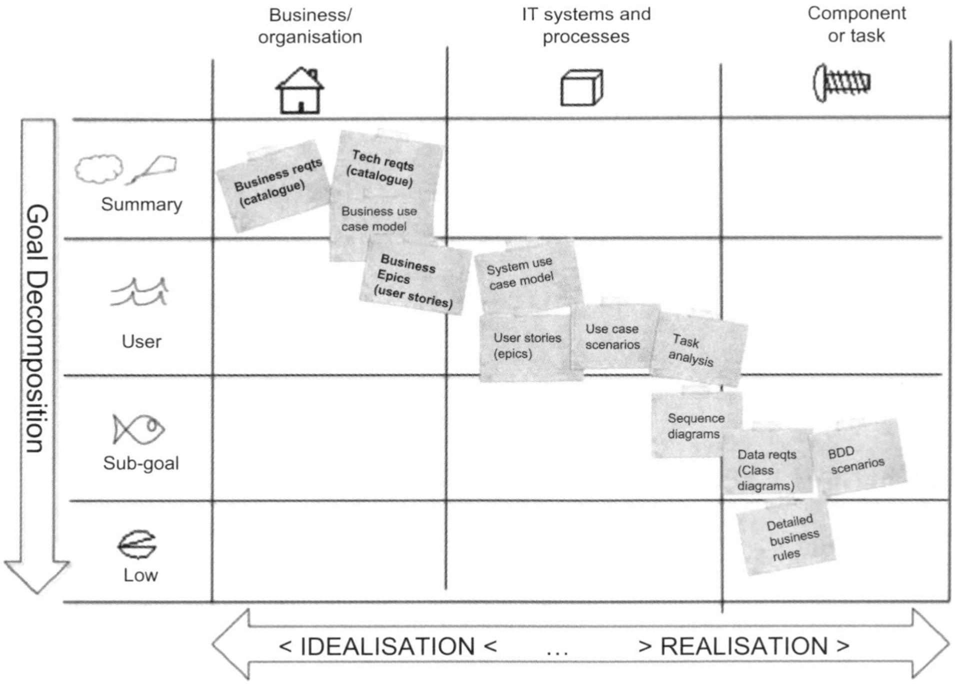

The simplified FMM is an excellent tool to plan how the requirements will be captured and recorded at each level. This will vary from project to project and will depend on factors such as the size and complexity of the project as well as the nature of the organisation. It is important to note that this planning must be done in conjunction with the development team, who will utilise the defined requirements, and the customer, who will need to collaborate to ensure that the delivered solution offers value to the business.

ISSUES WITH REQUIREMENTS ENGINEERING

Requirements engineering encompasses the core business analysis skills of requirements elicitation, analysis and definition. The term 'elicitation' is used advisedly in this framework, as it puts the onus on the analyst to work collaboratively with customers to uncover requirements rather than expect that they will be readily available. Most stakeholders will not know what they require without assistance, so requirements are elicited, rather than gathered, and this task needs considerable expertise. Requirements elicitation is the first stage in the requirements engineering framework in Figure 10.1.

It is very hard to express up front and in full detail something that you have never had or experienced. Sometimes stakeholders think they have a clear idea about what they want but often the focus is on a solution rather than the underlying requirements. It is part of the business analysis skill set to be able to challenge and analyse stated requirements, and assess the impact of proposed changes, to ensure that accurate and relevant requirements are defined. While it is possible to provide ideas initially, requirements tend to change as the project progresses and understanding evolves and deepens. For this reason, the requirements for an agile change project are not defined in their entirety at the outset; they are elaborated when required, typically in subsets that are allocated to an iteration for development.

The traditional approach to requirements engineering, shown here in Figure 10.4, can be ineffective for projects today.

Figure 10.4 Traditional approach to requirements engineering

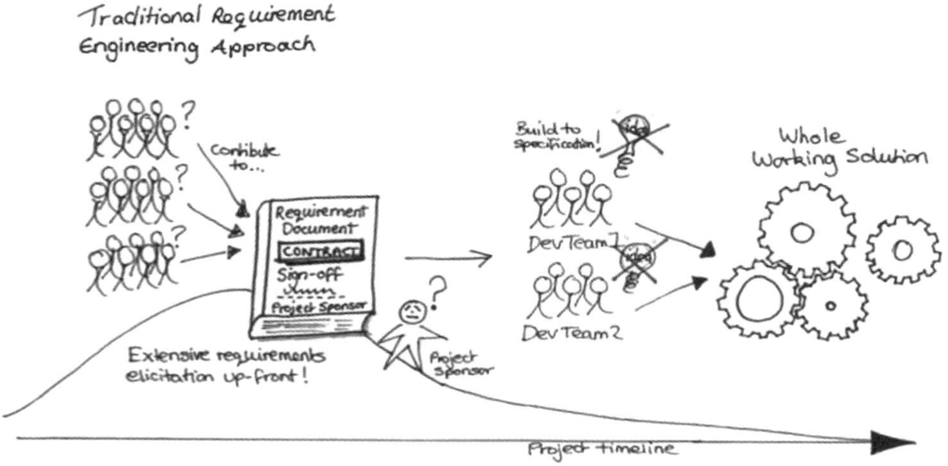

Figure 10.4 shows how requirements engineering may be concentrated at the beginning of a project and the results captured and signed-off in the requirements document. Not only is arriving at a complete, consistent and agreed specification difficult, but there is a high risk that much time will be spent changing and updating the requirements during the rest of the project. As requirements change, as many of the detailed solution requirements inevitably will, change control processes must be implemented to manage the changes and this can be very time consuming. If we analyse this approach to requirements definition and change control using three of the Lean 'wastes', we can identify the following issues:

- **Overproduction:** requirements are elicited, analysed and recorded too early and in too much detail.

- **Inventory:** there has to be an investment in time for recording and managing the requirements in order to keep them up to date.

- **Overprocessing:** applying tighter tolerances in the approval and sign-off procedures than is necessary. Getting formal approvals carried out, all of which may be in vain if/when the requirements change.

To combat some of these problems we need to consider a different approach to requirements engineering.

AGILE REQUIREMENTS ENGINEERING

For some agile projects, requirements definition can be straightforward, involving discussion and collaboration with one customer representative who is the 'voice of the customer'. Unfortunately, most projects are more complicated. As discussed in Chapter 7, there are typically many different customers and stakeholders to consider, all of whom have different views on what the solution needs to achieve. Understanding those individual views and forming them into something that customers and stakeholders can agree on requires extensive analytical and interpersonal skills. There is also a need for ongoing engagement to gain buy-in from the wider stakeholder group.

There may be problems with requirements engineering within agile development projects, as often the skills needed to do this work are lacking within the development team. One reason for these problems relates to the over-simplistic role titles, such as 'development team' or 'product owner', that are used in some methods. These titles do not help to clarify the skill set needed from those working on the project and can imply that the primary focus is on the software development. However, software features or software products should not be the focus of the development; as discussed in Chapter 6, the focus should be on the required business outcomes. If skilled business analysts are not available or involved, requirements engineering can end up being carried out by individuals who have the responsibility for this work but little practical experience. If the product owner has little or no business analysis experience or training and is left to conduct the requirements work, it is unlikely that the results will be satisfactory. Some typical issues that arise when agile teams conduct requirements engineering are:

- failing to undertake stakeholder analysis and missing key stakeholders;

- putting complete trust in one person to represent the 'voice of the customer';

- failing to engage with the wider stakeholder group and understand the different requirement viewpoints;

- focusing too much on eliciting functionality and features and ignoring the non-functional requirements;

- failing to analyse how the new solution will change current working practices, job roles, management structures and business processes.

Defining requirements for agile projects requires a different approach which is shown in Figure 10.5.

Figure 10.5 An agile approach to eliciting requirements

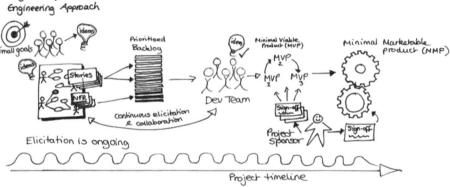

Figure 10.5 shows how the requirements elicitation and analysis needs to be ongoing, aligned to the iterations of the project and the requirements engineering horizontal slices described earlier. Sign-off happens at the end of each iteration and increment and it is the working solution, in the form of MVPs or the MMP, that are signed off, not the requirements document. This means that the requirements don't have to be fully specified in advance, but can be ideas that evolve and change over time. In this way, the requirements are emergent during the development process. The development team are responsible for building the solution that delivers the requirements, so will bring their skills and ideas to the development process. Within an agile project, they can engage and collaborate with the stakeholders and thus explore the potential and viability of these ideas. For example, do they offer positive outcomes for the customer?

Figure 10.5 does not show a specific business analyst role but there is an abundance of business analysis taking place; not all projects have designated business analysts, but they all need business analysis to be done. In this example, requirements engineering doesn't just happen at the start of the project, it is ongoing throughout because as the first ideas are formed, understood and prioritised, they give rise to new ideas that again need to be elicited and analysed. In this sense, requirements engineering is an iterative process that ebbs and flows along with the iterative and incremental heartbeat of the project.

REQUIREMENTS ELICITATION TECHNIQUES

It is important to employ elicitation techniques that will combat some of the problems that can arise during requirements elicitation on agile projects. Requirements elicitation helps business analysts to understand who to engage with, the problem to be solved, and which goals to prioritise and meet first. If this is not done, we could end up delivering a poor or limited solution. The use of facilitated workshops, involving a small group of business users with the aim of developing user stories, is an extremely popular approach for agile projects. However, this approach may not overcome the issues identified earlier and needs to be supported by other techniques.

Agile requirements evolve throughout the project and so it makes sense that we have a set of techniques for eliciting them that can be applied continuously. This is an iterative approach, where the high-level requirements are explored to uncover the detail needed to develop the solution. Table 10.1 explains the most useful techniques for evolving requirements iteratively.

Table 10.1 Techniques for evolving requirements iteratively

User interview	User interviews are still the most widely used technique in requirements engineering work; they provide a means of eliciting a great deal of useful information. While agile approaches focus on collaborative working, there is still merit in conducting one-to-one interviews to:
	• build rapport and trust with stakeholders;
	• identify individual stakeholder perspectives or even personal agendas;
	• highlight organisational politics;
	• understand how things work currently and where the issues lie;
	• understand the landscape for the change;
	• clarify the business goals to be achieved.
Survey/ questionnaire	Surveys can be useful to obtain specific information from a large group of stakeholders where interviewing individuals, or possibly running a series of workshops, would not be practical or cost effective. For example, where there is a user story that has a large user population, it can be helpful to use a questionnaire to research answers to a specific question or to gain user input on the level of priority.

(Continued)

Table 10.1 (Continued)

Observation	Observing the work in operation is an excellent way of clarifying or eliciting new requirements as follows: • understanding the order in which the work is done; • identifying where there are potential improvements in a process or software product; • highlighting where tacit knowledge exists.
Story-writing workshop	A story-writing workshop is probably the primary method of obtaining user stories and should include developers, users and the product customer. Business analysts may contribute to the story writing or facilitate the workshop. The story-writing workshop is the most effective way to quickly identify stories and is discussed further in Chapter 12.
Scenario	Scenarios draw out detailed requirements that include: • sequencing and order; • 'what if' analysis; • hidden business rules; • data constraints; • exceptional conditions. Scenarios are covered in more detail in Chapter 12.
Prototyping	Prototyping is one of the core techniques used within agile development to elicit new requirements. This is because prototyping is a way of visualising the requirements, whether using a low fidelity storyboard or working software. Prototypes help in the elicitation of requirements to improve or change the behaviour, look and feel or functionality of the solution. These are valuable requirements that would be hard to elicit in the early stages of a project. Prototyping is discussed further below.

Prototyping

Prototyping plays a large role in agile software development and can also be used to visualise other elements of the holistic solution. It is an elicitation technique because it unearths new requirements that are often identified through the use of the prototype. There are a range of prototyping approaches that can be used for different projects and deciding which one to use relates to the nature of the project and the solution under development. Where part of the solution involves a process, there may be a need to prototype forms or reports; where the prototype relates to a software solution, there may be prototypes of the user interface or of the internal functionality. It can be instructive to consider where the greatest risks lie and use prototyping to confirm or correct the proposed solution approach. There are two categories of prototype: throwaway and evolutionary.

Throwaway   The prototype is developed for the sole purpose of eliciting or analysing requirements where there is a lack of clarity, for example, where the project is in its early scoping phase. Throwaway prototypes can be low fidelity, perhaps a flip chart with sticky notes or a PowerPoint mock-up of a wireframe, or may be high fidelity using more sophisticated software packages. Whether high or low fidelity, the throwaway prototype is discarded after it has served its purpose.

Evolutionary The prototype evolves as the project progresses. Early working prototypes are used to gain more concrete understanding and are then further developed, tested, implemented and adapted as greater understanding develops.

Scenarios and prototyping are often used in tandem when eliciting and analysing interface requirements for software systems. Each step within a scenario represents an interaction between the user and the system. The interface displays instructions, captures data and presents information. The prototype helps in the elicitation of the presentational layout and the data requirements. A low fidelity throwaway prototype for a scenario where a customer registers an account is shown in Figure 10.6.

Figure 10.6 A low fidelity throwaway prototype

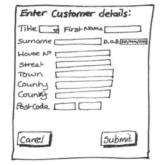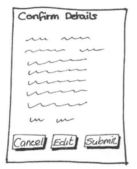

This type of prototype helps business analysts to present a visualisation of the scenario to the business user and work collaboratively to define the data, information and usability requirements. The additional benefits of a prototype such as this is that it is quick to create and change.

THE ROLE OF BUSINESS ANALYSIS IN ELICITATION

Not all organisations have dedicated and experienced business analysts. However, in every organisation and on every project, whether it is an IT or business change project, business analysis is needed to elicit requirements effectively. The business analyst role was originally developed to bridge the gap between business users and developers. However, where a collaborative team is working on an agile project, it is important that the business analyst does not act as a 'translator', speaking on behalf of the customers or the developers, as this has the potential to introduce bottlenecks or errors to the process. Figure 10.7 represents this situation.

Figure 10.7 Business analyst standing between customer and development team

Historically, there has been a separation between the technical staff and the user community on IT projects due to an assumption that communication between these two groups is problematic. While there may have been some situations where this assumption has been proven to be correct, agile development teams seek to engage T-shaped professionals (see Chapter 7) who work collaboratively towards a common business outcome. This approach helps everyone to develop a range of skills that will improve communication between the specialist disciplines. There is a role for the business analyst in this process, which involves facilitating discussions and clarifying any points of confusion. This role is represented in Figure 10.8.

Figure 10.8 The business analyst role in facilitating collaboration

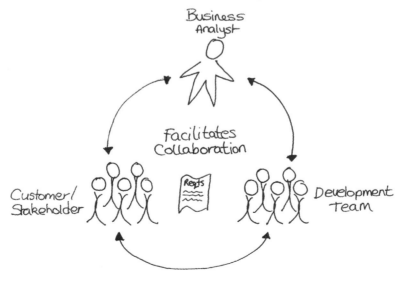

Where there are no dedicated business analysts on a project, this facilitation role will still be required. It may be performed by members of the development team (where they have the requisite skills) or it could be done by a business representative, such as the product owner or even the project sponsor.

CONCLUSION

It is imperative that the agile business analyst understands that a 'one-size-fits-all' approach to requirements engineering is not effective. Deciding the correct approach requires business analysts to understand the business requirements so that horizontal requirement 'slices' can be selected and elaborated in order to deliver increments of the working solution at an early stage. This will help to prove or disprove any assumptions and achieve the desired outcomes for the business.

Elicitation techniques help business analysts ensure that the right solution is developed and delivered. Without sound elicitation, the project could miss tacit knowledge, make assumptions and deliver solutions that meet what the customer wants, but not what the customer needs.

As individuals employed within agile teams accept that they need to become T-shaped professionals, there is a concern that business analysis skills may be overlooked. This would be to the detriment of delivered business solutions, as it is clear that customers need help to uncover and elaborate their requirements. This requires the support of professionals with business analysis skills but if there are no business analysts working on a project, the responsibility for this work will need to pass to other members of the development team. Whichever is the case, business analysis is needed to define the requirements to the extent needed by the project to ensure that working solutions that offer benefits to the business are delivered.

FURTHER READING

Cadle, J. (ed.) (2014) *Developing information systems*. Swindon: BCS.

Cadle, J., Paul, D. and Turner, P. (2014) *Business analysis techniques*. Swindon: BCS.

Paul, D., Cadle, J. and Yeates, D. (2014) *Business analysis: 3rd edition*. Swindon: BCS.

11 MODELLING USERS AND PERSONAS

This chapter covers the following topics:

- benefits of a modelling approach to requirements;
- modelling users and functionality;
- analysing users and roles;
- analysing personas and misuse characters;
- analysing the system context and scope;
- visualising user journeys.

INTRODUCTION

Change projects are usually instigated by managers but their impacts fall, in the main, upon the staff who carry out the operational work. The group of people in this category are usually known as the 'users' and this chapter examines the techniques that are used on agile projects to understand their needs and priorities. These techniques, which include persona analysis, use case modelling and user journeys, help to ensure that there is sufficient understanding of the user community before engaging in detailed analysis of the requirements. Whereas Chapter 6 focused on the business system models at the summary 'cloud' and summary 'kite' levels, this chapter is concerned with modelling the IT system and processes from summary level to user level.

BENEFITS OF A MODELLING APPROACH TO REQUIREMENTS

Chapter 6 explored the rationale for building models during business change projects. While that chapter focused on how we might model business systems, this chapter discusses modelling to understand the people who will need to use a new IT system. Techniques that model the user community offer a diagrammatical means of understanding the characteristics of the system users. This helps us to understand where there is the potential for problems or there are particular constraints that need to be taken into account when designing the solution.

Different models provide different perspectives on the problem being addressed. The simplified FMM shown in Figure 11.1 identifies three levels where models are relevant during agile business analysis. The levels show a direction of travel that includes three modelling perspectives: the business system, the solution and the system components.

Figure 11.1 IT systems and processes in 'the simplified FMM'

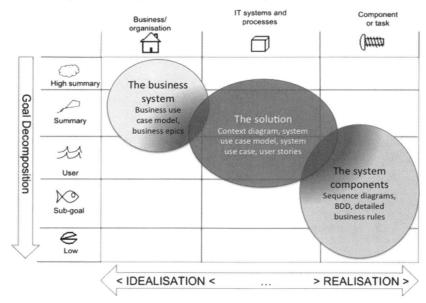

Some of the key benefits from building models on agile projects are as follows:

- they provide a canvas for exploring and discussing the scope of the system;
- they enrich the process of communicating information;
- they enable the analyst to conduct 'what if?' analysis and experiment with alternatives;
- they represent a clear statement of the information gained and help with the validation of understanding;
- they provide a means of investigating the existing situation, exploring options and conducting gap analysis;
- they offer opportunities for stakeholder collaboration.

Workshops can benefit hugely from the use of models. For example, a use case diagram provides a means of capturing collective understanding, providing a visual representation that provokes discussion and generates ideas. As a result, the process of discussing a particular aspect of the system, and developing the corresponding models, within a workshop environment, aids stakeholder engagement. While models offer benefits during the system development process, the collaboration activity required to develop a model is as beneficial. Where stakeholders have collaborated in the development of models, they are more likely to be committed to them.

The agile value of **Just Enough, Just in Time** also needs to be borne in mind as perfecting a model can result in diminishing returns from the effort deployed in doing this. If too much time is spent perfecting the model, then the value of the model is reduced. Similarly, the use of models needs to be considered, as this will help to determine whether or not they need to be kept up to date. If a model has been used for a particular purpose, there is little point in continually revising it once that purpose has been achieved. Scott Ambler has represented the 'point of maximal value' from models in the graph shown in Figure 11.2.

Figure 11.2 The value of modelling

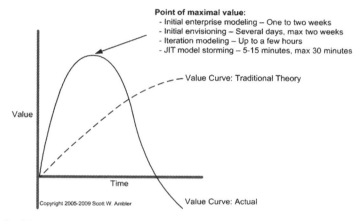

(reproduced with permission from www.agilemodeling.com)

The time axis represents effort rather than elapsed time. Therefore, a team may spend between 4 and 10 days of effort building models during the initial requirements envisioning work, but the effort may be spread over several elapsed weeks.

The Agile Manifesto is clear that documentation takes second place to the working software. It is important that agile business analysts bear this maxim in mind and ensure that models are only created when useful and updated when necessary.

MODELLING USERS AND FUNCTIONALITY

System use case diagrams show the scope of a proposed system and the actors (or job roles) who wish to interact with the system to achieve their business goals. Modelling the user interactions and the system functionality in further detail will often uncover that a system use case is very large or complex, so cannot be achieved in full in early releases. Modelling this level of detail can, therefore, be vital when adopting agile. Figure 11.3 shows a way to use modelling to move from the business context to the system delivery and iteration contexts, where working software will be delivered. While this example shows an IT project below the dotted line, the same approach can be used for business improvement or business change projects that don't have any IT components.

Figure 11.3 Using models to provide context from business to iteration

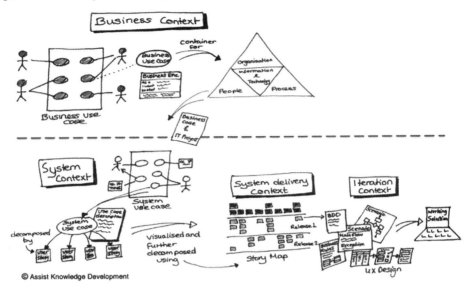

© Assist Knowledge Development

Usage and functionality are different. While it is great to know that an actor or role wants to undertake a particular function, there is also value in understanding who that actor is, and why that functionality is important to them. These two types of requirement are defined as:

1. **Usage:** the roles, actors and interfaces that interact with a system in order to achieve a goal.
2. **Functionality:** the functionality that the system performs in response to the usage request.

Functional requirements encompass usage and functionality but are not the only types of requirement. They must be balanced with non-functional requirements (NFRs) that define the quality characteristics of the solution and the constraints that limit functional feasibility. Requirement categories, including non-functional requirements, are covered in Chapter 13.

Available techniques

The development of online systems has meant that the user community is often large and encompasses many different perspectives and personalities. This makes the analysis of the users difficult and time consuming. User experience (UX) analysis is a technique that encompasses many aspects relating to the practical usage of a product, system or service including the functionality provided and qualities such as usability, look and feel, and accessibility. UX also considers the emotions and behaviours of users during the system usage. This requires the business analyst to understand the user community, the context within which the system is used, their interactions and their typical usage paths.

In this book we are going to consider two aspects relating to modelling the system and its users:

1. **The user community:** who are the users and what roles do they perform?
2. **The functionality:** which features and goals do the users want the system to deliver?

There are many techniques that may be used to model users and functionality. These are described in overview in Table 11.1 below and are explored in further detail later in this chapter.

Table 11.1 Techniques to analyse users and usage

User analysis matrix	A matrix showing the use cases required by each user role.
User roles	A list identifying and describing the user roles that will interact with the system.
Personas	A stereotyped user role that describes a particular set of characteristics. Personas are useful in gaining understanding about a category of user within a specific role, including their preferences and motivations. Personas are often used to understand user interface requirements. They also have a broader application to the entire solution as they are useful when analysing usage of business and IT systems. Understanding the users who fall into this category can help define usability and accessibility requirements.
Misuse characters	A particular category of persona focusing on users who might misuse the system either in error or on purpose. Understanding the users who fall in this category can help to define security requirements.
Context diagram	An overview diagram that shows the system boundary and the actors (user role or system) with which there will be an interface. Details of the system within the boundary are not shown. In effect, this diagram represents the system as a 'black box'.
Use case diagram	A diagram that represents both the external actors and the services they require the system to offer. Each service is shown as a use case, which is initiated by an actor external to the system. This diagram provides an overview of the functional requirements for the system.
User journeys	A model of the journey through the system when navigated by the user. Understanding the user journey can help to identify missing elements and identify usability requirements.

ANALYSING USERS AND ROLES

It is often helpful to undertake some sort of user analysis when developing a system. While the job titles will identify the range of actors, more sophisticated user analysis can extend understanding by defining sets of user characteristics, the events that cause them to use the system and the reasons for preferences and priorities. This information is highly relevant when collaborating with users in the development of a new system.

The size and complexity of both the change project and the user community will dictate how much emphasis should be placed on user analysis. For example, the introduction of a new expense claims system within the headquarters of a small organisation may require just a limited amount of effort to be spent on user analysis, whereas the introduction of a new human resources system across a multi-national organisation will require significant effort to be spent on user analysis if the delivered system is to be successful. Some change projects therefore are largely influenced by the users of the system and the job and tasks they perform. This is often referred to as the user role and is discussed further later in this chapter.

User analysis matrix

There are various aspects that may be analysed with regard to the user community, including the following:

- **Motivation and attitude of user:** What motivates users to make use of the system will inform not only requirements for the look, feel and usability of the product, but also how it is introduced and supported.

- **Skills of user and the skill requirements:** Does the task require the user to have specific numeracy, literacy or IT skills, or require in-depth knowledge of domain or terminology? What levels of skills are available within the community?

- **Frequency of tasks:** Are the tasks performed on a regular basis such as daily, weekly, monthly; or are they performed infrequently or by exception only and do they vary from one occasion to another?

- **Whether the task is performed alone or in a group:** Can the task be performed by a single user or are a number of users required?

- **Time criticality of tasks:** Does the task have to be performed at a set point in time, or does it take a set length of time to complete?

- **Safety criticality of tasks:** Are there any safety or security aspects associated with performing the task?

- **Is the user dedicated to the task or likely to be multi-tasking:** Is the user focused on performing this task, or will they be switching between a number of tasks?

One way of analysing usage is to consider the tasks and the issues listed above. Once understood, this information can be analysed using a graph such as a matrix. A user analysis matrix is the simplest and most popular way to represent usage. A usage matrix provides a means of representing the various users and aspects of their work.

For example, a matrix may represent a list of tasks, with the job titles of those involved in the work. This helps in the identification of user roles, as discussed later in this chapter. An alternative possibility is to use a matrix to cover aspects such as the frequency and optionality of use: how often the users are expected to use the system or the process; whether it is mandatory that they use the system or whether it is optional. Figure 11.4 shows an example of a usage matrix to see how often particular users may use or interact with the training provider booking system (described in Chapter 6).

Figure 11.4 User analysis matrix

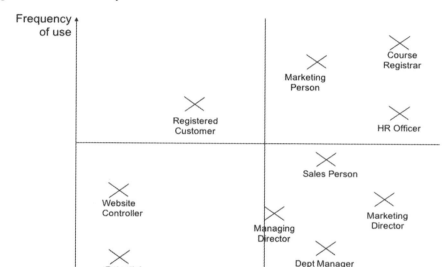

This example matrix does not distinguish between a manual or automated booking system. It may even be the case that the extent of automation is yet to be decided or that this analysis is to be used to determine whether an automated system is cost beneficial or not.

Other graphs could also be used to represent this data, such as bar charts, histograms or scatter graphs.

User roles

User roles are discussed in Chapter 7 and are particularly relevant when looking at system usage. Various techniques apply the user role concept: user stories begin from the perspective of a user role, and a user role is synonymous with an actor on a use case diagram. Therefore, understanding user roles is vital when eliciting and analysing the user requirements.

Essentially, a user role is a view of a system from a collective user perspective. User roles can be defined as a grouping or aggregation of users who require access to a particular set of system features. As discussed in Chapter 7, a user role may be viewed as a defined 'hat' that a user wears, which encompasses a set of tasks with defined access rights. A user role will have a designated set of responsibilities, which will relate to functional and non-functional requirements.

Understanding user roles is extremely important and identifying them usually begins with considering different job titles or groups of users. The jobs and users are then consolidated into 'views' required of the system by considering the different tasks to be performed or accessed. A matrix setting out the job titles and the potential tasks is a good starting point for a user role discussion.

Within an agile team, user roles are typically identified in collaboration with the customer and development team within a workshop setting. Techniques such as the job title/task matrix can be used during the workshop to initiate the user role discussion. An overview process for planning and organising a role development workshop is provided in Figure 11.5.

Figure 11.5 Approach for user role development workshop

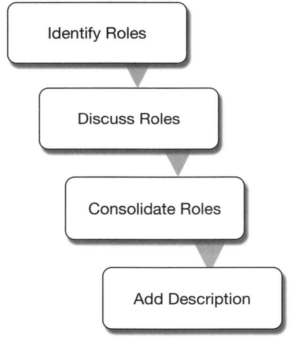

There are several techniques that may be used within the workshop to elicit information and ideas. Brainstorming is often used but has some disadvantages, as those less comfortable with the 'shout out' approach may contribute little, if anything, to the discussion. Brainwriting is an alternative technique that can be used to overcome this issue during a user role development workshop. Brainwriting requires workshop attendees to write down ideas which are shared with the rest of the group. This approach helps to generate further ideas during the timebox allowed for the brainwriting exercise. Guidelines for using this technique are shown in Table 11.2.

Table 11.2 Guidelines for brainwriting

Area	Guideline
Timeboxing	The time allocated to each brainwriting activity should be timeboxed. Using this techniques lots of ideas can be generated quickly; 10–15 minutes is usually enough time.
Sharing ideas	During the timebox, ideas must be shared as they are identified. This may be done in two ways, either by participants writing on individual sheets of paper or by creating a central list on a flip chart or whiteboard. When using sheets of paper, each participant should take a sheet, write an idea on it, put the sheet into the centre of the table, take another sheet and so on. This results in everyone reusing each other's sheets of paper and having the opportunity to build on each other's ideas. A central list requires each participant to add their ideas as they arise and also results in people sharing and developing thoughts. Discussions regarding the ideas should be deferred until after the timebox has ended.
Discussing ideas	Once ideas have been generated and the timebox has ended, time should be allocated to discuss the results. This is the opportunity to talk about the ideas and to organise them.

The brainwriting technique, if used according to the guidelines above, can bring the following benefits:

- The silence can help people to think. Especially those who prefer to reflect on the question at hand and do not appreciate the pressure of a required instant response. They may also feel distracted by the noise generated when lots of people share ideas.

- Everyone gets a chance to participate. Some will produce several ideas and some only one idea but everyone gets an opportunity to share their thoughts.

- The ideas generation process is not dominated by the 'loudest voice'. During brainstorming it is possible that one or two participants will dominate and this can prevent others from participating.

- Less confident participants who don't like speaking out in large groups are more likely to participate, as they don't need their voice to be heard over others or worry about their idea being criticised.

- The idea generation process is not distracted by lengthy discussions that waste time.

Once the initial roles have been identified, another timebox should be set to organise the roles. A central record should be compiled of the roles identified in the earlier timebox and there should be a discussion about how they might be organised and described. Aspects to consider when organising user roles include the following:

Look for overlaps	It is useful to analyse the roles identified and suggest or group roles that are similar or overlap with each other. They should be recorded (possibly on sticky notes) and placed near or overlapping each other. The more similar they are, the more they should overlap. This kind of analysis is referred to as affinity analysis and it's a data analysis and mining technique used to discover relationships among activities or tasks performed by individuals or groups.
Consolidate roles	Overlapping roles should be consolidated through discussion and clarification. Where user stories for one role are likely to be the same as those for another role, then the roles can be consolidated or one can be removed. This often results in a new role name being identified.
Add a role description	Once an organised set of user roles has been created, a short description that captures information about the role and the tasks it performs should be produced. This may include information that distinguishes one role from another.

A role card, such as that shown in Figure 11.6, is useful to record the user role descriptions so that they can be used later during the software development work.

ANALYSING PERSONAS AND MISUSE CHARACTERS

Personas are a way to form a view of users based on their perceived patterns of use of the system. They include the values held by users and the behaviours they display. They are captured in short descriptions that define characteristic behaviours, goals, skills, attitudes and environments. Fictional personal details are used to present the persona as a realistic character. A persona may be allocated a name in order to increase the sense that it is describing a real individual. This can help the project team to empathise with the users represented by the persona and gain a deeper appreciation of their needs and priorities.

User roles provide useful input when developing personas; they also enable the identification of individuals who may fulfil a user role and act in a way that is detrimental to the system and the business. These roles are called misuse characters and are important to understand if there are potential implications for performance or security.

Figure 11.6 Role card description

> **User Role:**   *Course registrar*
>
> *The course registrar receives and manages the scheduled course bookings on a daily basis. Is responsible for updating the course schedule spreadsheet and storing and managing customer details through the customer database. Other tasks include sending out joining instructions and course booking confirmations to customers*

Personas

Some of the user roles will be highly important within the context of the system, possibly because they work on critical tasks or because there are large numbers of people in the role. It can be extremely helpful to generate one or two personas to help characterise and understand the different aspects of the user roles. Personas were developed by Alan Cooper in his book, *The inmates are running the asylum* (1999) as a practical interaction design tool. They are created through researching the types of user that might assume a user role. A great deal of information and statistics, available on the internet and within organisations, provide insights when developing personas and help to ensure that they are representative of the user roles we are analysing.

Personas are widely used in marketing and user interface design, and are used extensively in retail. Within a retail environment, products are promoted to certain categories of customer and personas are used to help explore the behaviours and expectations of these customers. For example, a company selling package holidays may have personas as shown in Figure 11.7 below.

Personas are very useful in helping us to understand the features required by customers and prioritising the work required to deliver the business goals. For example, there is a project goal to provide new features on the holiday company website that will help to achieve a business goal of increasing sales. Research has shown that 60 per cent of the customer base is composed of retired couples, so the persona for 'Steve' is useful to direct and prioritise work. Personas can also help the company to develop multiple features that will appeal to particular user groups and to identify impacts from environmental changes. In this situation, there may be demographic changes and 'Steve' may become more, or less, strategically important to the business.

The persona shown in Figure 11.8 below is for 'Bill', who attends courses provided by the training provider company that has been discussed throughout this book.

Figure 11.7 Personas for customers of a holiday company

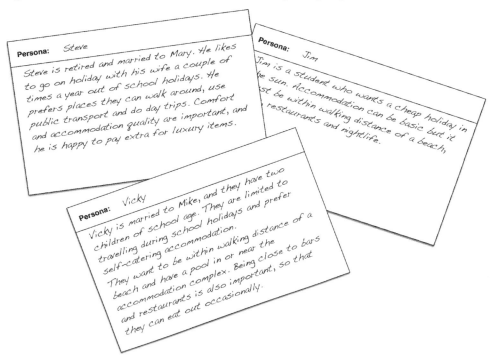

Persona: Steve

Steve is retired and married to Mary. He likes to go on holiday with his wife a couple of times a year out of school holidays. He prefers places they can walk around, use public transport and do day trips. Comfort and accommodation quality are important, and he is happy to pay extra for luxury items.

Persona: Jim

Jim is a student who wants a cheap holiday in the sun. Accommodation can be basic but it st be within walking distance of a beach, restaurants and nightlife.

Persona: Vicky

Vicky is married to Mike, and they have two children of school age. They are limited to travelling during school holidays and prefer self-catering accommodation.

They want to be within walking distance of a beach and have a pool in or near the accommodation complex. Being close to bars and restaurants is also important, so that they can eat out occasionally.

Figure 11.8 Persona for a customer of a training provider

Persona: Bill

Bill is an independent consultant who wants to attend certified training courses to improve his consultancy opportunities. He has to spend his own money and time when attending courses and so a shorter course, or weekend course, are preferable so he can minimise loss of earnings. Certification schemes through reputable organisations are important to him, as it looks better on his CV and sounds more credible.

It is often the case that more than one persona will be required to describe a user role, as there may be a range of characteristics to be represented. Some teams add pictures to their personas to provide an enhanced visualisation of the target audience for the system.

Misuse characters

Misuse characters are becoming increasingly important in today's cyber world, where everything and everyone seems to be connected. One of the issues that the interconnected world brings is the possibility for people to misuse systems for unlawful gain or mischief. Misuse characters provide a way of considering people who are not archetypal users and who might seek to sabotage the system or use it in a way that it was not intended for. They are sometimes referred to as the 'abuser' role.

Like personas, misuse characters are not real people. However, unlike most personas, they are exaggerated characters. Analysing misuse characters can help to elicit nonfunctional requirements, such as security requirements, or can help with the information assurance of systems. Examples of misuse characters with criminal intent might be people who:

- install card readers onto an ATM in order to obtain card details illegally;
- trawl social media to discover when people are on holiday so they have an opportunity to burgle their house;
- use a contactless machine to scan radio-frequency identification (RFID) bank cards through handbags or pockets.

Like personas, misuse characters should be captured on role cards. An example misuse character for the training provider company is provided in Figure 11.9. It can also be helpful to indicate the level of risk associated with a misuse character.

Figure 11.9 Misuse character card

Misuse Character: *Assured Training Company (ATC)*

ATC is a relatively new training company that tries to undercut other training companies in order to maximise their business opportunities. ATC regularly view other training provider websites looking for course prices that they can undercut. They also look for courses that they can copy from other providers.

ANALYSING THE SYSTEM CONTEXT AND SCOPE

Roles, personas and misuse characters are essential to understanding the system. However, it is how they interact with the system, and why, that really helps to clarify the context in which the system is being used or is required. Without understanding the context, it is easy to lose sight of what the change project is trying to achieve and how this relates to the broader business goals and objectives. Change projects that don't invest effort in understanding scope and context can run into problems later when making priority decisions, only to find the context of the project was not agreed or understood. Investing time in analysing the system context doesn't mean that the scope and context will remain fixed for the duration of the project. Rather, it provides a context by which the goals set for the project can be tested and are achievable. Using context diagrams is a way to achieve this understanding.

Context diagram

The context diagram provides a backdrop from which further modelling can evolve. Understanding the actors needing to interact with the system under development is necessary and helps in the elicitation of the features to be provided by the system; a context diagram illustrates this. It provides clarity when considering the actors and their interactions because the analysis is not clouded by the detail of functionality. The clarity of the contextual view enables further exploration of the required functionality. An example of a context diagram for the course booking system is shown in Figure 11.10.

In line with most agile techniques, the context diagram should be developed during a workshop with relevant stakeholders involved. Ideally this should not take more than an hour. If after an hour there is no agreement, then it is possible that participants are attempting to develop a model that is too prescriptive rather than considering it as a starting point from which to develop deeper understanding. The business analyst can play a valuable role in facilitating this work and managing the expectations of those involved.

When developing context diagrams, it can be useful to indicate the key interactions required by some user roles; an example is shown in Figure 11.11 below. However, it is important not to represent too much information on the context diagram as this could provide a muddled view, resulting in confusion and delay.

Context diagrams are typically used as a basis for developing use case diagrams. The use case diagram provides an elaboration of the context diagram by expanding upon the interactions and features required of the system.

Use case diagrams

Use cases, originally developed by Ivar Jacobson, have been used since the 1960s, but did not become widely known until the 1980s. Use case diagrams show the actors wishing to access the system, the use cases they require in order to achieve their goals, and the boundary of the system. A use case is a description of a particular feature that is created at varying levels, depending upon aspects such as complexity and priority. Use case descriptions can be a rich source of detail, containing information about the alternative paths required to deliver the goal of the use case.

Figure 11.10 Context diagram for course booking system

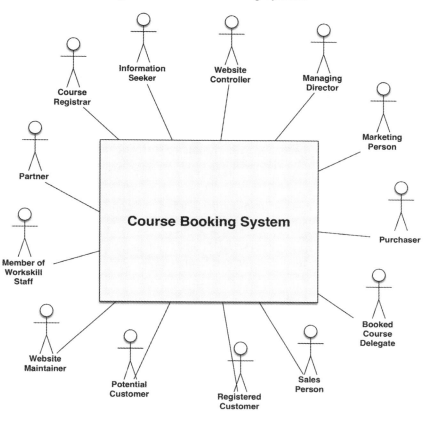

Figure 11.11 Showing 'use' on a context diagram

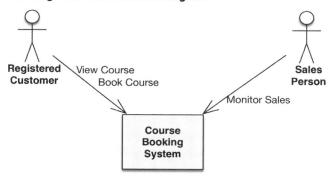

Agile teams often avoid use cases because there is a misconception that they need to be described in extensive detail before the development work can commence. This is not the case. Use cases are intended to evolve iteratively and there are several levels of documented use cases. For example, a use case can begin as a defined goal, which then becomes more and more detailed as and when the detail needs to be understood. It is also possible to document a use case using a user story; at an outline level of description, a use case and a user story have much in common. Use cases illustrate the multiple flows required to achieve the overall goal and each flow may be recorded using either a use case description or as a user story.

In 2011, Ivar Jacobson, Ian Spence and Kurt Bittner, wrote *Use-case 2.0: the guide to succeeding with use cases*. In this publication, they demonstrated how use cases work with agile development projects and they introduced the concept of use case slices. This concept is concerned with the identification, prioritisation, development and delivery of parts of use cases (the 'slices').

Use case models can be invaluable in understanding and capturing scope and context; they can help to avoid the fragmented view that can result from relying solely on user stories. The development of 'use case slices' and the application of different levels of use case elaboration can be extremely useful when eliciting and analysing the required features and goals of a system. Bittner and Spence (2003) in their book, *Use case modelling*, define six levels of detail for a use case. These levels are represented in Figure 11.12 below.

Figure 11.12 Use case levels

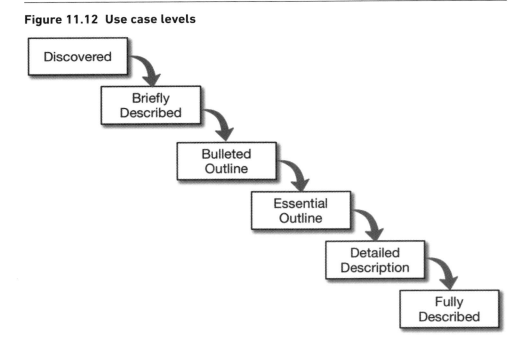

It is important to reiterate that use cases do not have to be elaborated through all these levels. Some use cases may offer **just enough** detail at the briefly described level, for example, if creating use cases to provide scope and context for the solution being developed and then using user stories to support the work of the development team. In other situations, it may be better to describe the use case in full. For example, where there are many alternative pathways to be handled by the use case, it is necessary to understand these in depth to inform decisions regarding which will be automated and which will be handled manually.

Use case templates vary from organisation to organisation. UML publications offer standard templates but the format is adaptable and may be changed to meet the needs of a project. The customary use case levels are 'discovered', 'briefly described' and 'fully described', and these are discussed below.

Discovered

A use case that has been identified on a use case model can be considered as 'discovered,' as shown in Figure 11.13.

Figure 11.13 Discovered use case

Briefly described

This should be created soon after the use case is 'discovered' and provides an initial, outline description (see Figure 11.14).

Figure 11.14 Briefly described use case

Actor	Registered customer
Use case name	Book course
Brief description: This use case will allow registered customers to book course places through the website.	

The use case can then evolve through the 'bulleted outline', 'essential outline' and 'detailed description' incarnations, gradually increasing in detail.

Fully described

A fully described use case contains extensive detail as shown in the example below (Figure 11.15). This includes the trigger for the use case, the main and alternative flows through the use case and characteristics such as concurrency of use, performance and security.

Figure 11.15 Fully described use case

Actor	Registered customer
Name	Book course
Brief description	This use case will allow customers to book course places through the website.
Goal/name	Book a course
ID	R/018
Scope	Course booking system
Level	System
Trigger/event	Registered customer has logged onto the training provider website and decides to book an available course.
Preconditions	Registered customer is registered and has checked that the course is available to book.
Success guarantees	Registered customer is booked onto the course, customer details are accepted and confirmation of the course booking is shown.
Basic flow	1. Registered customer selects course to book 2. System shows available dates 3. Registered customer selects date they wish to attend that course 4. System confirms booking details and requests payment 5. Registered customer enters payment details 6. System confirms payment and provides booking confirmation
Alternate flows (or extensions)	2a. Course requested has no available dates 3a. Course dates not suitable for customer 4a. No availability for that course now 5a. Registered customer decides to book via telephone 6a. Registered customer enters invalid payment details 6a1. Registered customer payment not authorised
Performance	Confirmation must take no more than 1 minute from submitting payment details.
Security	Only registered customer and training provider admin staff can amend or change the booking once confirmed. Only a registered customer can make a booking.
Volumes	100 concurrent users

The basic flow embedded within the use case shows the detailed interaction between the customer and the system and the sequence in which this interaction needs to occur.

The basic flow shows the primary and successful path through the use case. Often referred to as the 'happy path' or 'main success scenario', the basic flow should describe the series of interactions that should take place, and in what sequence, between the actor and the system in order to achieve the goal for the actor. The use case in Figure 11.16 represents the interaction between the registered customer and the course booking system that is required to achieve the goal of booking and paying for a course place.

If the basic flow details the successful path, then the alternate flows capture error handling or secondary paths required to achieve the goal of the use case or to exit from the interaction. To identify the alternate flows, it is a good idea to apply 'what if analysis' to the steps of the basic flow. For example, what would happen if the registered customer selects a course to book and there are no available dates; how should the system respond? The steps associated with this situation would be captured in the alternate flow 2a in the use case description.

For many, the textual description can be hard to digest and so modelling the pathways may be preferable. This can be done using a UML activity diagram as shown in Figure 11.16.

Figure 11.16 Activity diagram for use case

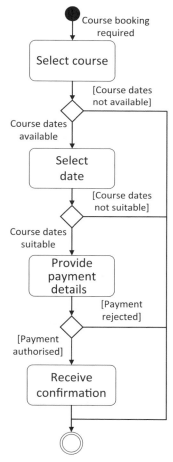

Fully described use cases help to capture valuable details concerning business rules, sequencing and the detailed requirements needed to build the system. The format provides an excellent basis for discussion and collaboration and they are an important tool in the business analyst toolkit. Additionally, 'what if' analysis can elicit information on flow and user expectations, and help in the development of prototypes and achievement of good UX design.

VISUALISING USER JOURNEYS

A useful way to analyse users is to look at their user journey. A user journey is a set of steps that a user might take to access a system. The journey could represent the way the users currently work ('as is'), or how they could work in the future ('to be'). Either way, the steps and sequence that a particular end user takes can be valuable in understanding the scope of the work, user behaviour and system functionality.

A user journey should start with a user role or a persona and should include:

- the goal that the user is aiming to achieve (could be a user story or a process task);
- the steps that they undertake to achieve the goal;
- mechanisms or processes utilised (i.e. manual process, system or interface);
- emotions or pain points experienced through the journey.

The purpose of the 'as is' user journey, as shown in Figure 11.17 below, is to understand the current process, which helps to identify any disconnects or 'pain points' that a future solution will need to address. In contrast, the purpose of the 'to be' user journey is to show how the journey might look in the future and what benefits that might bring to the user or the organisation.

Figure 11.17 'As is' user journey

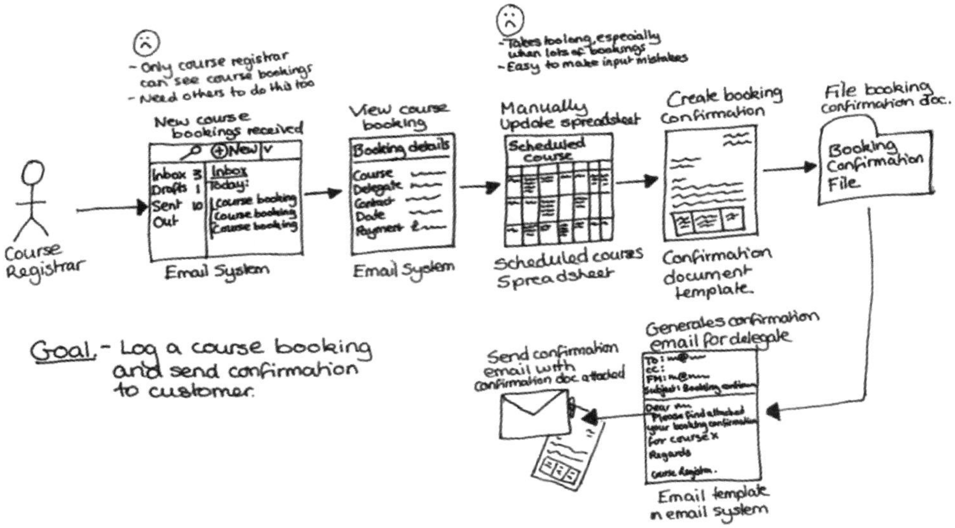

The format of a user journey can vary depending on the intended audience. Many user journeys are represented visually, as shown in Figure 11.17, but this can depend upon the ability and confidence of the analyst in building a free-format, hand-drawn representation. If preferable, a series of boxes and lines drawn using a drawing package may also be used. The important point is to represent what the user wishes to do and achieve during this journey.

CONCLUSION

Collaborating with the user community is an essential part of an agile project. However, discussions are greatly enhanced by applying frameworks and techniques, such as those set out in this chapter, to elicit and analyse information that may otherwise be overlooked. For this reason, the models explored in this chapter are extremely useful additions to the agile business analyst's toolkit.

REFERENCES

Bittner, K. and Spence, I. (2003) *Use case modelling*. Boston, MA: Addison Wesley.

Cooper, A. (1999) *The inmates are running the asylum*. US: Sams Publishing.

Jacobson, I., Spence, I. and Bittner, K. (2011) *Use-case 2.2: the guide to succeeding with use cases*. Ivar Jacobson International. Available from: www.ivarjacobson.com/publications/white-papers/use-case-ebook [20 December 2016].

FURTHER READING

Cooper, A. (2008) The origin of personas. Alan Cooper website. Available from: www.cooper.com/journal/2003/08/the_origin_of_personas [20 December 2016].

Mears, C. (2013) User journeys – the beginners guide. The UX Review. Available from: theuxreview.co.uk/user-journeys-beginners-guide/ [20 December 2016].

12   MODELLING STORIES AND SCENARIOS

This chapter covers the following topics:

- modelling system usage;
- user stories;
- scenarios;
- Behaviour driven development;
- story mapping.

INTRODUCTION

Over the last decade the adoption of user stories as an approach to capturing require-ments has increased considerably. So much so, that in some projects user stories have been used as the sole format for requirements. Using user stories alone carries risks, and different requirement formats should be considered for different types of require-ments. In other words, projects should avoid a one-size-fits-all approach to eliciting, recording and analysing requirements.

While user stories are effective in capturing the essence of functional requirements, further techniques need to be employed to draw out the detail of the functionality or to provide a coherent view of the, often numerous, user stories.

This chapter discusses user stories and considers the alternative techniques that can be used alongside them.

MODELLING SYSTEM USAGE

Understanding the actors and roles, described in Chapter 11, for the solution under development is vital. Systems need to provide functionality that can enable users to perform the work required by the business. Making sure the right functionality is built is an essential aspect of agile software development, but needs business analysis input.

Outline functional requirements can be captured in many ways, but the best way to define the detail of the required functionality is to work iteratively so that the detail emerges over time. Where functionality is defined in detail early in the project life cycle, it often becomes out of date as the project progresses. This can lead to more time being spent changing and managing the requirements definitions rather than ensuring that the required functionality is delivered. Agile is clear that priority should be given to the delivery of working software rather than the maintenance of documentation, as it is the software that offers potential value to the organisation. An agile business analyst needs to ensure that 'just enough' detail is captured in the requirements documentation so that priorities can be allocated and decisions made about where analysis efforts should be deployed. Business analysts also need to work collaboratively with their customers to decompose requirements and goals such that priorities can be allocated at both goal and sub-goal levels. This helps the analysis and development work to move from an idea or concept, into something that can be realised in working software.

We have referenced the simplified Functional Model Map (FMM) throughout this book as it represents the required direction of travel from concept to solution. Figure 12.1 below shows the FMM as the analysis work begins to move from the solution to the internal components.

Figure 12.1 The simplified Functional Model Map

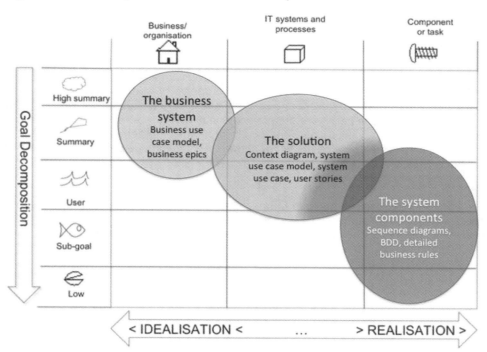

No two projects are the same and so it makes sense that the approach to capturing functionality may change from project to project. Having different formats available is an essential part of the business analyst toolkit and many have already been discussed in earlier chapters. Table 12.1 sets out different approaches and techniques for describing and capturing user stories that will be discussed in this chapter.

Table 12.1 Techniques for modelling stories and scenarios

User story	A short story describing a user role (who), what the user role wants to do and why they want to do it.
Scenario	A sequence of steps initiated by an event that will deliver an outcome.
BDD	A set of event-driven scenarios to be tested on the delivered system from the perspective of a user role.
Story map	A visualisation of the ideas and concepts for a solution (usually using user stories) to define what the solution needs to do, and the order in which it should be delivered.

USER STORIES

User stories were first developed with XP and were described as being 'like use cases'. As time has gone on, the difference between user stories and use cases has become more apparent; however, both techniques are still relevant and useful, and can be used together on a project. User stories are small fragments of business value that can be delivered within a project iteration; this is usually a period of between two and four weeks. In contrast, use cases are project-wide goals that the solution needs to deliver and so will inevitably take longer than two to four weeks to deliver. The advantage of use cases is that they provide the wider context. The advantage of user stories is that the focus is on smaller goals, thus enabling small amounts of software functionality to be delivered within an iteration.

User stories, popularised by Mike Cohn in *User stories applied* (2004), seem to have become the de facto standard for requirements on agile projects. Each user story represents a slice of functionality that concerns the achievement of a business goal and can be divided up across iterations. Although a user story sets out a requirement, it does not represent a formal requirements document in the sense that a user story is not signed off and does not represent a formal contract between the customer and the development team. Rather, a user story is a placeholder for a further conversation that will help to elicit understanding and further details of the requirement.

User stories are often considered to have a hierarchy. This is not the same as the requirements hierarchy that has been traditionally assigned to requirements developed using a linear approach, whereby the high-level requirements break down into lower-level requirements and so forth, while traceability between them all is maintained and controlled. The terminology used to define user stories is considered more as a way of describing and managing the decomposition of user stories and is explored here in overview to help in understanding the level at which user stories should be defined.

Further information on how stories can be managed and organised using this terminology is provided in Chapter 13.

During the initial development work user stories, which have been derived from use case models, will often be too large to deliver within a project iteration. Due to this they will need to be decomposed as described in Chapter 8. Managing user stories through decomposition has been the subject of much talk amongst business analysts and project teams. This has led to the development of a hierarchical structure for user stories that helps in their decomposition and allocation to iterations. The terminology used in agile to discuss the size and level of user stories consists of three main categories: themes, epics and user stories. These are described in Table 12.2 below.

Table 12.2 Levels in a user story hierarchy

Theme	The best way to think about a theme is as a logical heading given to a group of user stories. When user stories were captured on cards it made sense to put a rubber band around a collection of cards that were logically related. That way, if the functionality could wait until a later release, the cards could be kept together. Also, if the cards were dropped on the floor they would still remain in logical groupings. So, a theme is a heading given to a set of user stories that helps to organise them. The logical grouping could be based upon user roles (e.g. priority customer) or could be around features (e.g. online payments). Themes tend to be at an overview level and, in some situations, can represent high-level goals. Once a theme is decomposed, only the logical heading remains. Themes, therefore, should not be written as user stories; they are simply a heading under which user stories reside.
Epic	Epics are the name given to large user stories and are usually easy to identify as they are hard to estimate because of their size or they do not have a defined outcome or end point. An example epic from the training provider case study used throughout the book is 'Manage course booking'. Epics need to be decomposed into smaller user stories as the time approaches when they will be used to develop software. In this sense, epics are transitory in that they only exist to be broken down. Jeff Patton (2014), in his book *User story mapping*, describes epics as resembling big rocks. Once a big rock has been broken down into smaller rocks, the big rock no longer exists. Instead, it is represented by lots of smaller rocks that if pieced back together make up the bigger rock. Similarly, once an epic has been decomposed into smaller stories, it no longer needs to exist. If there is an overwhelming urge to maintain the detail contained in the epic, then a theme should be used as a logical heading.

(continued)

Table 12.2 (Continued)

	It should be noted that the term 'epic' is sometimes used more widely to identify large pieces of work. For example, in Chapter 6 we refer to the 'business epic' as a container for work concepts that will require significant funding and consider all of the elements needed to deliver the business outcome using the POPIT™ model. Epics are also referred to in SAFe (Scaled agile framework n.d.) for the enterprise, where they are described as 'a significant initiative that helps guide the value stream towards the larger aim of the portfolio ... they drive much of the economic value for the enterprise'. When discussing epics, it is helpful to clarify whether you are talking at a portfolio level or referring to a large user story in a development project.
User story	A user story is a description of desired functionality told from the perspective of a user or customer and which, once delivered, should provide value to the user or customer. User stories need to be small enough to be delivered within an iteration. User stories are the only category in this hierarchy that is realised by working software.

When writing user stories, there are six main attributes to consider in order to ensure that they are good stories. The suggested acronym is INVEST, which was devised by Bill Wake (2001) in his book *Extreme programming explored*. These attributes are:

Independent	Each story should be independent in that it should not be dependent on other stories. If it is not independent, problems can occur later when planning and estimating. Each user story should therefore represent a goal and offer value to the user.
Negotiable	The user stories should not be contracts or requirements that software *must* implement. They are short descriptions of functionality to be explored and negotiated in a conversation between the customer and development team.
Valuable	The user story should be valuable to an end user or customer. It must represent a goal or outcome of value that an end user or customer can understand. User stories that are only valued by the developers are not user stories. User stories should be written so that the user understands the consequences of not including them.
Estimatable	All stories must be given an estimate. If they cannot be estimated, they are either too big or the team lacks the technical or business knowledge to calculate the estimate.

Small	Each user story should be small enough such that an estimate to deliver the functionality can be calculated and the work may be planned. In the early days of a project, stories may be large and represent high-level goals for the solution. As the project progresses, stories should be decomposed so they are small enough to be delivered within an iteration (typically two to four weeks in duration).
Testable	Each story must be testable. It is this step that verifies that the working software is complete. The tests should be written from the user story confirmations and additional tests written that arise as the detail of the story is uncovered during the iteration. Within agile, as much testing as possible should be automated so that tests can be run again and again as the software develops through the iterations. BDD is used to identify the tests that can be automated.

Splitting and decomposing stories

Splitting stories can appear to be a simple process. In reality, it is a very difficult thing to get right as the stories need to be split and decomposed on the basis of achieving smaller goals and not sections of functionality. Goal decomposition was discussed in detail in Chapter 8.

> The term 'splitting stories' is common, but in fact we should actually refer to this as splitting epics. A user story is the correct term for a story that is small enough to be estimated and delivered within an iteration. If this is true, then it does not make sense for a story to be split further as there is no requirement to do so. With this in mind.

The term 'story' is used in this book as a way of referring to the format (e.g. 'As a ... I want to ... so that'), which is common for both a user story and an epic and is discussed further in this chapter. Where the author requires this to be specific, it will be made clear.

When splitting and decomposing stories there is a tendency to do this along technical lines. While this may make sense for the development team, it makes no sense to the customer as the story now describes technical functionality. Each piece of functionality could be developed across different iterations and therefore nothing of value can be demonstrated to the customer in an individual iteration. The value to the customer derives from the delivery of the whole story not the individual technical aspects of how it is built.

When splitting stories, Mike Cohn (2004) describes how big stories (i.e. epics) fall into one of two categories:

1. the compound story;
2. the complex story.

A **compound** story is an epic that has not yet been decomposed into user stories. For example, a web booking system may include the story, 'As a customer I would like to book a flight.' While this is fine during initial planning, when deciding what needs to be built, first further discussions with the customers may uncover that this story actually means:

- each customer can book themselves one seat on one flight;
- each customer can book multiple seats on one flight for multiple people;
- each customer can book multiple seats on multiple flights;
- each customer can reserve an 'extra leg room' seat;
- each customer can order a meal during the flight.

Each of the above will become an independent story that can be prioritised differently.

Another way to split a compound story is to use the create, edit, delete framework such as:

- create a customer booking;
- edit a customer booking;
- delete a customer booking.

The **complex** story is a large story that is harbouring uncertainty. In this situation, the team may need to spend some initial time understanding the problem in order to reduce the uncertainty. Once they are clearer about what needs to be done, further stories can be generated. An example of this may be the story 'As a sales person I want the customer to receive discounts on their course price so that they can be rewarded for customer loyalty' but the developers are unsure of how to implement this on the website as they do not know the rules associated with applying discounts. They may choose to split the story so that initially they include a story such as:

- As a developer I want to investigate the business rules and technical solution for applying discounts so that we can estimate the work required for future iterations.

This story is a 'spike', which is a story that cannot be estimated without timeboxed research. This story, often referred to as a technical story, will be allocated to one or more of the development team to research during a timebox. If the uncertainty cannot be resolved within the timebox, the project will need to consider whether it is worthwhile continuing with this story. After completing this investigation, the original story can be further split into the following:

- As a sales person I want to know which registered customers have signed up to bulk course booking schemes so that I can know they are entitled to a discount code.
- As a sales person I want to apply a discount code to a registered customer who has signed up to bulk course booking schemes so that their discount can be automatically applied.

- As a registered customer I want my bulk course discount to be automatically applied when I book a course through the website so that my loyalty is recognised and obtaining the discount is simple for me.

The patterns set out in Table 12.3 below provide useful approaches when splitting compound user stories. The examples given relate to the training company case study used throughout this book.

Table 12.3 Patterns for splitting compound user stories

Task steps

As a web maintainer, I want to post a new course description to the company website	• as a formatted pdf • as a reviewed Word document

Business rules

As a purchaser, I want to book course places	• on one course • across several courses • for multiple delegates

Simple or complex

As a reseller, I want to pay for a course place	• by credit card • by purchase order, invoice and remittance

Data sets

As a course delegate, I want to receive joining instructions	• in English • in Welsh • in French

Data/content entry

As a web controller, I want create news and events	• through links to other sites • by uploading formatted pdfs • by creating HTML pages

CRUD

As a purchaser, I want to	• create a course booking • change a course booking • cancel a course booking • check the course booking details

The 3Cs

When defining user stories, Ron Jefferies (2001) came up with the 3Cs to describe the three critical aspects of user stories: card, conversation, confirmation.

Card	User stories are written on cards or sticky notes. The card does not contain all the information that makes up the requirement. Instead, the card has just enough text to identify the requirement, and to remind everyone what the story is. The card is a token representing the requirement. It is used in planning. Notes are written on it, reflecting priority and cost. It is often handed to the developers when the story is scheduled to be delivered, and given back to the customer in the form of working software, when the story is complete.
Conversation	The requirement itself is communicated from customer to developers through conversation: an **exchange** of thoughts, opinions and feelings. This conversation takes place over time, particularly when the story is estimated (while planning for the release) and again at the iteration planning meeting when the story is scheduled for delivery. The conversation is largely verbal, but can be supplemented with documents. The best supplements are examples and are executable. These examples are called confirmations.
Confirmation	No matter how much discussion or how much documentation we produce, we cannot be as certain as we need to be about what is to be done. The third C in the user story's key aspects adds the confirmation. This component is the acceptance test.

These 3Cs are discussed in detail below.

The user story card

The user story card is either a small card or sticky note used to capture the story itself. The card or sticky note is purposefully small in order to encourage the capture of the minimum detail. The user stories should be written by, or for, the project customers and should drive the development of the software. User stories should describe functionality that will be useful to a customer.

A typical user story format is as follows:

> **As a** ... (role or actor) (**Who**)
> **I want** ... (what capability or feature do they need) (**What**)
> **so that** ... (why is it of business value or benefit) (**Why**).

The 'Who' and 'What' are essential to the story, but the 'Why' only helps with clarity and determining the acceptance test. The 'What' is the actual goal of the user story. It is the thing of value that the role or actor wants to achieve. When splitting stories it is the 'what' that should be the focus of the goal decompostion. Stories help developers to ask relevant questions about the context and reason for the request, examining it from the perspective of the stated user role. Figure 12.2 contains an example of a user story for the course booking system.

Figure 12.2 Example user story

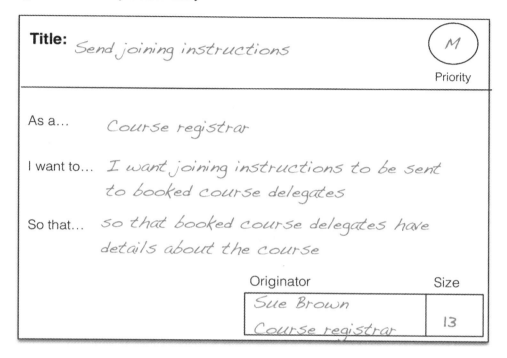

Title: *Send joining instructions*

M

Priority

As a... *Course registrar*

I want to... *I want joining instructions to be sent to booked course delegates*

So that... *so that booked course delegates have details about the course*

Originator	Size
Sue Brown *Course registrar*	13

The conversation

The simple format of the story card aids communication between the various parties involved in the agile development work. Throughout the project, a series of conversations takes place between the customer and the development team and these conversations may be captured as additional documentation that will be attached to the card along with any discovered acceptance test criteria.

Although the card is a visible representation of a user story, the greatest value is derived from the conversations needed to develop the user stories from their inception to the delivery in working software.

A workshop is the primary method of obtaining user stories for agile teams and should be attended by the development team, a business or product owner, customers (including end users) and any other parties who can contribute to the story writing.

These workshops bring together all the stakeholders concerned with a particular system and should aim to achieve consensus and ownership with regard to the decisions that are made. Techniques, in particular brainwriting, described in Chapter 11, should be used to encourage the identification of innovative ideas during the workshop.

Cohn suggests the following format for story writing workshops as follows:

- Select two to three high priority user roles.

- Identify high-level goals for each role.

- Decompose the high-level goals into smaller stories using the user story format: 'As a ... I want to ... so that ...'

There are some important aspects to be considered when developing user stories, as discussed in Table 12.4 below.

Table 12.4 Guidelines for writing user stories

Write for one user role	Write stories from the perspective of one user, for example, as a registered customer (**not** all registered customers). Also, stand in the shoes of the user role and look at the system from the role's viewpoint. For example, if I were a registered customer what would I want to do on the course booking website?
Ensure that user stories are valuable	Ensure that the user stories offer value to a user role rather than defining sub-goals or tasks that need to be undertaken during development. The user stories shown below are sub-goals, as logging on to the system and entering payment details are steps that the customer would need to complete in order to book a course. On their own they are not valuable to the customer as they define the user interface.

- As a registered customer I need to log on to the course booking system.

- As a registered user I need to enter my payment details criteria.

This level of detail should not be captured as separate user stories. Instead the user story should read:

- As a registered customer I need to book one training course for myself so that I can attend.

(continued)

Table 12.4 (Continued)

User stories have a meaningful end	Ensure that each story has a meaningful end. Consider the following user story: 'As a registered customer I want to manage my bookings.'
	How is it possible to know when a registered customer has finished managing course bookings? This would better be described as multiple stories such as:
	• As a registered customer I can view a course booking.
	• As a registered customer I can update a course booking.
	• As a registered customer I can cancel a course booking.

The workshop facilitator plays a key role in the user story workshop by keeping the workshop on track, applying the guidelines in Table 12.4 and ensuring that each participant contributes. Business analysts are often well placed to facilitate the workshop on behalf of the development team.

It is during the conversation that the detail of the story is revealed, so the user story itself is not a specification of what the solution needs to do. Therefore, user stories should not be 'signed off' nor should they form a contract for the software to be delivered. User stories should enable the development team to respond quickly, and with fewer overheads, to rapidly changing real-world requirements. The detailed requirement emerges as the user story is developed and the artefacts to define this detail may take many forms, for example, models, designs, business rules definitions and prototypes.

The confirmation

A user story remains an informal statement of the requirement until the corresponding acceptance test criteria are produced. Appropriate acceptance criteria must be written during conversations with the customer. These criteria will be used to ensure that the goals of the user story have been fulfilled in the resulting solution. The conversations uncover the detail of the requirement, which is developed within the working software and accepted once it is agreed that it delivers the confirmations agreed during the user story conversations. This is the main difference between a formal requirement, which forms a contract, and a user story, which provides a basis for collaboration. The intention of the user story is to be able to respond faster and with fewer overheads to rapidly changing real-world requirements.

The acceptance criteria for a user story are written as confirmations, usually on the back of the user story card as shown in Figure 12.3. It may be helpful to write confirmations for the large or high-level user stories described earlier (e.g. epics) as this helps to test business processes, and identify business rules or constraints. This can support the work to split the user stories and may provide a useful starting point for BDD scenarios (BDD is discussed later in this chapter).

When writing confirmations, it is useful to consider criteria such as SPAM:

S: security
P: performance
A: availability
M: monitor/measure

Figure 12.3 Example user story 'confirmation'

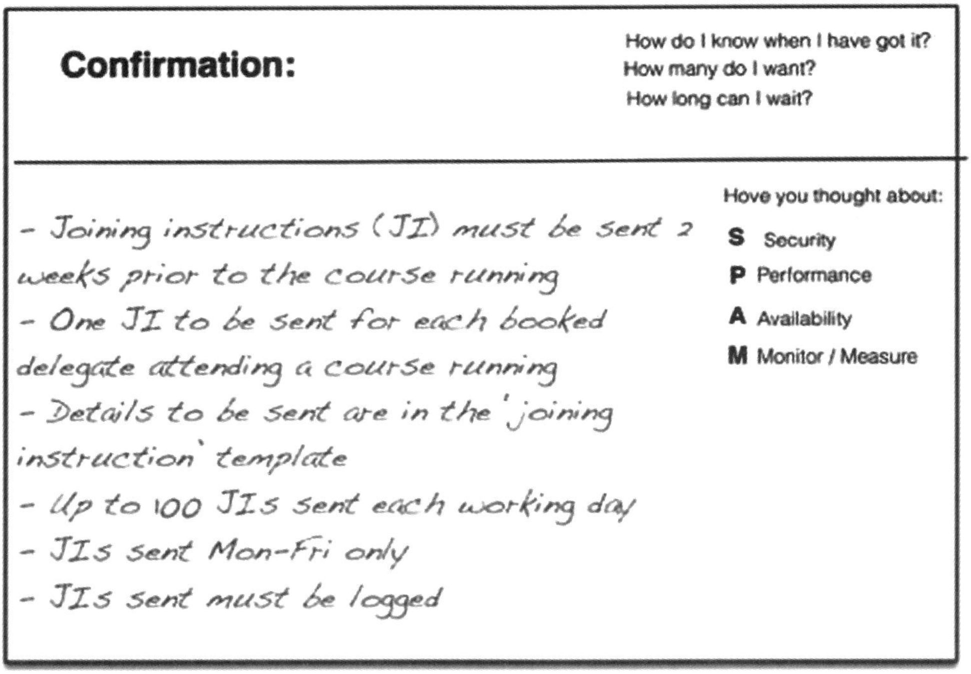

Once a user story has been agreed for inclusion in an iteration backlog, formal acceptance tests must be written to ensure that the goals of the story are met.

For example, the user story 'As a registered customer I want to cancel a course booking so that I don't have to pay for a course I can't attend', may have the following confirmations:

- Verify that only the registered customer can cancel a course that they have booked.

- Verify that only cancellations made 24 hours or more before 09:00 on the course date can be cancelled without incurring a fee.

- Verify that delegates cancelling courses on the day of the course are charged 50 per cent of the course fee.

A story can have any number of acceptance tests depending upon what is needed to ensure that the software functionality works correctly. A user story is not considered complete until it has passed its acceptance tests.

Where a user story is at an atomic level, in that it complies with 'INVEST' rules and is small enough to be delivered within an iteration, the acceptance tests should be written in a format compliant with testing. BDD is a popular approach for writing acceptance tests and is described later in this chapter.

Relevance of user stories

User stories are not appropriate for all types of requirements nor are they appropriate for all organisations, especially those who have a strong cultural bias towards formal sign-off of documents in order to release project funding. Other requirement formats exist for non-functional, general or technical requirements and these are discussed in Chapter 13. Adopting the user story format in a project, but then following stringent sign-off procedures for the stories in order to formalise a contract between the customer and the development team is not in line with the agile approach.

In his book *User stories applied* (2004) Cohn states that,

> while user stories are a very flexible format that works well for describing much of the functionality of many systems, they are not appropriate for everything. If you need to express some requirements in a form other than user story, then do so.

Agile is a philosophy underpinned by principles and values. User stories help in the application of the agile philosophy by providing a basis for collaborative discussions between developers and customers regarding the functionality to be delivered by working software.

SCENARIOS

Scenarios are used frequently in many aspects of business. They may be used to describe the different ways actors interact with a software system, a functional area of a business or the organisation itself.

There are many different definitions of scenarios, but in its simplest form a scenario describes a sequence of activities performed in response to a real-world event. The event could originate from outside the business or system, an external event, or could be an internal event originating from inside the business or system. Alternatively, an event could be based upon a particular date and time. Examples of events are:

- a person calling on the telephone to make a complaint;

- a customer placing an order for a product online;

- an internal user raising an invoice through the invoice system;
- a librarian checking whether a book is available to borrow;
- a customer going into a store to buy a product.

In each of the above cases, the event would trigger a sequence of activities that would result in an outcome. The outcome is sometimes referred to as the scenario goal.

Scenarios are particularly useful as they help to uncover the detail of how work is carried out. This detail includes:

- **interaction:** the interaction between the software/business system and a customer;
- **sequence:** the order, or steps, in which things are carried out;
- **acceptance:** the checks to ensure that the scenario is working as it should.

Scenarios help to identify where assumptions have been made and define necessary detail. They help to avoid issues such as business rules being misunderstood, data requirements not being identified or the wrong things being tested.

Additionally, scenarios enable 'what if analysis' to ascertain what would happen in a specific situation or if something unexpected happens. This is particularly important to elicit non-functional requirements or to derive tests to prove that a system or process is functioning correctly or within the limits expected. For example, what would happen if we raised 200 invoices concurrently; or if we expected to have a surge of users logging onto a system at the same time? The system needs to be tested to make sure it can cope with these possible situations.

Scenarios are developed using the approach shown in Figure 12.4.

Figure 12.4 Approach to developing scenarios

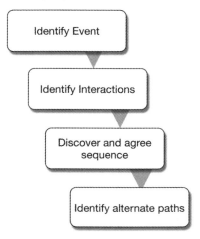

Scenarios can apply at various stages during system development and may be created using many different formats, both textual and diagrammatic; further information regarding documenting and modelling scenarios is presented in Chapter 11. Some of the typical formats used within agile approaches are described in Table 12.5.

Table 12.5 Scenario formats

Use cases	Originating from the UML, use cases describe the interaction of an actor with a system (both business or IT system). This technique is discussed in Chapter 11. Use case development begins by clarifying the basic flow or main usage scenario. Once this is understood, alternate flows are identified and documented. A use case may contain many flows. Each flow through a use case is a scenario.
Usage scenario	A derivative of use cases is defined in www. agilemodeling.com which uses specific examples of actors to represent the interaction and behaviour of that user in a given situation. This tends to make it more personal than the impersonal approach adopted for use cases. Other differences are that usage scenarios tend to follow just one path of logic rather than considering the basic and alternative paths defined within use cases. This is because usage scenarios tend to be developed 'just in time' and focus on a particular pathway that handles a specific combination of circumstances. They are usually discarded once they have served their purpose.
BDD scenario	BDD originated as a technique used in testing but has a lot of similarities to usage scenarios in that BDD scenarios are written from the perspective of a user with specific characteristics. BDD scenarios are defined for small individual user stories and represent the acceptance criteria for a story. BDD scenarios use a specific language called Gherkin and are defined below.

BEHAVIOUR DRIVEN DEVELOPMENT

Many agile projects are starting to adopt BDD as a technique for writing acceptance tests that can be automated. BDD is a collaborative exercise between the developer, tester and business representative, who is often the business analyst. It ensures that development projects remain focused on delivering what the business actually needs.

BDD was originally developed by Dan North (n.d.) in early to mid-2000. It addresses the problem that can occur when business analysts write a detailed specification that is then translated into software requirements by the developer and translated into test cases by the tester. This approach can lead to misunderstanding and miscommunication. BDD brings these roles together, as shown in Figure 12.5 below, so discussions are collaborative, thereby minimising the opportunity for miscommunication or misunderstanding. It should be noted that the roles may be perspectives that are adopted for the discussion rather than specific roles within the agile development team.

Figure 12.5 BDD collaboration

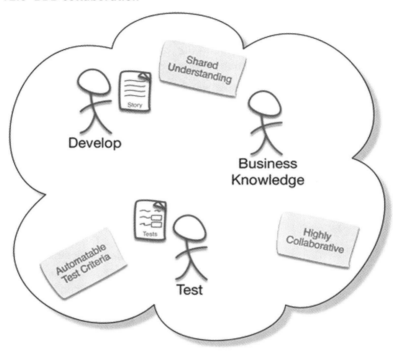

BDD can be very beneficial when used to develop acceptance tests in that it helps to ensure:

- shared understanding amongst the business and development team;
- traceability as development work can be traced back to business objectives;
- delivery of software that meets the business needs;
- improved quality of code.

There are two main elements to BDD, which are:

- the practice of writing examples of what the business needs to do in a language that both the business and development team can understand;
- the use of written examples as the basis of automated tests, providing a means of checking functionality to ensure that it works as required by the business.

Table 12.6 provides the structure used in BDD with a worked example.

Table 12.6 BDD structure and example

Feature	Title	A title and a description that encompasses the different scenarios. The description is often written as a user story.	Booking courses As a registered customer I want to book a course so that I can be more skilled.
Scenario	BDD heading	The actual scenario for the feature. Features will usually have multiple scenarios.	Booking a standard available course on the website.
Given	Context	The context for the start of the story. For example, I am a registered customer and I have searched for course details.	**Given** the 'agile business analysis' course is scheduled for 8 May, and I am a registered customer, and there are >1 places available to book
When	Action	The action they carry out	**When** I make a booking for 8 May.
Then	Outcome	The outcome that is achieved from carrying out the action	**Then** I will be confirmed on the course and places available to book will be reduced by 1.

STORY MAPPING

Story mapping is a technique introduced by Jeff Patton (2014) to explore the broader picture for the system under development. This helps to provide a context that may be missing when using a backlog of stories. A story map can be used to visualise any backlog and therefore is not restricted to IT development projects. For example, it could be used with business epics (Chapter 6) to visualise process improvements. The story map provides several views of the system, including:

- the broader picture of what the project is trying to achieve;
- the end-to-end process of the system told from the user's perspective;

- the stories required to meet the end-to-end process;
- the proposed delivery of the project in terms of the releases;
- dependencies between stories and processes.

There are different approaches to creating story maps. One approach is to identify high-level user stories as a starting point. To create a story map, the following steps are suggested:

- **Step 1:** identify user roles and user stories.
- **Step 2:** discover logical groupings.
- **Step 3:** place in a narrative flow (backbone).
- **Step 4:** analyse for breaks in the workflow.
- **Step 5:** decompose stories.
- **Step 6:** create a first release.

These steps are covered in more detail below.

Step 1: identify user roles and user stories

Before creating a story map, it is important to have done preliminary work to define the scope of the system and identify the user roles and user stories. A business process could also be helpful to provide a contextual view and determine the logical sequence of tasks. Both views are important to consider within the story map. It is worth sketching out existing business processes if they do not exist as these provide a better understanding of the 'as is' system.

Step 2: discover logical groupings

Analyse the user stories and group similar user stories under logical headings. For example, user stories such as 'register bookings', 'cancel bookings or 'update bookings' may be logically grouped under a heading such as 'manage bookings'. These logical headings are essentially 'themes' and will help to communicate the broader picture and help to order and prioritise the story map.

Step 3: place in a narrative flow (backbone)

The next step is to determine the narrative flow setting out the logical progression of the story map. This is sometimes called the 'backbone'. Creating the backbone requires the themes (Jeff Patton (2014) refers to these as 'activities') to be arranged in a logical flow from left to right (horizontally) along a board or wall. The backbone must represent the flow of work of the business, reflecting the 'tasks' to be conducted and the order in which this should be done. For example, it is not possible to confirm a booking before the booking details have been received. Placing these in a logical flow helps the customer and the development team to visualise a workflow and identify any gaps.

Under each 'theme' place the epics (the high-level user stories), or tasks if using a business process model, for that theme. For example, if the theme is 'manage payments' then some of the epics might be 'make payment' or 'process payment'. Figure 12.6 provides an example of a story map backbone showing themes and tasks/epics.

Figure 12.6 Story map backbone

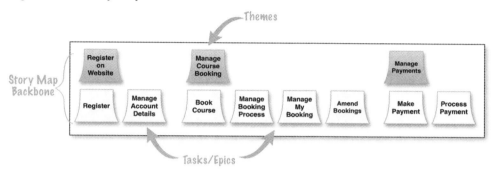

Step 4: analyse for breaks in the workflow

The tasks in the story map backbone may be carried out by different roles and where this is the case it may be worthwhile showing the roles on the story map backbone. It is important to pay particular attention to points in the sequence where the themes transition to a different role, as this is where gaps may occur.

When using a business process model, it is worthwhile using it to validate the sequence of the themes and tasks on the story map backbone. Where there are differences between the story map and business process model views, there will need to be discussions about these differences to identify where changes need to be made. This may result in revisions to the business process model or may highlight missing aspects within the story map. This may result in the identification of additional epics and, ultimately, user roles and user stories.

This step helps to instil confidence in the story map, as it ensures that it is in a logical sequence that reflects the processes and working practices of the business.

Step 5: decompose stories

Once the story map backbone has been confirmed it can be populated with user stories. The user stories created during step 1 should be placed underneath the relevant themes and tasks defined within the story map backbone. When placing the user stories onto the backbone it is possible that a user story doesn't fit under any of the themes or tasks currently identified within the backbone. In this situation, there are two possibilities: a new theme or task may need to be added to the backbone or the user story may be out of scope. This will require customer and product owner discussion to decide which is the case.

When placing the user stories onto the story map the level of criticality should be considered. This is represented on the vertical axis of the story map, which should be labelled 'used frequently' at the top and 'seldom used' at the bottom. An example of this is shown in Figure 12.7 below. User stories that are used more often should be placed higher up the story map than those seldom used.

Figure 12.7 Story map populated with decomposed stories

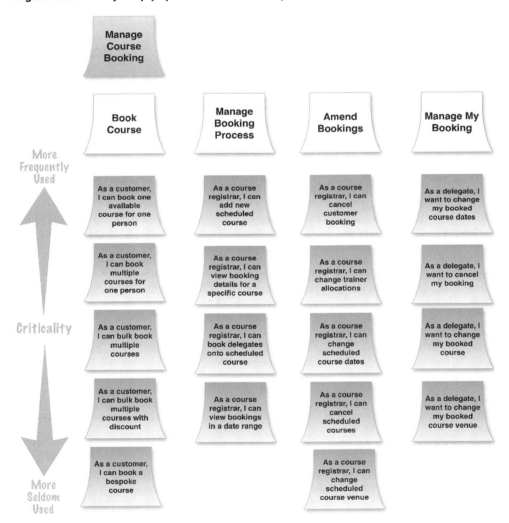

It is likely that the user stories identified so far are all epics and will therefore require further decomposition in order to uncover the lower-level user goals that can be delivered within an iteration. Decomposing stories was discussed earlier in this chapter.

Another technique for splitting stories is described by Jeff Patton (2014) and is called 'Good, Better, Best'. This technique also helps to clarify the criticality of the story. The technique is concerned with asking the following questions, within each of the three categories, for each story.

Good

What would be just **good** enough for this story? For example, what would be enough to demonstrate the functionality but probably not enough to make a customer happy? Write down the characteristics that would make a story just good enough and then treat each characteristic as a separate user story. Place the new user on the story map according to the level of criticality.

Better

Then ask, what would make it better? This might include things such as speed of use, or improved navigation of screens or improved search ability.

Best

Finally ask, what would make it fabulous? This is where you can be really innovative. You don't need to worry too much about feasibility or acceptability, as all stories are just ideas until they are agreed within an iteration.

Step 6: create a first release

Once the story map is created it can be used to decide what should be built first. Some teams focus straight away on the first iteration, where others focus on a first release that will contain numerous iterations. The first deliverable may be an experimental prototype that is demonstrated to customers in order to test an idea or reduce a recognised risk. This is often referred to as an MVP or Minimal Viable Solution (MVS). Feedback collected through the early deliverables will enable the customer and development team to learn from the process and create further user stories for future iterations and releases.

The early deliverables should facilitate and validate learning, so they may be low-fidelity prototypes that do not use or generate actual data. They may be prototypes that aim to address risk and test assumptions concerning functionality and usability, so they may not be appropriate for delivery into a live business environment.

Once ideas have been tested and risks reduced, future deliverables may focus on being complete enough for release to the live business environment. This is sometimes referred to as the MMP and should address the prioritised user needs and fulfil expectations of user experience.

Jeff Patton (2014) suggests drawing a horizontal line across the story map to identify the first deliverable. Everything above the line is in the first deliverable, and everything below the line will be done in subsequent deliveries as shown in Figure 12.8 below. Each deliverable, whether an MVP or MMP, should attempt to encompass the minimum set of stories required to meet the needs of the business. Patton's technique of 'Good, Better, Best', combined with MoSCoW prioritisation (Chapter 9), may be used to define the minimum set of stories to be delivered. The earlier the deliverable is demonstrated, the quicker learning can take place. This will help to avoid wasting money and time – after all, initial ideas may turn out to be wrong!

Figure 12.8 Using the story map to define deliverables

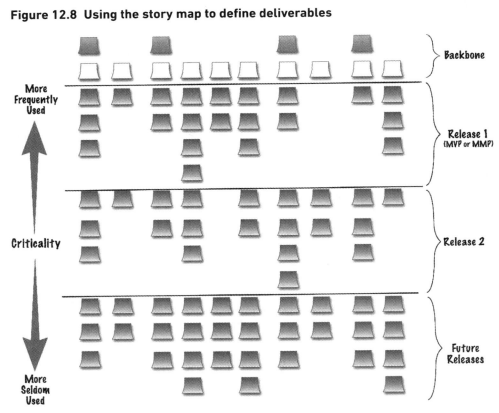

Creating a solution with just the right amount of features sounds like common sense. After all, why would a project want to deliver more features than are necessary? However, determining the right amount of features can be difficult, so sometimes projects deliver over-engineered solutions that contain unnecessary features. Where this is the case, the additional features can clutter the user interface, making the system difficult to use, and can also increase maintenance cost. This is why the MMP is an important concept, as it helps the project team to focus on developing the features that matter to the customer.

CONCLUSION

This chapter has looked at a range of techniques that are relevant to agile projects, primarily where the focus is on software development but business application is also possible. Business analysts are well aware of the need to expand their toolkits in order to ensure that they can adapt to the range of situations possible on a change project. The techniques discussed in this chapter are beneficial in exploring requirements with customers such as end users and enabling the evolution of detail during the development process.

REFERENCES

Cohn, M. (2004) *User stories applied*. Boston, MA: Addison Wesley.

Jefferies, R.E. (2001) Essential XP: card, conversation, confirmation. Ron Jefferies. Available from: http://ronjeffries.com/xprog/articles/expcardconversationconfirmation/ [20 December].

North, D. (n.d.) Introducing BDD. Dan North & Associates. Available from: https://dannorth.net/introducing-bdd/ [20 December 2016].

Patton, J. (2014) *User story mapping*. Sebastopol, PA: O'Reilly Media.

Scaled Agile Framework (n.d.) Available from: www.scaledagileframework.com [19 January 2017].

Wake, W.C. (2001) *Extreme programming explored*. Upper Saddle River, NJ: Addison Wesley.

FURTHER READING

Agile Alliance (n.d.) User Stories. Agile Alliance. Available from: www.Agilealliance.org/glossary/user-stories/ [20 December 2016].

Agile Inc. (n.d.) SAFe 4.0 for Lean Software and System Engineering. Agile Inc. Available from: www.scaledAgileframework.com [20 December 2016].

Ambler, S. (2002) *Agile modeling: effective practices for eXtreme Programming and the unified process*. New York: John Wiley & Sons.

Ambler, S. and Lines, M. (2012) *Disciplined Agile delivery: a practitioner's guide to Agile software in the enterprise*. Upper Saddle River, NJ: IBM Press.

Bittner, K. and Spence, I. (2002) *Use case modeling*. Boston, MA: Addison Wesley.

Cadle, J. (ed.) (2014) *Developing information systems*. Swindon: BCS.

Cockburn, A. (2000) *Writing effective use cases: the Agile software development series*. Boston, MA: Addison Wesley.

Jacobson, E. (1995) *The object advantage: business process reengineering with object technology*. New York: Addison Wesley.

13 ORGANISING TASKS AND REQUIREMENTS

This chapter covers the following topics:

- types of requirement;
- the requirements catalogue;
- the itemised backlogs;
- requirements catalogue or solution backlog?
- recording non-functional requirements;
- hierarchy of requirements.

INTRODUCTION

Business analysts may be involved in many different types of project. For example, software development, process change, capability uplift or hybrid projects that encompass many different aspects. Whatever the project, there will be a business context that provides a rationale for the change and some high-level business requirements that form a backdrop for the project against which more detailed requirements may evolve. Prioritisation (see Chapter 9) plays an important part in determining which projects within the analysis portfolio are enacted and, within projects, which business requirements are included within the initial solutions delivered to the business.

Understanding the business context for a change project is vital. Without business analysis to determine the nature of the problem to be solved or the opportunity to be grasped, and without understanding of the high-level business requirements, there is a risk of a myriad of detailed requirements being raised in a fragmented and inconsistent manner. To overcome this possibility, there has to be some early understanding and documenting of the business context and the business needs to be addressed. This does not mean that every last detail of every business requirement has to be documented and cross-referenced; it does mean, however, that an agile business analyst needs to ensure that there is sufficient documentation containing the required level of detail. This requires business analysts to work closely with their business customers, using their domain knowledge and analytical skills to uncover where effort needs to be expended and at what point.

Managing the requirements is also important so that those with the potential to offer value at an early stage or overcome an urgent problem are progressed first, while other aspects to be tackled at a later stage are recognised and not overlooked. Also, changes to the high-level scoping requirements need to be expected and processes to handle such changes must be embedded within the project approach. Having said this, it is also important to recognise that there is little point in documenting and managing requirements purely for the sake of producing and controlling documentation; there has to be a genuine need to be addressed and the approach adopted has to be sufficient to address this need. Understanding the levels of requirements definition, the different ways in which requirements may be documented and the alternative governance mechanisms will help business analysts to deliver beneficial solutions at the earliest stage possible. This is explored further in Chapter 11.

This chapter looks specifically at the different types of requirements and the requirements hierarchy and explores their value in an agile change project; it also discusses the different ways requirements can be recorded and managed.

TYPES OF REQUIREMENT

One of the commonly used structures distinguishes between the four different types of requirement shown in Figure 13.1 below: general, technical, functional and non-functional requirements.

Figure 13.1 Types of requirement

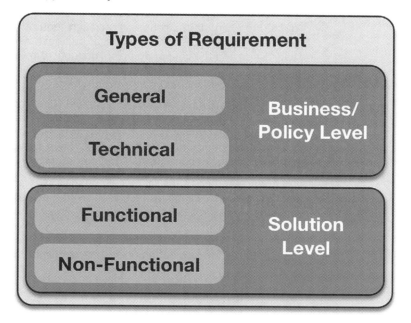

The rationale for these categories is that each one focuses on different aspects of a solution, with the business and technical requirements providing strategic and architectural contexts for the solution. The four types of requirement are described below.

General requirements   These are the overview general requirements to be addressed by the solution. Some of these requirements may be enforced by law, for example, regulatory requirements. Others may be internal policy, for example, marketing or branding requirements. Other general requirements may concern requests from senior business managers, for example, for a new service offering. Some general requirements offer a composite view of desired features or functional requirements and need to be decomposed when considering the solution in further detail.

The general requirements set out the context for the change project. Some – such as those setting out compliance or policy requirements – may have been defined for the entire organisation during a previous project and therefore may be reusable. However, these requirements are still subject to prioritisation and it is often the case that they are the most important requirements to prioritise because they indicate where effort should be focused and at what point. Some of these requirements may have been suggested by stakeholders without consideration of cost or feasibility or impact. It is vital that business analysis is conducted to examine the rationale for each requirement and to determine whether there is a real business need to be addressed and the cost of doing so, the goal to be achieved in delivering the requirement and the urgency with which the requirement should be delivered.

Technical requirements   Most organisations have defined technical standards of one sort or another; the larger the organisation, the greater the likelihood of extensive technical standards. However, even the smallest of organisations is likely to have standardised on software for documentation and communication.

An understanding of the technical constraints is an important aspect of a change project, as it could mean the difference between success and failure. There may be an entire technical infrastructure with selected hardware and software, networking and communication suppliers. There may be standards for data definition and transmission. Failing to understand these requirements could cause serious problems and delays. However, many of them are reusable so they should not have to be defined for each project. An agile business analyst needs to be aware of these requirements and ensure that previous definitions of technical constraints are used where possible.

Functional requirements

The functional requirements set out features and goals that should be met by the solution. A fundamental aspect of agile business analysis involves considering the most appropriate way to elicit, elaborate and record functional requirements.

Functionality may be explored and documented in many ways, as set out in Chapters 11 and 12. For example, it may be helpful to analyse and model functionality using techniques such as use cases and user stories. These artefacts may be created at different levels, providing a clear link between the business need and the proposed solution. They also offer a means of recording the required features and the goals to be achieved by the solution. They show a clear link between the business and solution requirements when using these techniques.

However, in some cases, a catalogue of requirements may be the most relevant approach. For example, if a project has a strong contractual basis, it may be necessary to list the requirements in a catalogue and clearly identify aspects such as the owner, the rationale and any cross-references to other project documents.

Non-functional requirements

Non-functional requirements define the level of service quality to be provided by the solution. They cover a range of areas, in particular:

- access and security;
- capacity and scalability;
- availability, robustness and maintainability;
- business continuity, backup and recovery;
- performance and response;
- deletion and archiving;
- compatibility and interfacing;
- accessibility and usability.

These requirements may be recorded within the functional requirements documentation, such as where a non-functional requirement – for example the speed of the response – relates to a specific functional requirement to provide some information or take some action. An example might be in a restaurant, where an order must be taken within ten minutes of seating customers at a table. A non-functional requirement that is embedded within the description of a functional requirement is sometimes referred to as an associated non-functional requirement or could be written as detailed acceptance criteria using techniques such as BDD, as discussed in Chapter 12.

Other non-functional requirements apply to several functional requirements and may be relevant across the entire solution. For example, wherever information or data is recorded or accessed, there may be an overarching requirement setting out the level of access available to different user roles. These requirements are sometimes referred to as system-wide or solution-wide non-functional requirements.

The means of recording non-functional requirements needs to be considered carefully whatever the development approach to be used. However, this is particularly the case when working in an agile environment. This subject is considered in further detail later in this chapter.

THE REQUIREMENTS CATALOGUE

A catalogue is a central repository of information. It may encompass a list of services or products or any other item that needs to be listed and organised centrally. A requirements catalogue provides a central repository for requirements that have been identified for a particular change project and is typically organised such that requirements that have similarities are located together.

Each requirements catalogue entry records the information about a specific requirement. This information may include some of the following aspects for each requirement:

- unique identifier;
- name and description;
- type of requirement;
- owner with responsibility for decisions about the requirement (for example, the level of priority);
- source who identified the requirement;
- designated level of priority;
- related requirements (such as non-functional requirements) and other documents;
- rationale justifying the inclusion of the requirement;
- version history for the requirement.

One of the frequent misconceptions about the requirements catalogue is that each entry has to be definitively and rigorously complete before the catalogue can be agreed. This misconception needs to be challenged, as in many circumstances it is not desirable, or even possible, to provide a detailed definition. A general requirement may be a high-level statement such as 'the solution must use company branding standards'. In this case, there would be little point in spending time recording links to the potentially numerous related requirements; it just needs to be accepted that this will be applied whenever relevant to the solution. Similarly, technical constraints and some non-functional requirements, such as those related to accessibility and usability, have a solution-wide application and could be cross-referenced to many functional requirements. However, to do this would be a waste of time; understanding that these requirements are relevant to each development iteration would suffice.

It may also be the case that the requirements catalogue is used to record high-level functional requirements where the detail is defined using modelling approaches. So, we might define the following requirement: 'the solution must record customer details', but then use a data model to define what is meant by 'customer details'. In the past, requirements catalogues have been used to contain as much narrative information as possible; information that has then been duplicated (and sometimes contradicted) in business process, use case and data models. This has meant that time has been spent on activities of little value and often areas of very low priority have been explored to the same level of detail as those that are absolutely essential. If we want to use a requirements catalogue, we need to ensure that it is used in an informed way, recording relevant information to support the development of the required solution.

Agile business analysis is founded on applying business analysis in line with the agile philosophy and principles. Documentation that is sufficient to the situation is a key element of this approach and the use of the requirements catalogue should be considered within this context. Agile projects may find it helpful to use a requirements catalogue for some categories of requirement – for example, the general requirements – because they provide a contextual view. However, it may be more beneficial to use an alternative approach such as a backlog of user stories to record areas of functionality requested by customers.

THE ITEMISED BACKLOGS

The concept of a backlog derives from the Scrum approach to software development. Each backlog provides a means of listing the work items to be conducted by the project during the development of the product. Hence, Scrum calls the backlog the 'product backlog'. However, a software product is not sufficient to improve business; it needs to be deployed in conjunction with the other required changes to processes, jobs, skill enhancements and organisational changes.

Business analysis has always taken a holistic view, moving beyond focusing on software products to think about multi-faceted solutions to business problems or opportunities. In some situations, there may not be a need for software at all. For example, a simplification to a process might address a particular business problem and deliver the required benefits. Therefore, looking at the concept of a backlog from a business analysis perspective, a solution backlog containing a list of itemised requirements to be met, is more relevant. The solution backlog might relate purely to a software product but, in our experience, the chances of such a limited solution generating business improvements are low.

While the solution backlog contains the entire set of required work items, we also need to consider the use of backlogs in driving the solution development. There are two other backlogs to consider: the release backlog, which contains the work items that form the set of changes that are to be deployed into operation; and the iteration backlog, which lists the items to be worked on during a specific iteration. The release backlog contains the minimal set of items from the solution backlog that will offer value when delivered to the stakeholders. These three versions of the backlog are represented in Figure 13.2 below.

Figure 13.2 Three different views of the backlog

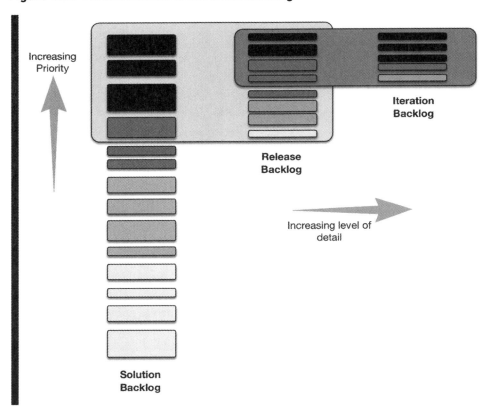

The solution backlog

The term 'solution backlog' reflects the business analysis world view that change projects focus on providing a solution that addresses a problem or grasps a business opportunity. The solution may involve a software product but invariably, for a business change to be successful, it may also encompass broader aspects such as people, process and organisational changes. Each of these aspects needs to be considered when scoping the proposed solution.

When the project is focused on software development, the backlog items drive the work of the software development team; this is the focus of agile methods such as Scrum and XP. However, as described in Chapter 3, business analysts are often involved in different aspects of change projects so may need to apply a broader, more holistic focus. In these situations, the backlog should reflect the need for the solution to encompass a range of areas. Business epics (discussed in Chapter 4) may be used to describe these work items. For example, where the project is concerned with business process change, the backlog items may include the following:

- As an expenses administrator, I need to have a set of common instructions for staff so that they can provide the information and receipts I require.
- As an internal auditor, I need to have access to the relevant audit guidance so that I can produce an accurate report regarding the audit status of a department.

Once these items reach the level of priority where they are allocated to an iteration for further development, there will need to be collaboration and communication with business stakeholders in order to elaborate on the requirement and ensure that the needs are met. In doing this, business analysis is needed to investigate the requirement and ensure that there is a clear justification for the changes. This may involve challenging some of the detail provided by the business stakeholders to ensure that the root causes of any problems are uncovered and the actual issues, rather than the manifest symptoms, are addressed by the solution.

The solution backlog allows business analysts to think holistically about the elements to be included in the backlog and extend their focus beyond software development. The solution backlog has similarities to the requirements catalogue in that it provides a prioritised master list of the items to be considered for inclusion in the solution. It is also a living document in that it develops over time, beginning with an initial set of items and evolving as more detail of the required features emerges. It is prioritised using an approach to rank or categorise the items. Chapter 9 sets out the different prioritisation approaches that may be used to do this.

An accepted feature of the solution backlog – and possibly one of the key differences with the requirements catalogue approach – is that there is not a sense that the backlog is 'signed off' as a complete record of the requirements for the solution. Instead, it is accepted that there is further understanding needed and more details to uncover. The solution backlog should be maintained, and priorities adjusted, using a collaborative approach that involves the project team and the key business stakeholders.

The items recorded in a backlog may be of different types. For example, they may be functional requirements that set out what the solution must enable the customer to do. Or, they may be non-functional requirements that define the levels of quality to be offered by the solution. The functional features to be delivered as part of the solution may be defined using techniques such as use cases or user stories; the exact technique used will depend upon the situation as discussed in Chapter 11.

Ordering and reordering the solution backlog

The development of the solution requires the project team to explore the work items documented in the backlog. This work may cause additional items to be identified as the team explore the solution in further detail and this will require re-prioritisation of the backlog.

Where the work items are recorded user stories, they are used by the project team to evolve the understanding of what is to be delivered. This work may cause additional user stories to be generated, which are added to the backlog. The new user stories may be large or may be of a more manageable size and complexity. Adding new stories will require the re-prioritisation of the backlog so that the most important items are highlighted; this will ensure that they are incorporated within the next release or iteration. Therefore, there is an ongoing, iterative approach to prioritisation that will require collaboration with the business stakeholders. The aim of a business change project is to improve the work of an organisation or produce a marketable product that may be sold by the organisation. The work to achieve this requires ongoing awareness of the business context into which any solution will be delivered. As a result, business analysis is essential if decisions regarding prioritisation, ordering and selection of the backlog items are to be effective and in line with business needs. This 'ordering and reordering' of the backlog is also described in Chapter 15 and referred to as 'product backlog refinement'.

The timing of the backlog ordering activity can be critical. It is possible to do this during an iteration, but this approach may deflect the project team from the work they are undertaking. However, if the business analyst is involved in the reordering activity, this would allow the work of the project team to continue while ensuring that the basis for deciding upon the next iteration is in place. A further benefit of the business analyst involvement in this activity is that it helps to ensure that the development work remains consistent with the original goals and business case for the project.

The release backlog

Solutions developed using an agile approach will be delivered in releases, or increments, and each increment may comprise a set of software features, process improvements and organisational changes. An increment may be developed during one or several iterations but essentially is delivered into operation once there is a set of changes that is internally consistent and will offer value to the customer organisation.

The release backlog is an important concept because it sets out what is to be delivered in the next increment. Therefore, it must be internally consistent and complete – there is little point in introducing a partial solution that requires significant effort to be spent on workarounds.

The iteration backlog

Each iteration needs to have a designated package of work items. These items should be subject to analysis, development and testing within the iteration and result in functionality that has the potential to be deployed. The backlog for the iteration needs to contain a set of items to be worked on during the iteration. While the time to deliver the items will have been estimated (Chapter 14) and the team velocity will have been calculated (Chapter 15), it is always possible for the estimates to be incorrect or for the team to work more slowly than predicted. As a result, it is useful to include items that have not been prioritised as 'mandatory' within the iteration backlog in order that there is some contingency should delays occur.

For example, if using MoSCoW prioritisation, the iteration backlog might contain several 'must have' items, some 'should have' and some 'could have'. This set of items provides a basis for ensuring that the urgent mandatory requirements are addressed and that there is the opportunity to work on the lower priority 'should have' and the optional 'could have' features. Where items take longer than originally conceived, perhaps because greater complexity emerges during the development team's work and delays are encountered, the lower priority requirements provide a means of ensuring that no time is wasted in the iteration and that the urgent mandatory requirements are delivered. The inclusion of different priority levels provides contingency and reduces risk. The iteration backlog is a key element in iteration planning and is considered in detail in Chapter 15.

REQUIREMENTS CATALOGUE OR SOLUTION BACKLOG?

It is important to recognise that the focus of the requirements catalogue is different to that of the backlog. For this reason, it may be helpful for an agile change project to have both documents, each providing a specific set of information as follows:

- a requirements catalogue setting out certain types of requirement, in particular the general business requirements and technical requirements. It may also be useful to catalogue non-functional requirements; this is discussed further in a later section of this chapter;

- a solution backlog setting out the work items for the project team, in particular any functional requirements to be delivered by the solution.

The importance of pre-project analysis, where a proposed initiative is investigated and options evaluated, was discussed in Chapter 6. This work is unlikely to benefit from the development of a solution backlog because at this stage it is not known whether a solution is required or feasible. However, it will always be important to record the business requirements, as they form the basis for understanding why a change project is needed and the key aspects to be included. There may also be some technical issues or constraints that need to be considered when evaluating the feasibility of a proposed solution. A requirements catalogue is a useful document to record these types of requirements.

The nature of some of the requirements, for example, general requirements and technical requirements, may mean that they need to be viewed separately from the functional features to be delivered. A data protection requirement, for example, may need to apply across all the features of the solution and the different elements, whether software, process or people. These requirements need to be defined so that they provide a context for the rest of the work, and techniques such as use cases or user stories do not offer an efficient way of doing this. It is preferable for the solution-wide requirements to be recorded as a distinct set. A requirements catalogue setting out any solution-wide requirements and used in conjunction with a solution backlog formed of work items to be delivered would meet several needs. This approach would:

- distinguish those requirements that need to be considered during every iteration and ensure that they are visible to the project team;

- provide a means of grouping the contextual requirements that set out the business and technical constraints;

- enable the work on the various elements of the solution (software, process, people and organisational changes) to have access to a unique definition of the solution-wide requirements;

- provide a basis for thinking about the best way to record requirements rather than trying to force them into an unhelpful format.

It is useful to distinguish between the work items to be delivered during an iteration and the requirements that must be applied to the entire solution. The solution backlog is an excellent tool for recording work items to be undertaken on a change project. It provides an effective means of driving the release and iteration backlogs, and helps to ensure that prioritisation work is focused on meeting immediate needs. However, a requirements catalogue provides an extremely useful structure and format for the broader requirements that are not best defined using feature-based techniques such as use cases and user stories. Using a requirements catalogue in conjunction with the solution and related backlogs will enable a change project to ensure that work is governed effectively and conducted to address business needs.

RECORDING NON-FUNCTIONAL REQUIREMENTS

Non-functional requirements are often the most difficult requirements to define. There are several reasons for this, including:

- the wide range of non-functional requirements to be considered;
- there is often a lack of focus on non-functional requirements until later in the project;
- the complexity surrounding some of these requirements.

Another issue is that some non-functional requirements only apply to a specific feature or a small area of functionality, whereas others apply much more widely. A response-time requirement may relate to just one user story – for example, the time to provide a quotation for a service – while another such non-functional requirement – for example, the time to return information following a query – may apply across the entire solution.

Some non-functional requirements, such as archiving and deletion, relate closely to legal and business policy needs and may be concerned with areas of data rather than functional requirements. Others, such as availability, may apply to every aspect of a system. Some of these purely relate to an IT system, some to a combination of manual and automated processes, while others may be completely manual. As this indicates, there are a lot of reasons why non-functional requirements require considerable analytical work if they are to be defined clearly.

Where a non-functional requirement has a very specific purpose, it may be included within the relevant user story. If we take as an example the response time requirement mentioned above, we might develop a user story as follows:

- As a theatre-goer I want to find out the availability of tickets **within 5 seconds** so that I can decide whether or not to make a booking.

The bold section comprises the non-functional requirement relating to response time. As this is documented within a user story, it provides enough information for further discussion but does not set out the requirement in detail.

However, if there is a non-functional requirement that applies solution-wide, then documenting it within each user story would be impractical and confusing. Instead, it may be preferable to document it within a requirements catalogue section that is dedicated to non-functional requirements. A good example of this would be a security requirement where there are several different levels of security across different areas of data, one way of recording this succinctly is to use a matrix. An example setting out the access permissions and limitations for a ticket sales website is shown in Figure 13.3 below.

Figure 13.3 Example requirements catalogue definition of access requirements

Limitations to be placed upon the following website usage categories:

- control data, for example, passwords, registrations: level 1
- customer data: level 2
- sales order data: level 3
- website management system: level 4
- content information deemed to be valuable: level 5
- content information not within level 5:   level 6

Website controller	Band A (levels 1, 3, 4, 5, 6)
Marketing director	Band B (levels 2, 3, 5, 6)
Marketing assistant, sales assistant	Band C (levels 3, 5, 6)
Information seeker, potential customer, purchaser	Band D (level 6)
Registered customer	Band E (levels 5, 6)
Website maintainer	Band F (levels 4, 5, 6)

Another possibility is to highlight non-functional requirements at an outline level but using a more visible form. For example, as shown in Figure 13.4, it can be useful to create sticky notes that provide the essence of the non-functional requirements that are particularly relevant to a current iteration. The specific details may then be recorded formally in the catalogue where they can be accessed when needed and the notes ensure that the relevant non-functional requirements are kept visible to the agile team. This approach is particularly useful for non-functional requirements that apply across the solution and could also be used for constraints related to general and technical requirements.

Figure 13.4 Visible non-functional requirements and constraints

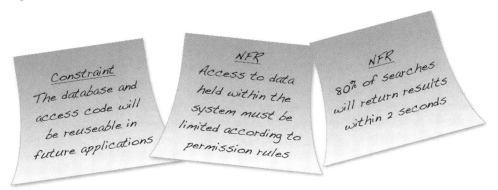

Note: NFR = non-functional requirement.

Each non-functional requirement should be considered separately to identify the best recording mechanism. A general rule is that solution-wide, non-functional requirements are best documented in a catalogue, although it is advisable to couple this with the more visible approach described above. The catalogue will provide a means of describing each requirement in the most appropriate way; the access requirements example shown above is an example of one approach but others will be required for different types of non-functional requirements. A textual description of the requirement may also be useful where it applies to just one feature or user story but contains significant rules and complexity.

HIERARCHY OF REQUIREMENTS

The different types of requirement form a hierarchy that is invaluable during business analysis, particularly within an agile environment. This hierarchy is shown in Figure 13.5 below.

Some of the general requirements, as discussed earlier, may state legal regulations or policies with which the solution must comply. Some requirements are raised by stakeholders who know what they want the solution to include to achieve a business goal. These are all within the general requirements category and are at the top of the requirements hierarchy. The general requirements set the context and the high-level goals for the solution. They also provide the basis for further analysis and definition, and thereby support the elicitation and elaboration of the more detailed functional and non-functional requirements to be provided by the solution. The technical requirements have a different role in that they set constraints within which the functional and non-functional requirements must operate. Therefore, there is a hierarchical link with both general and technical requirements, each with a different focus.

The general and technical requirements must be understood if the delivered product or system is to offer value to the organisation. Without this understanding, the customers may request features or quality characteristics that would meet local needs or support

Figure 13.5 Hierarchy of requirements

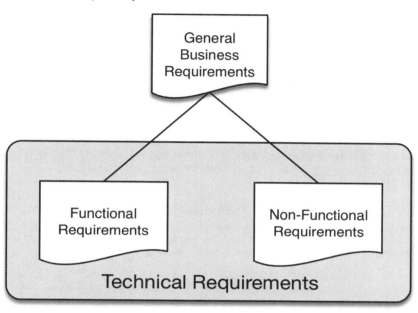

individual experiences but not address broader organisational requirements or consider the impact of such requests on timescales or costs. A recent report (Luftman et al., 2012) emphasised the importance of the alignment between the business and the IT function, and the concerns chief information officers have about the lack of such alignment. This is where business analysis can offer insights that are necessary if requests for services, features and characteristics are to be considered advisedly. One way of ensuring this is to consider the rationale for a requirement – in particular how it links to aspects such as the business strategy and CSFs for the organisation. In some situations, asking the customer why a particular requirement is needed can be vital in eliciting the real nature of the business need and ensuring that root causes of problems are addressed rather than symptoms just being masked.

Deriving detailed requirements

Where an overarching business requirement or need has been expressed, it is often possible to analyse the requirement to derive more specific solution requirements. For example, a business policy regarding customer support is likely to generate several usability and accessibility non-functional requirements; data protection regulations concerning confidentiality of personal data will give rise to non-functional requirements regarding access permissions and restrictions, deletion timescales and so on; a business process requirement regarding a new service to be offered to a customer may cause the creation of functional requirements covering aspects such as information provision, service registration and service delivery.

Understanding the hierarchy places any customer requests firmly in the business context and enables the business analyst to understand the rationale for the requests. It also provides a structure for understanding overarching business goals that may then be decomposed into lower-level goals (see Chapter 8).

Hierarchy of use cases

Business use cases, as described in Chapter 6, provide an excellent basis for setting out the overall context and scope for a change or development project. They provide a means of identifying user roles and reflecting the needs expressed by senior managers within the organisation. They can also be used to relate business events (or triggers) to a business process and to the achievement of a business goal. They provide a means of prioritising at a business need level and allow the customers to clearly show which areas of the solution are considered to have the most potential value.

Use cases can be decomposed from a business to system level where the solution is an IT system; this is reflected in Figure 13.6 below. This also provides a hierarchical structure whereby decomposed business goals and the corresponding functional requirements can be represented. Ensuring that the hierarchy and the links between the levels reflect the needs of the business is a key business analysis task.

Figure 13.6 Decomposed business use case into system use cases

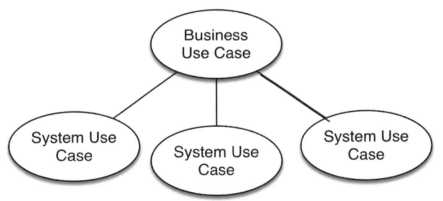

An alternative decomposition may form a hierarchy that includes system use cases, reflecting the functionality to be provided by an IT system, plus other actors providing services or conducting work that is outside the system under development. The business use case may incorporate work that needs to be performed manually by the business staff or may require services to be provided by an external organisation (see such as a requirements Figure 13.7). A typical example is the use of online payment services from specialist organisations, such as Worldpay or PayPal.

Figure 13.7 Decomposed business use case showing external actor component

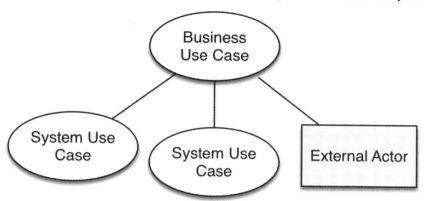

One of the major limitations of use cases is that they document functions to be provided by a business or IT system. So, business requirements such as complying with data protection legislation or applying organisational branding, are not well recorded using a business use case approach. Similarly, the majority of technical constraints and non-functional requirements are recorded more accurately using alternative approaches such as a requirements catalogue or matrix.

Hierarchy of user stories

Agile practitioners have long created user stories as a means of recording and defining the features required in a solution. A user story is a statement of desired software functionality told from the perspective of a user role. A user story should be of a sufficiently small size to be delivered within an iteration. Chapter 12 describes the structure and format of user stories, explaining that in themselves they do not contain enough information to deliver the finished product or solution; they form the basis for further analytical and design work.

However, user stories may be developed at different levels of granularity. Sometimes the business stakeholders identify user stories that are at an overview level, requiring the delivery of a business goal; often these user stories cannot be developed within an iteration because of their size. Such user stories are known as 'epics' and are typically too large and complex to estimate with any degree of accuracy. Epics need to be split into smaller user stories that can be delivered by an iteration. It is possible that some of the smaller stories within an epic may be delivered by the manual processes supported by the software rather than by the software product itself. Again, we can form a hierarchy, using the user story technique, to move from high-level business stories and goals to more detailed and specific stories with smaller goals.

User stories are used during both the analysis and the planning process for agile software development projects. They provide insights into the features to be included in a software product and provide a means of breaking down functionality to a granular level.

One of the criticisms often levelled at user stories is that they can present a fragmented picture of the solution and, when this approach is used, it is difficult to see the whole picture. One way of dealing with this issue is to combine the development of use cases and user stories such that a holistic view of the required functionality is obtained. The user roles are the key sources for both use cases and the user stories so these techniques work well together to identify and define functionality. Two possible approaches to avoiding fragmentation are:

- Build a hierarchy of use cases, from business to system. These diagrams will enable the analyst to gain a contextual view of the situation under investigation and help to ensure that all aspects are considered. The system use cases can then be explored using user stories. This hierarchy is reflected in Figure 13.8 below.

Figure 13.8 Hierarchy of use cases leading to user story development

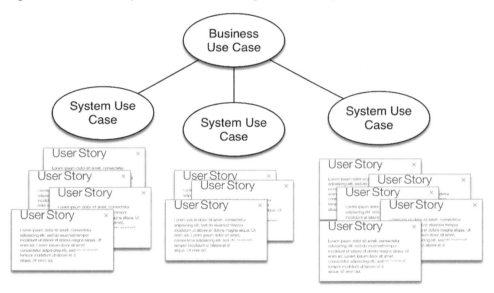

- Use a context diagram (as discussed in Chapter 11) to define the set of user roles prior to identifying the user stories. This will separate out the discussion about user roles, providing a means of focusing on them and building a good set before beginning to identify user stories.

Whichever is the case, it is useful to recognise that the higher-level, more complex user stories are typically identified first and then decomposed to reveal specific user stories focused on achieving more detailed sub-goals. The user stories are recorded in the solution backlog and prioritised to indicate which features are the most important. The effort to develop each user story is estimated. A set of estimated, prioritised user stories can then be selected to form the basis for the work of an iteration.

Business analysts may be needed to explore the user stories, particularly if there are more detailed aspects such as tacit knowledge, data, business rules or interactions to be uncovered. These more detailed areas are not recorded in the backlog but form the models associated with the original user story.

CONCLUSION

There are several different approaches to recording requirements, each of which may be helpful according to the particular circumstances. This chapter has looked at some of the standards that may be adopted to record and manage the features to be included in a solution.

Business analysts should have expertise in applying a toolkit of approaches to elicit, analyse and document business needs at different levels and across a range of aspects. For this reason, they are well placed to offer support to the project, helping to record, prioritise and investigate the solution requirements, features and goals. Identifying the most relevant and useful approach to adopt when recording these items is a key element of business analysis. It is particularly important when working in an agile development environment, as following documentation standards blindly or recording unnecessary levels of detail at an early stage can result in wasted efforts that could have been expended elsewhere to deliver greater benefit.

REFERENCE

Luftman, J., Zadeh, H.S., Derksen, B., Santana, M., Rigoni, E.H. and Huang, Z. (2012) Key information technology and management issues 2011–2012: an international study. *Journal of Information Technology*, 27 (3): 198–212.

FURTHER READING

Cockburn, A. (2000) *Writing effective use cases: the Agile software development series.* Boston, MA: Addison Wesley.

Cohn, M. (2004) *User Stories applied: for Agile software development.* Boston, MA: Addison Wesley.

Paul, D., Cadle, J. and Yeates, D. (2014) *Business analysis: 3rd edition.* Swindon: BCS.

14 ESTIMATING AGILE PROJECTS

This chapter covers the following topics:

- agile estimation approaches;
- why and when to estimate;
- estimation techniques.

INTRODUCTION

Accurate estimation is essential to all types of change projects, but the **Just Enough, Just in Time** concept presents new challenges for business analysts working alongside or within agile teams. When the detail of project scope is not known up front, how can the team provide useful estimates?

This chapter introduces the key principles that underpin most agile estimation techniques, and puts them into context. Examples demonstrate how agile teams use estimation in practice and highlight how these techniques can be utilised effectively by business analysts.

AGILE ESTIMATION APPROACHES

Business analysts will be familiar with estimation, and there are many well-documented techniques and methods. Estimation on agile projects is just as important as in other types of project, but there are a few differences and a few new techniques. These techniques apply to all types of project, not just those involving software development.

Agile approaches are different to traditional approaches and it is important that business analysts understand these differences if the agile values and principles are to be upheld.

The agile values promote **'Responding to change over following a plan'** and **'Customer collaboration over contract negotiation'**, and there is a principle that **'Working software is the best measure of progress'.** Some sources have now replaced 'software' with 'product', which accepts that elements of a product, other than software, should be considered.

Consequently, these agile values and principles suggest that estimates should be treated in a somewhat different way from traditional projects. Specifically, agile teams approach estimation with an assumption that the factors that contribute to the estimate will change, and hence the estimates will change. This means that it is vital to understand what is being estimated, and why. An estimate is a best guess, based on the knowledge that the team has at the time. It should also have a tolerance, or margin of error. This might be quite large at the start of a project, because so many things have the potential to change. As the project proceeds, more things become certain, risks are reduced and the estimates can be more precise. In addition, more of the work has been completed, leaving less work still to be done.

This is, in some ways, similar to what happens on traditional projects – the initial estimates may be updated as the project progresses, usually at the end of the project stages. The difference with agile estimating is that it is done on an ongoing basis, and there is a focus on preparing detailed estimates only for elements that are required in the near future and not on estimating elements that may never be developed.

It should be noted that all estimates made during the course of the project are **acceptable**; it's just that early in a project, the estimates are less *precise* and more subject to change. Figure 14.1 below illustrates the estimation cycle used in an agile project.

Figure 14.1 Estimation cycle

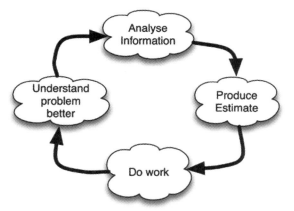

WHY AND WHEN TO ESTIMATE

Estimation is required at all stages of an agile development cycle, and will serve different purposes at each stage.

- At the very start of a project, the team may have to estimate how long the whole project will take, or how much work can be expected in a given timescale.

- As the product backlog is developed, estimates of the size of the backlog items are required, but should not be too detailed in case they are not required.

- At the start of an iteration, the team must estimate how much work they think they can deliver in the iteration.

- As the user stories are broken down into tasks, the amount of time each task should take is sometimes estimated.

- Throughout an iteration, the team may estimate whether they are on track to deliver the user stories with which they started.

- At the end of an iteration, the velocity of the team is re-estimated, based on the evidence from the just-completed iteration. This may lead to re-estimation of the project or release milestones. Velocity is explained in Chapter 15.

ESTIMATION TECHNIQUES

Agile estimation approaches mostly rely on the whole team contributing to the estimate (Wideband Delphi), because the whole team (including business analysts) will be delivering the project; and on some form of relative sizing, because humans are much better at comparing things than at calculating actual numbers. These approaches allow agile teams to come up with helpful estimates that are accurate **enough** without attempting to be highly precise.

Wideband Delphi

Wideband Delphi was developed in the 1970s by Barry Boehm and John Farquhar. The technique relies on obtaining estimates from suitably qualified people and then synthesising them to produce the final estimate. Most agile estimation techniques rely on the theory of Wideband Delphi and some form of relative sizing.

General process

- Each estimator is given a specification of the work (activity, task or deliverable) and is asked to provide their estimate for it. These estimates are compiled anonymously.

- The estimates are then summarised (still anonymously) and the summary is circulated to all the estimators.

- Estimators reconsider their own estimates in the light of the summary and provide a revised estimate if they wish.

- The above process is repeated as many times as necessary to achieve a reasonable consensus.

The participants bring different experience and knowledge to their estimates and, because the estimates are anonymous, personal disagreements are avoided and the estimates can be considered objectively.

Relative sizing

Most people have difficulty in defining precise estimates for complex tasks. However, they find it much more straightforward to make comparisons between estimates for different tasks.

Relative sizing is a way of using experience to gauge the size of something using historical information or judgement. It can allow very precise estimates, quickly, without requiring complex analysis.

The concept can be illustrated with the jar of jelly beans shown in Figure 14.2.

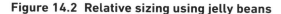

Figure 14.2 Relative sizing using jelly beans

Trying to estimate the number of jelly beans is a surprisingly difficult task, because there is no reference point upon which to base the estimate. However, if the number of jelly beans in a full jar is known, the problem becomes much simpler. This is because humans are very good at judging relative sizes – we find it quite straightforward to tell that something is twice as big or four times as long. Therefore, being told that a full jar contains 440 beans makes estimating how many are in the jar in Figure 14.2 much easier, and results in a much more precise and accurate estimate.

This is fundamental to agile estimation; comparing the requirement or item being estimated to previous items results in a much more accurate estimate.

The things being compared don't have to be exactly the **same**, they just need to be similar **enough** that they can be compared. For example, being told how many smarties were in a full jar should still result in a reasonable estimate of the number of jelly beans in the half-full jar.

Estimation units

Teams can estimate in any unit that helps them. The advice is generally to try to avoid using actual time units (like days or hours). Some commonly used units are shown in Table 14.1 below.

Table 14.1 Commonly used estimation units

User stories, epics or number of requirements	Especially useful at the 'whole-project' level as they are relatively easy to count. However, since stories are not all the same size it can be misleading. You can use epics or separate stories in small, medium or large stories to make the process more granular (for example, a 25 epic, 40 story project).
Story points	A very commonly used abstract unit. What one point means will differ between teams, so it is important that everybody's view of a point is the same.
Ideal developer days/ hours	This assumes a developer could spend all the time on the work. Can be helpful to provide consistency, but it is easy to underestimate the non-coding time in real life, especially when deciding how much work can be done in an iteration.
Days/hours	Seemingly logical, and easy to map into available time, but notoriously difficult to get right. Common in non-agile projects but, really, only good for simple, well-understood tasks.
Abstract units	Non-numeric and abstract representations of size. Examples are small, medium, large, extra-large. Or using more abstract terms: animals, area, volume and so on. Like story points, they abstract away from real life, but the whole team needs to know what they mean and how they relate. Sometimes called Nebulous Units of Time or NUTs.

Up-front estimation

At some point in almost every project, usually around the start or before it begins, somebody wants to know what will be delivered, when and at what cost. Given what we know about agile projects, this is a hard question to answer. There is usually more work to do than the team will have time to complete, and the customer is rarely certain on scope and detailed requirements at the beginning.

To estimate how long a project might take, a traditional team may try to break down all the requirements, estimate all the parts, add up the days and add some contingency. An agile team might approach that differently:

- Get together and spend some time understanding the project.

- Think about what kinds of work will be involved.

- Try to compare the work to previous projects.

- Come up with a rough idea of how long it might take, perhaps as a number of iterations, taking into account factors such as team size, familiarity with the problem space and so on.

- Once the team start work, they will get a feel for how fast they are going, and can revise their estimate.

Taken at first glance, that seems a very bad way to come up with an estimate. However, because the agile team will be delivering the product in a prioritised way, the most important work will be delivered first. So, even if the estimate is too low, and the project has to stop before all the requirements are delivered, the missing requirements will be the lowest in priority. It requires trust between the project sponsors and the team and, for teams working in a commercial context, the contract and commercial terms need to be carefully considered.

This type of approach follows many of the agile core values and principles – it is iterative, involves the whole team, uses just enough detail, and focuses on value to the customer. It is also a good way to access the team's tacit knowledge in a way that an analytic breakdown of the problem isn't able to do. Business analysts play an important role here, particularly with their ability to think more broadly than just about the tasks of the team, and to consider people, process, organisational and facilities aspects in addition to software.

This overall approach can be applied to all kinds of estimation with agile teams, including non-IT projects. The key thing to remember is **Just Enough, Just in Time**. For example, items on the product backlog aren't committed to at this point, so only need rough sizing, and low level tasks during an iteration might not need an estimate at all.

Relative estimation (bucket method)

In this technique, a small set of estimation categories or buckets (perhaps 3–5) are chosen as the estimate results. The team start with a story and decide which bucket it should belong in. The next story is then discussed, compared with the first, and a bucket chosen for it, and so on.

This is a good way to roughly divide up a backlog, and it can be particularly effective when used at product backlog level. Because there are only a small number of possible values, and they must cope with the smallest to largest story, the results can be a little coarse for some types of estimation.

Examples of this include 'T-shirt sizing', where the 'buckets' are T-shirt sizes, such as extra-small, small, medium, large and extra-large. Other teams use groups of animals (small animals, medium sized, etc.) or measures of volume (shot, half, pint, etc.). This method can also be used with a very limited number of choices (big/small).

Ordering

Sometimes called **Relative Mass Estimation**, this technique uses an intermediate ordered stage. This means it can also be used for prioritisation, and can be used for ordering and estimating other attributes, not just work. It is applied in the WSJF prioritisation technique used in some agile methods (see Chapter 9).

To begin, all the items being estimated should be on cards that can be moved around a large table.

- The first story is discussed and the team decides roughly how big they think it is and place it somewhere on the table – on the left, if it is small; on the right if it is big; or somewhere in-between.
- The next story is discussed and the team decides if it requires more or less work than the first story. It is placed on the table in the appropriate place.
- This continues with each story placed somewhere on the table depending on how easy or hard it is relative to the existing cards.

This results in a very visual representation of the work the team has to do, with the hardest work at one side and the easiest work on the other.

Finally, the stories have a numeric estimate placed on them. This can be done by starting at the easiest story, allocating it 1 point. The team members then work their way up through the stories, allocating each story 1 point until the team reaches a story that they think is twice as difficult as the first story. This gets 2 points, and so on. Any numeric sequence could be used, including Fibonacci, or one of the relative sizing methods mentioned above. The important thing to remember is that it is a rough estimate and not to dwell too much on the value.

This technique can also be used to assess priority of stories, and can be gamified where players take it in turns to move cards around the board, challenge decisions or add a new card.

Divide to size

This method aims to get all the items the same size as one another. The team begins by deciding what size that should be (say, 5 points, or 1 ideal developer day). After that:

- A story is discussed.
- If the team believes it is the right size or less, it stays.
- Otherwise, it is divided into more than one story, and they are discussed. This is repeated until all the parts are the ideal size or less.
- The team them discusses the next story.

Planning Poker®

There are several variations of planning games that agile teams use at various times to help make estimation more fun. The most well-known is Planning Poker®, which was developed by Mountain Goat Software. This game uses special cards to limit the choice of estimates to promote discussion and help to reach consensus more quickly.

The game is played by the whole team, and can be used for estimating anything with a numeric unit. It is commonly used to size user stories for the backlog. The game uses sets of cards (See Figure 14.3) with a sequence of numbers printed on them. The numbers usually follow a modified Fibonacci sequence (such as 0, 1, 2, 3, 5, 8, 13, 20, 40, 100).

There is a lot of uncertainty in estimation, so having discrete choices forces teams to converge on a single number. Discussions about the uncertainty are encouraged as the gaps between the numbers increase. Some packs of cards add in ½, infinity, 'don't know' and a request for a break. The numbers can represent any numeric unit.

Figure 14.3 Planning Poker® cards

Playing Planning Poker®

The game is played in an estimation workshop or planning meeting. For each story to be estimated, the team goes through the cycle shown in Figure 14.4.

Figure 14.4 Planning Poker® process

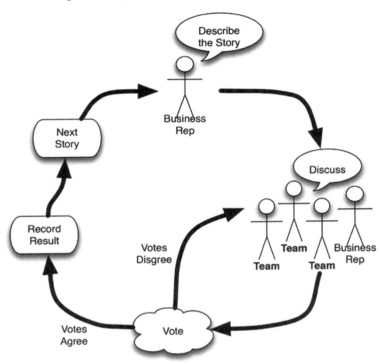

- The story is described (often by the customer) and the team discuss it. This lets them ask questions and clarify any assumptions or risks.

- Each team member privately chooses their estimate for the story and deals their card, face down.

- At the same time, all the estimates are revealed.

- If they are all the same, the estimate is recorded.

- If they are not the same, the high and low votes are discussed and the reasons behind them explained.

- The team vote again.

- This process is repeated until the team agree on an estimate.

- The next story is chosen, and the entire process is repeated until all the stories have been estimated.

The process should involve the whole team, and it is preferable that the team members are co-located. However, there are electronic versions of the cards available to allow remote participation. Before the meeting, the team must have a common understanding of what the values mean. Typically, they will pick a story everyone is familiar with from an earlier iteration and agree how many points that story represents. They can then apply relative sizing judgements to estimate the new stories. The numbers matter – an 8-point story should be about four times as difficult as a 2-point story.

This game can be modified in a variety of ways. Teams can choose their own numbers or number sequences, or even choose non-numeric votes such as different sized shapes or animals (for example, flea to elephant).

One of the problems with using numbers is that people naturally relate them to days' effort. This can be misleading because different people work at different rates, particularly in a multi-disciplinary team of generalising specialists. Using days as a unit can also be easily misinterpreted by other stakeholders, particularly where the estimates have not taken account of other activities like holidays, training or management meetings and there is confusion between the concepts of effort and elapsed time.

The game is usually (but not always) used to judge story size and the relative time a story will take to deliver. Business analysts have an important role to play, as they can often bring insights to the team that will affect their estimates. For example, a business analyst might point out that user experience testing will require more users than the developers thought, or that a business process will require updating, which is additional work. They may also be aware of complex business rules that underlie some stories.

CONCLUSION

Estimation is not an exact science: estimates are almost always at least a little bit wrong; and sometimes a lot wrong. Agile projects expect and anticipate change, so agile estimation must also expect change. Largely, that means doing as little work as possible to get to an answer that can be used.

There are many different ways to estimate. Most rely on collaboration and the experienced expert principles of Wideband Delphi. They also apply a form of abstract relative sizing.

The key things to focus on are that the whole team has the same understanding of the units being used and to apply the **Just Enough, Just in Time** principle.

FURTHER READING

Ambler, S. (2009) Dr Dobb's Journal. *Lies, great lies and software development project plans*. UBM. Available at: www.drdobbs.com/architecture-and-design/dr-dobbs-agile-update-0709/218700176 [20 December 2016].

Ambler, S. (n.d.) Agile Modelling. Ambysoft Inc. Available at: www.agilemodeling.com [20 December 2016].

Boehm, B. (1981) *Software engineering economics*. Englewood Cliffs, NJ: Prentice Hall.

Cohn, M. (2005) *Agile estimating and planning*. Upper Saddle River, NJ: Prentice Hall.

15 PLANNING AND MANAGING ITERATIONS

This chapter covers the following topics:

- the iteration;
- iterations and goals;
- planning the iteration;
- managing and monitoring the iteration;
- reviewing the iteration;
- the role of business analysis in agile iterations.

INTRODUCTION

This chapter explores the work conducted within the iteration, the fundamental element of an agile project. There are many aspects to understanding how an iteration works, including planning, monitoring and reviewing the work. The techniques and approaches used during these activities are discussed below. The key artefact for an agile project is the backlog. In Chapter 13, we discussed this in the context of a solution so referred to the 'solution backlog'. Here, the focus is very much on the delivery of the software product so we refer to the 'product backlog' or often, simply, the backlog. However, the concept of a central repository of work items, such as requirements and user stories, remains the same. As such, the backlog is an artefact that business analysts in agile teams will become very familiar with.

THE ITERATION

Many agile methods are described as iterative and incremental, so it is important to understand what these terms mean.

- **Iterative:** the work evolves through elaboration and successive refinement.
- **Incremental:** the product is delivered in several parts, with each part building on the last, usually adding new features or qualities.

Often, the delivery of the increment coincides with the end of an iteration, but in some projects, particularly where they are large or complex, it may take several iterations before an increment is ready for delivery. This is where the working software delivered at the end of an iteration does not offer sufficient functionality for it to be deployed.

The iterations defined by the various agile methods share many common features, though they may use different terminology. This chapter will define and discuss the features of an iteration in a method-agnostic way, and will describe a range of techniques and practices to plan, manage and track the iteration. Business analysis has an important role to play throughout, and, in some cases, active business analyst involvement is critical to success.

Iterations have a set of typical attributes that are described below.

- **Goal:** some reason or purpose for the iteration to exist. The iteration should **do something** and have something to show for the work at the end. There should be clear business value.

- **Plan:** the steps required to meet the goal should be clear and agreed with the team, the customer and other important stakeholders. This includes how the work will be tested and accepted. By planning only this iteration in any detail, the team is mitigating against the risk that future requirements (or goals) will change.

- **Implement:** the steps agreed are done by the team, with a focus on achieving the goal. For software products, this may appear like a mini-waterfall of steps for each work item, with all the activities from requirements capture to integration and testing required.

- **Monitor and review:** even within an iteration, progress is reviewed, often daily, and the team should know whether the goal is still achievable, and desirable. This progress should be visible and transparent, and often uses physical components like boards, sticky notes and wallcharts. This means that both the team and other stakeholders can monitor progress.

- **Review the iteration:** continuous improvement is a critical element of agile development, so agile teams take every opportunity to identify things to do better, but especially at iteration boundaries. This includes acknowledgement of things that went poorly, but it also means understanding that the project itself will change and evolve; and that may require the team to change its behaviour or composition.

- **Decide the next iteration:** the team, with the customer, decides whether there will be a further iteration and, if so, how it should happen. This may include making changes identified in the review.

A simplified iteration cycle incorporating these attributes is represented in Figure 15.1.

Figure 15.1 Cycle of an iteration

Iteration

This cycle may be familiar to business analysts as it is a variation on the Shewhart Cycle, popularised by W. Edwards Deming (1982), with his Plan-Do-Study-Act wheel developed in the 1950s. Agile teams often work at a high level of intensity during an iteration and are focused and optimised to react to change.

Figure 15.2 shows a slightly different view of an iteration, identifying some of the activities common to iterations using more familiar terminology: 'prepare backlog' and 'iteration planning meeting' are forms of planning; 'daily stand-up meetings', 'show and tell' and 'retrospective' are types of review. These activities are described in further detail later in this chapter.

Figure 15.2 Iteration activities

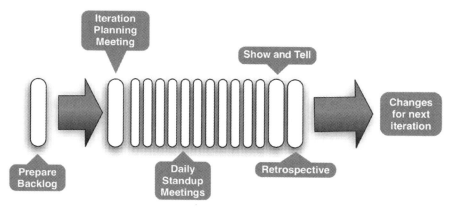

In agile projects, the iterative process is often layered and iterations can be considered to exist at several levels of abstraction (see Figure 15.3):

- micro-increment level (for example, daily iterations);
- delivery level (for example, two week iterations);
- project or architectural level (for example, phases like business case development; inception or construction, that could take several weeks or months);
- strategic or release level (for example, major product releases).

Figure 15.3 The layered approach to iterations

Several approaches (particularly those focused on scaling or enterprise-level projects like SAFe, DAD or the UP) address some of this layering specifically. But even those that do not (such as Scrum or XP) still provide some approaches and practices that teams can use at any level of iteration.

This chapter covers the most common level of abstraction – the delivery layer, which is shown in Figure 15.3 above. This typically involves short iterations (two to four weeks), each of which delivers a version of the overall product and culminates in a final increment or release after several iterations. These iterations are called 'sprints' when using Scrum.

ITERATIONS AND GOALS

Each iteration must focus on achieving a goal that will provide business value to some degree. As the iterations progress, they contribute to an increment that may be deployed for use in the business. As increments progress, they contribute to delivering the overall solution for the project and, in turn, this contributes to the delivery of the predicted business benefits. How these iterations, increments and goals interrelate is shown in Figure 15.4.

Figure 15.4 The relationship between iterations, releases and goals

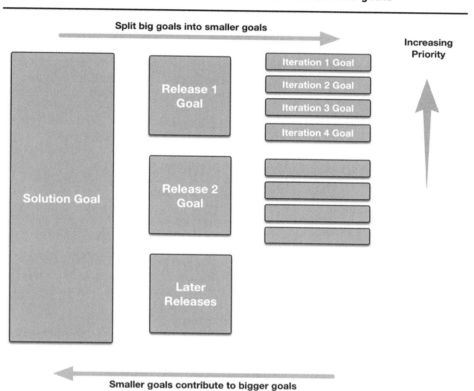

Although the overall release plan may be decided at the start of the project, it is important not to plan too much detail into later iterations, as they may change. All changes should always be tested against higher-level goals to ensure that they are being met.

The benefits of goals

Goals serve to focus the team on what is important. Even with a prioritised backlog as described in Chapter 13, it can be easy for teams to lose focus on what will offer value to the customer. This is where a business analysis perspective can be very helpful. Where possible, goals should be described in line with what is deemed valuable to the customer. Decomposing and working with goals is explained in detail in Chapter 8.

Goals are also helpful when naming iterations. For example, calling the iteration 'Allow credit card website purchases' instead of 'iteration 4' means that is it very clear that the purpose of this work is to make the credit card purchase section of the website work. There may be other tasks on the backlog, but if those that relate to the credit card processing have not been completed, the goal cannot be met.

The iteration goal also needs to be aligned with the project and release goals. This alignment helps to ensure that the iteration contributes to the goals of the release, the release contributes to the goals of the project, and the intended value to the business is delivered. Agile methods embrace and anticipate change, but sometimes changes that happen during development can mean that the project becomes slightly misaligned with the original intent. When this begins to happen, it is critical to recognise it straight away and decide if further action needs to be taken.

This is especially important where the iteration goals have been set by different stake-holders or customers from those involved in setting the project goals. Indications during early iterations that the project goals are wrong or will not be met, need to be commu-nicated to the stakeholders responsible for the higher-level goals immediately. This is particularly critical where project goals have other purposes (such as being linked to contract payments or dependencies on other projects).

This cross-checking between iteration goals and project goals is one of the ways that agile methods can provide early warning of project issues. Early warning means that there is time to correct, or, if the changes are catastrophic, that the cost of cancelling the project is reduced – it is always cheaper to cancel a project earlier rather than later!

It is not always the case that the iteration goal is decided first. Often, the prioritised user stories will determine the goal. However, the converse is also true – knowing the overarching goal of the iteration may cause some user stories to be 'promoted' because it becomes clear that they contribute directly to the goal.

What is important, however, is that the user stories that are delivered provide features that are valuable to the business. This upholds the agile value of '**working software over comprehensive documentation**'.

When setting goals, possible pitfalls to look out for are:

- goals set by the development team, not the customer;
- goals that only cover a small amount of the work of the iteration;
- iteration goals not well aligned with project or release goals;
- different stakeholders having different views on what the goals are (or should be).

PLANNING THE ITERATION

Simplicity–the art of maximising the amount of work not done–is essential[1]

Before work can begin on an iteration, a degree of planning is required and this should be in line with the agile maxim of '**Just Enough, Just in Time**'. Starting with a properly ordered backlog, the team must agree which backlog items should be selected for this iteration. This means that they must know what resources they have available, and must have sufficient understanding of the work that will be required to satisfy each requirement. The team must have enough information to answer these questions, but as discussed in previous chapters and in the agile principles, there should not have been a lot of up-front work in case a requirement changes or isn't required. This can be achieved in several ways:

- **a product backlog refinement session:** during the previous iteration to confirm the priority of the requirements and add just enough detail to allow them to be estimated;

- **an iteration planning meeting:** at the start of the next iteration, for the whole team to size the highest priority requirements and provide estimates on which ones can be completed during the iteration. This work can often commence towards the end of the previous iteration in preparation;

- **a requirements elaboration step:** as soon as the team starts working on a requirement, to ensure that they understand the necessary detail, and to agree the acceptance criteria for success.

Several factors can affect iteration planning. Many arise at the start of projects, particularly when using approaches that do not cover the whole project life cycle. Scrum, for instance, expects several preconditions to be met before it can begin: there must be an ordered backlog of requirements in place and the team must have the environment, facilities and skills to begin delivering working software in less than one month in duration. In practice, this is rarely the case and teams require time to reach this stage. The backlog needs to be created and there may be technical or architectural risks to be mitigated. There may also be structural or architectural elements required that simply take longer to build than allowed for in a typical sprint. These must all be understood **enough** before release or iteration planning can begin.

The phase where these essential factors are put in place is often called 'sprint 0', but it isn't a formal part of Scrum and there isn't a great deal of guidance on how to do it. This means it can be easy to fall into some of the bad practices of traditional development. Business analysis is an important skill at this stage of the project, and the business analyst must ensure that the agile values and principles are still adhered to. The most important thing to remember is that the goal of 'sprint 0' is just to be able to start 'sprinting'; and this requires 'just enough' work to be done.

Team velocity

Teams work at different speeds from one another. Velocity is the term used to predict how much value a team can deliver during a defined time frame, based on knowledge about how they have performed in the past. Various measures of value can be used, but a popular approach involves user story points. These are discussed in Chapter 14, along with further detail on estimation techniques and measures.

Knowing the velocity of a team is important for two reasons: first, to be able to give a rough idea of how long in total a project may take to complete; second, to be able to work out how much work should be attempted in each iteration.

To calculate the duration of simple projects, the basic technique is:

- guess how many points of value the team can deliver during the first iteration;

- use the first iteration of representative work to establish a baseline for velocity;

- based on initial velocity and an idea of the size of the whole backlog, the team works out how many iterations should be required to deliver the whole backlog;

- after the second iteration, the velocity of the team is re-estimated.

Figure 15.5 Calculating team velocity

Figure 15.5 shows an example of estimation using story points.

Since units, like story points, are subjective different teams may estimate the same value differently. In other words, one team's 8 story points could be another team's 13 story points. This means that story point sizing and therefore team velocity are unique only to that team.

If the agile team is a highly performing team, estimates of velocity can be very accurate, particularly when estimating work with which the team is familiar. However, if the team changes, the velocity needs to be recalibrated. So, to maintain predictable velocity, teams need to remain constant. This doesn't mean that teams cannot change, but it does mean that when there is a change to the team, we cannot expect the velocity to remain the same.

This method works well for simple, well-understood projects and once projects are well underway. It can be an excellent way to understand team capability and predict future deliveries. However, it fails if the backlog gets too big, where the project is not well understood at the outset or where it is likely that the requirements will change. This is for the following reasons:

- To obtain an accurate estimate, a whole release worth of user stories must be estimated.

- Even assuming that's possible, while the team is doing this, they aren't working on anything that will offer value to the customer and they are delaying the time when something valuable may be delivered.

- It is likely that things will change to invalidate the estimate, for example, team behaviour, new and changed requirements, false assumptions.

- To estimate large, complex or high-change projects, the concept of team velocity is not as helpful and alternative approaches should be used.

The same approach can be used to track how much value the team is able to deliver each iteration, and to help predict the right amount of stories to plan for the next iteration. This can still be helpful when the overall project size is not known, as it helps to optimise the work done preparing stories for the next iteration.

Since velocity is a measure of the volume of valuable software produced within a given timebox (i.e. an iteration), only work that offers value to the business should be included when calculating velocity. Other work carried out by the team, such as technical spikes or management activities should not be counted as velocity. In practice, however, iterations often include other tasks, such as spikes, refactoring, fixing defects, management activities or partially completed stories. Where these tasks deliver genuine value they should be included, but often they aren't.

A good approach is to allocate 60 per cent of the available effort for story point delivery and ensure that any activities that don't generate business value are in the remaining 40 per cent. Over time, the amount of non-value-generating work will average out, and the team will have a reasonably accurate estimate of the amount of value they can deliver in an average iteration.

Iteration planning meeting

The iteration planning meeting is a critical meeting for the team and must involve the whole team, including the business analysts. This is important because it is the whole team who will be doing the work so it is critical that they all contribute to the meeting and commit to the outcome. The key business stakeholders should also attend, particularly a business representative such as the product owner. Business analysis skills are important to the success of this meeting; they ensure that the team is delivering the right requirements, and that the project team and business stakeholders understand one another. The purpose of the meeting is to:

- agree the goal of the iteration;

- agree which items from the product backlog will be included in the iteration backlog, and their priority;

- get commitment from the team members that the iteration plan is achievable and that they have the skills to deliver it.

The iteration planning meeting is usually held at the start of the iteration and is considered as part of the iteration. It should be after the review meeting for the previous iteration so that any changes can be incorporated within the new iteration. It is an important meeting and, as such, should have sufficient time devoted to it. Founder of Scrum, Ken Schwaber, recommends that 5 per cent of the overall iteration duration should be spent on planning and preparing for the iteration (Schwaber and Sutherland 2014). The meeting is usually divided into two parts.

Part 1

This part focuses on identifying which backlog items[2] should be included in the iteration. Since the product backlog should already be ordered, the team should start at the highest priority item, estimate how big they think it is and work out whether they have the effort to complete it in this iteration. If so, they continue down the list until there is not enough effort left in the iteration. Some of the estimation techniques discussed in Chapter 14 can be used if necessary.

When deciding which backlog items to put into the iteration, teams must also consider what will happen if all the work planned isn't completed. Since iterations are often timeboxed, the iteration will sometimes end before all the tasks for a backlog item are finished. For this reason, it is helpful to consider the priorities of the work of the iteration and ensure that the mix of priorities provides some contingency, as discussed in Chapter 9. For example, using the MoSCoW prioritisation approach might mean allocating mainly backlog items with a priority of 'M', but also including some with a priority of 'S'. In the situation where some backlog items need to be dropped, it is possible to defer the 'S' backlog items until a future iteration. A good rule of thumb is to ensure that 'M' backlog items account for no more than 60 per cent of the total backlog items set for the iteration.

Following this approach also allows teams to include backlog items with a 'C' level of priority where they are linked to higher priority backlog items and need little additional effort to deliver, or where they are mitigating risk for higher priority backlog items in later iterations. Since the MoSCoW priority is revisited in each iteration, this is also a way of bringing forward backlog items that will be 'M' or 'S' in later iterations for the team to start on if they have time left toward the end of this iteration.

During Part 1 of the planning meeting, it is likely that there will have been little work on the backlog items. Accordingly, it is usual at this point for some backlog items to be too big to be completed in a single iteration. Where this is the case, the backlog items (usually user stories) are decomposed in line with the goal decomposition approach described in Chapter 8. Since this involves discussing, adjusting, breaking down and estimating backlog items, it is essential that the product owner and any other significant customers are present. Given the need to collaborate with stakeholders, business analysis skills will be extremely helpful during this work.

At the end of Part 1, the team has an agreed and prioritised backlog of work, and they should be confident that they can achieve them all in the time available. However, the selected backlog items remain at a high level of abstraction so the underlying tasks, and who will complete them, may not be clear.

Part 2

During Part 2 of the iteration planning meeting, the team must further decompose the stories to allow them to start work. However, since there is a prioritised list, the high priority stories should be worked on first and the lower priority stories can be left until later.

For each story to be broken down, the set of individual tasks should be identified and estimated. If individual tasks are being estimated, it is good practice for the team to be responsible for the estimate. Consequently, the estimate can accommodate different skill or experience levels and so the collective expertise of the team responsible for completing the tasks adds to the accuracy of the estimate. At this level of estimation, it is common practice to use hours, days or 'ideal' developer days as the unit of measure.

At this stage, it is common for some requirements to be vague and for the team to struggle to break them down fully. Perhaps there is uncertainty about what exactly is involved or perhaps the right technical solution is not clear. To address this, teams create specific tasks to gather information. These types of tasks are often called a 'spike' – a short, usually time-bound, task that results in additional information to help the team estimate stories (for example, deeper requirements elaboration or technology investigations). Spikes can exist on the backlog in their own right or they can be added in iteration planning meetings when it becomes clear that they are necessary. The results of spikes will allow existing stories to be progressed or new stories to be added to the project.

The problem with spikes is that they consume effort from the team during the iteration, yet they deliver no business value themselves. For this reason, it is important to ensure that spikes are **Just Enough, Just in Time**, and are only planned for high priority or high-risk stories.

Possible issues during iteration planning

Issues may arise that cause problems during the iteration planning meeting. Some of the potential issues are:

- lack of involvement from the whole team or over-dominance from a small number of team members;
- poor customer involvement or non-attendance;
- functional, rather than goal, decomposition of stories;
- over-optimistic estimates that lead to too much work being accepted for the iteration;
- poor documentation of what previous iterations have delivered;
- difficulty estimating because of a lack of knowledge about the story;
- a poorly ordered or poorly maintained backlog leading to the wrong work being done;
- over-optimistic velocity, or forgetting to include holidays or training courses;
- failure to incorporate lessons learned from the retrospective/review meetings.

Product backlog refinement

One of the most important artefacts of any agile team, particularly for business analysts, is the backlog. As described in Chapter 13, there are two main backlogs: the product backlog and the iteration (or sprint) backlog.

The product backlog is first created at the start of the project and comprises the list of requirements that the project stakeholders think they want the project team to deliver. Although theoretically an ordered list, product backlogs are frequently long and, in reality, it tends to just be the stories towards the top that are properly ordered or prioritised.

At the start of an iteration (in the planning meeting described previously), the team should examine the product backlog with the product owner and assess the top items – those of the highest priority – to create the iteration backlog that will shape the work for the forthcoming iteration.

However, that implies that the product backlog is still up to date and accurate, and, sadly, that's not always the case. The project team concentrate on the iteration; the product owner helps them (and often has other responsibilities) and the poor old backlog can get a bit neglected.

This is where the process of 'product backlog refinement' is needed. This is the practice of preparing the product backlog for forthcoming iterations, by doing some or all of the following things:

- reassessing the relative priorities of stories (techniques like WSJF can help here (Chapter 9);
- removing stories that are no longer required;
- adding and prioritising new stories that have come to light;
- identifying possible 'spikes' and prioritising them;
- checking the estimates for the higher priority stories and considering splitting into separate stories. For these stories, elaborate the requirement with additional detail in preparation for the discussion at the planning meeting;
- ensuring product and goal coherence. Consider whether the changes proposed affect other requirements for the product, including any already delivered, and that the agreed goals are still being met.

These backlog refinement activities are shown in Figure 15.6.

This task should be carried out with the product owner and business stakeholders, but does not always need to involve the whole team. It is a task that is ideally suited to business analysts. However, there some constraints are important to consider:

- Suggested changes to the backlog must not alter or extend the overall agreed scope of the project (particularly where this has a financial impact).

Figure 15.6 Backlog refinement activities

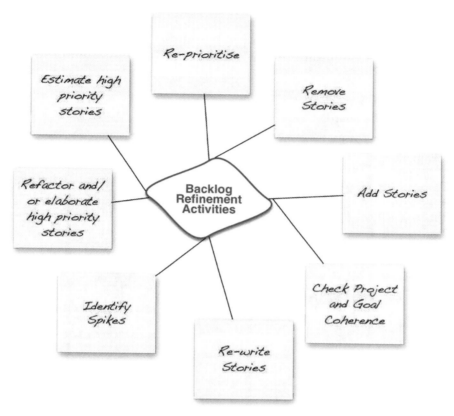

- Changes must not compromise the project and release goals.

- Where the project has committed to an overall amount of work (for instance, through a contract) then adding new work must be balanced by taking out similarly sized work.

Where these constraints need to be broken or challenged, then a more formal and classic approach to change management or change control needs to be applied.

Managing and visualising progress

In order to properly plan, manage and track the work of the team, it is important to communicate what is happening. Agile boards are a popular technique derived from Lean manufacturing to help visualise and manage workflows. They can be physical boards or tables, or may be implemented using software tools.

The board is constantly updated through the iteration by team members, allowing them to self-organise, spot problems early and help one another. It is the focal point for the

245

team, providing the raw material for daily meetings and helping to provoke discussion. Since boards are often on display in the team area, they also enable transparency within the team, which is a core pillar of Scrum (Chapter 5).

The agile board is particularly important for Kanban and its derivations, but can also add value to other agile methods. An agile board for an iteration is shown in Figure 15.7.

Figure 15.7 Agile board

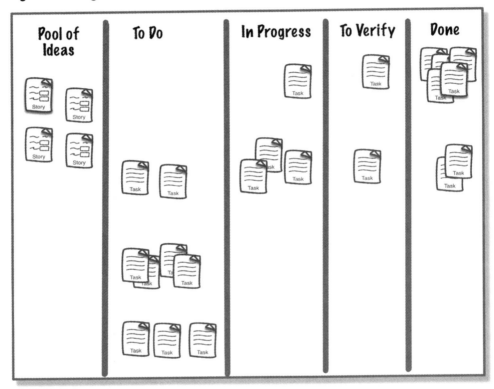

Each row on the agile board is a user story, taken from the product backlog and agreed by the team to be developed in this iteration during the iteration planning meeting. Each user story is turned into multiple task items, which all start in the 'To do' column and gradually migrate toward the right as they progress. In some methods (for example, Kanban), the number of tasks allowed to be in each column is limited, and team members work from the right to the left to unblock columns and encourage flow.

The columns typically found on an agile board are:

Stories This means the user story to be delivered ('As a user I want to ...').

To do This is the set of tasks identified to complete the user story.

Work in progress This refers to any task that is currently being worked on by a member of the agile team.

To verify Once complete, tasks must be tested or reviewed. In some teams, this is a formal 'approval' stage. For software, the test stage could be a separate task.

Done Task cards move into this column when they are done. A user story can only be considered done once all the task cards within the row for that story have been moved into the 'done' column, and it is agreed that the 'Definition of Done' for the story has been achieved.

Projects often customise their boards, and can use colours, shapes, codes or extra columns to add information.

Agile boards also support other elements of agile development. Since all the tasks outstanding are visible, team members are encouraged to choose their own tasks. They should first look for tasks that will create space on the board (the tasks toward the right, such as testing or reviewing), but should also select tasks that suit their own skills and development requirements. This is central to the **'whole team'** concept, and the **'self-organising'** nature of agile teams.

The board should help the team members to see if there is a skill shortage within the team or whether the team is unbalanced in some way. This may require others to join the team, possibly to provide additional skills.

At the end of the iteration, the stories that have been completed – those that have **all** their sub-tasks in the 'done' column – can be added up and, if accepted by the business owner, can be used to update the team velocity.

Agile boards also support methods without timeboxed iterations. In those methods, increments are released when a set number of stories are complete. This might be important in support life cycles, where the cost and impact of updating a version will need to be worth the potential benefit.

It is common for new tasks to be identified as the work progresses and the team learns more about the stories. This is why it is important that the team works on the higher priority stories before starting lower priority stories.

Dealing with change

The second agile principle states: **'Welcome changing requirements, even late in development.'**

Change is inevitable, even with simple projects. Many agile practices and techniques have evolved specifically to make dealing with change easier, and more likely to result in increased value to the customer. That's why it's important that agile teams are prepared for change, seek it out and help to harness it for the benefit of the customer.

This is embodied nicely in another principle: **'Simplicity – the art of maximising the amount of work not done – is essential'**, and the maxim **Just Enough, Just in Time**. When things change, work done against the old requirement is wasted and represents unnecessary time and/or cost.

Agile teams have many factors at their disposal to cope with change, such as iteration length. Given that teams try hard to do as little work as possible on requirements until they formally enter an iteration, it follows that changes to things not yet started will have low impact on the team. With short iterations, it will never be terribly long before the customer has an opportunity to change the team's focus. And in the worst case, where the change is so significant that the iteration must be scrapped, the maximum amount of time lost will be limited to the time already spent on this iteration.

Setting a clear focus on iteration goals is also critical to coping with change. At the end of an iteration, the customer should be able to use the product that has been delivered. That means that it should be sufficiently tested, integrated, documented and supported. While the Agile Manifesto values working software over comprehensive documentation, there still needs to be **enough** documentation and support to allow the software to be used by the customer.

Agile teams should be able to make a clean break at the end of each iteration, even when it isn't **planned** to be the final iteration. That means that if the customer decides that the version demonstrated meets their needs, then the project can finish. There and then. Not after another three iterations while we finish off the documentation, write a support guide and fix all the bugs we didn't have time to fix during the last iteration.

This gives the customer the ability to stop work early, potentially saving money, but in larger organisations, it also allows business calls on priority to be acted on quickly. If there is a higher priority project for the agile team to work on, it makes sense that they can complete their existing commitments quickly and move on.

Non-timeboxed Iterations

Most of this chapter focuses on iterations that are time bound, and the team decides what work can be done in the available time. That's because most agile methods work on some kind of timeboxed iterative model. However, this isn't true of all methods, and some, such as Kanban, are bounded by other factors, such as Work Completed.

However, many of the techniques and situations described are just as applicable to non-timeboxed iterations. They are still agile methods, so still place value on the same manifesto statements and principles as the others do.

With non-timeboxed iterations, the team must decide what criteria they will use to decide when to release a version to the customer. This could still be goal based (and each goal may take a different amount of time to be delivered) or it could be based on the number of stories that are 'Done'.

One advantage of goal-based iterations is that goals themselves are rarely the same size. That means that time-bound teams will find themselves either stretched at the end to fit everything in, or will have completed some stories that aren't really helping the goal. Goal-driven teams deliver when the goal is complete, which could be quicker or slower than other goals. On the other hand, the continuous, production line nature of some methods can make it feel like the work never ends.

MANAGING AND MONITORING THE ITERATION

Agile teams use a number of techniques and approaches when managing and monitoring their iterations. These approaches typically have some attributes in common: they embody one or more of the Agile Pillars of Transparency, Inspection and Adaptation (see Chapter 5); they require **Just Enough, Just in Time**; they encourage continuous improvement; and they involve the whole team.

Some common techniques are daily stand-up meetings and burn charts.

Daily stand-ups

A common agile practice is the daily stand-up meeting. This meeting, which originated from Scrum and XP, is one of the more popular techniques for managing ongoing work and has been widely adopted outside agile development. It is fundamental to maintaining the heartbeat and rhythm of the iteration, and is a way of ensuring that pace is being maintained and regular communication is also taking place.

The daily stand-up is facilitated by the Scrum master (in Scrum) or by the iteration lead or team leader, however, the facilitation skills of a business analyst can prove very useful in these meetings. It is crucial that the whole team is involved and, to encourage participation, the meeting is usually limited to 15 minutes and conducted standing up – partly to ensure it is kept short, but also so that there are fewer reasons to prevent it happening. You don't need to book a room if you can stand around the agile board to have your meeting! Each team member is asked the following questions:

- 'What did you do yesterday?' or 'What have you completed since the last meeting?'
- 'What will you do today?' or 'What do you plan to complete by the next meeting?'
- 'What impediments are you facing?' or 'What will stop you completing what you plan to?'

There is some debate about what the 'best' questions are (and there are many more versions than those stated above). However, the intent of the daily stand-up meeting is to focus the participants' attention on whether they are making the progress that is expected, and on asking for help for anything that might delay or prevent progress. It is a meeting of peers, not a management progress report, and should feel like an important part of the team's day.

The meeting focuses on the identification of issues not the solving of them. In Scrum, it is the responsibility of the Scrum master to remove any impediments, and they focus on that following the meeting, not during it. Similarly, if one member of the team has dependencies or issues regarding the tasks of another team member, they should discuss these with each other following the meeting. If they cannot resolve an issue, it can be escalated to the Scrum master as an impediment to team progress.

Monitoring and reporting progress

The use of agile boards has already been discussed as a good way to record and present progress, but they only show the present situation. Burndown and burnup charts are also used to communicate team progress. Burn charts can have value at several levels, within iterations, for particular increments or across the whole project. Typically, burndown charts show progress within an iteration, while burnup charts show progress across iterations towards project or release goals. However, this is not a hard and fast rule.

Burndown charts

A burndown chart plots the amount of work, usually in the form of stories, tasks or story points, that has been delivered by the team as they move through the iteration. Unlike an agile board that just shows current status, burndown charts show when the work items were delivered, and can provide useful information on how the team is working. Figure 15.8 shows an example burndown chart.

Figure 15.8 Example of a burndown chart showing story points

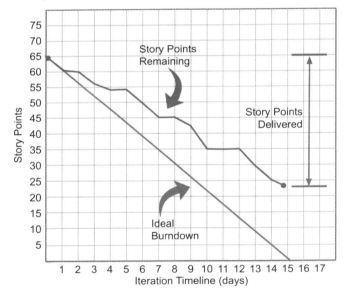

The Y-axis shows what has been delivered and the X-axis shows the iteration timeline, usually in days. Teams use their burndown chart for three main reasons:

- to capture some metrics that allow them to calculate their velocity and ensure that future iterations are loaded with the right amount of work;

- to give themselves a sense of making progress, and give them increasing confidence that they will meet the iteration goal;

- to share with their customers that they are making progress, and that the customer can expect their goal to be met.

There may be problems when the user stories are quite large and take most of the iteration to complete, as it looks like the team is making slow progress and no stories are being delivered. This is made worse where a story is not **quite** finished by the end of the iteration because it shows on the chart that the whole story has not been delivered rather than that the team had completed most of the work. This situation may be avoided if user stories are appropriately sized and are small enough to show progress.

A second issue that burndown charts can expose, even with correctly sized stories, is where the priority of the customer (product owner) is being used to drive team behaviour. This is evident where the agile team is not working on the higher priority user stories first, moving towards the lower priorities as the iteration draws to a close. This approach shows regular deliveries on the burndown chart, and the customer knows that the work already completed was their highest priority work.

However, it is common (particularly with teams who are struggling to adopt the agile mindset) for teams to start the iteration by breaking down all the stories and sharing them out amongst the team. Early on, most stories have someone working on them. Because there are fewer team members in each story, each story will take longer. At some point (perhaps quite late in the iteration) some stories will be completed, and show as progress on the burndown chart. But, since the stories were all started at the same time, the first stories to be completed might not be the highest priority ones. As the iteration draws to a close, some stories might not be completed yet and it is possible that they are the higher priority ones.

Burndown chart showing work remaining

An alternative approach to recording progress and reporting burndown, is to burndown tasks rather than stories, and to record work remaining rather than stories completed. In this method, tasks are identified and estimated in hours during the iteration planning meeting. These tasks are then totalled and the estimated hours of work for the iteration plotted on the Y-axis as shown in Figure 15.9.

This approach offers some benefits. If tasks are sized relatively small but not too small (3–12 hours), then team members see progress frequently. Tasks smaller than a couple of hours are too small to bother recording, though of course they do add up.

The downside to this approach is that it requires the whole iteration to be broken down to quite a detailed level at the start of the iteration, and since tasks do not represent the delivery of customer goals, it is less clear whether the team is on track or not. It is important for the team to update the time remaining on each task at the end of each day.

Figure 15.9 Example of a burndown chart showing remaining effort

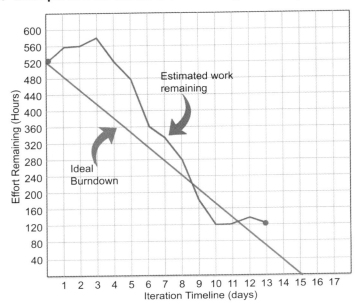

Iteration Timeline (days)

While the burndown chart may not show any progress, this approach provides a more accurate indicator of how close the work is to completion.

Burnup charts

Another representation is a burn chart that tracks progression towards a release goal. The same measures of velocity can be used but the number of iterations is used instead of days along the X-axis. The Y-axis is typically some measure of progress, such as stories or story points, but the chart starts at 0 and works up rather than down. An example is shown in Figure 15.10.

This chart of velocity scores throughout the life cycle and also allows for the validation of up-front estimates and the correction of final delivery targets. The target line shows what the customer expects to be delivered. As the iterations proceed, the angle of the progress line can be extrapolated to see whether the target line will be hit when expected. The accuracy of the prediction will depend on the accuracy of the velocity recorded in previous iterations.

This can be helpful for two reasons:

1. if the team experiences problems, the impact on the final delivery can be predicted; and
2. if the customer wants to change the scope (up or down) the new delivery date can be predicted.

Figure 15.10 A burnup chart showing progress of iterations

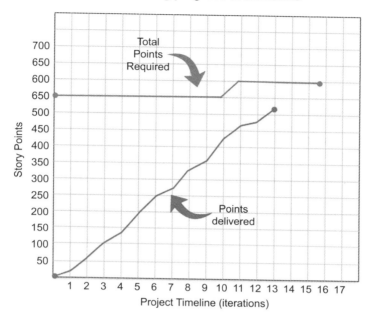

Either situation allows an early indication that a project may require some intervention: typically additional resources (velocity), additional time or a reduction in scope.

REVIEWING THE ITERATION

At the end of the iteration, two important things happen:

1. The team shows their progress to the customer.
2. The team reviews the iteration and decides on any changes they want to make.

Iteration review (show and tell)

The 'show and tell' meeting is a critical milestone for the team and customers. The purpose of the session is for the development team to present back to the customer or product owner what they have delivered during this iteration; and for the customer to decide whether the acceptance criteria for each backlog item has been met.

The customer gets to see progress so far and can provide feedback, thoughts and ideas to the team to help them in future iterations. This may result in changes to the backlog or the creation of bug reports for defects in the current version.

These meetings are mainly for the benefit of the customer, so care must be taken by the team not to get bogged down in technical detail. The team should **'show'** the product in action, demonstrate the functionality, and **'tell'** them what the customer or user experience will be like. The aim is to make the development work come alive in the user's eyes. They are intended to be interactive, with the customer feeding back what they are thinking. All feedback should be captured and responded to.

An experienced business analyst can play a critical role here, helping the customer to understand what they are being shown (especially if it is an early, unpolished version) and helping the development team to avoid too much technical detail.

The whole-team practice of agile means that the person closest to the development is often best placed to present the detail; the ability to take pride in your work and be recognised for your contribution is an important motivating factor. It should not be the team lead or project manager claiming all the glory!

Show and tell sessions are an important part of the agile process but can often fail due to a lack of planning or poor facilitation – areas where contributions from a good business analyst can be invaluable.

Retrospectives

One of the most important meetings in agile iterations is the iteration retrospective meeting. It directly addresses the core agile value of **responding to change** and the principles of **reflecting** and **becoming more effective**.

The realities of agile projects are that very little is completely predictable or already perfect. Retrospectives give teams the opportunity, in a safe environment, to reflect on how they performed and decide on any changes they wish to make. To provide a safe environment for honest reflection and feedback, only the direct team members should attend.

Retrospectives should take place after each iteration and all team members should attend. Retrospectives should also be held following major releases or at the end of the project. These retrospectives are often longer and more intensive. They can occasionally be helpful if an unexpected event changes the situation, for instance, if an iteration has to be abandoned.

A well-conducted retrospective can help the team to focus on the significant events and help them to remember what happened. This can require good facilitation, so business analysis skills are particularly helpful.

Running a retrospective

Many development teams simply discuss some variation of these three questions during retrospectives, as shown in Figure 15.11.

This is a good start, but more structured approaches can lead to far greater value. In their 2006 book, *Agile retrospectives: making good teams great*, Derby et al. define a simple framework for conducting retrospectives that draws on many of the skills possessed by business analysts. They recommend a focused facilitation approach to

Figure 15.11 Common retrospective questions

create the right environment to elicit the right data, analyse what the team are saying to establish patterns and trends, and identify a small set of high-impact but manageable changes. The key is to pick two or three important changes rather than try to fix everything possible.

There are two further questions that should be asked, but are often omitted:

1. Is the team the right shape for the next iteration? And, more critically;
2. Should the project continue at all?

As projects mature, the precise mix of skills and experience required may change. This could mean that the team is too big or too small for the next iteration, or perhaps the team was struggling with some technical detail and would benefit from some consultancy or specialist training.

One key advantage of agile approaches over traditional methods is the ability for agile teams to finish early. Because they focus on delivering working solutions and highest priority work first, it is possible to reach a stage where the project could continue into the next iteration, but the customer is actually quite happy with the product as it is. Where this is the case, the team should be able to stop, resulting in a cheaper product for the customer.

This feature of agile teams is especially important in larger organisations, where the main benefit is that the team can now start on new, higher priority work earlier – they are not committed to the original end date. This does, however, depend on the team being disciplined enough to have completed all necessary non-functional requirements, general and technical requirements.

Why retrospectives fail

The biggest danger in a retrospective is that is becomes accusatory and defensive rather than supportive. Team members become more concerned with protecting their reputation than honestly examining how the team performed. The single most effective thing that can prevent this is to adopt a no-blame culture during the retrospective – and to mean it. That might mean excluding managers or team leaders from the meeting, or finding ways to permit anonymous feedback.

Some pitfalls to watch out for:

- **Poor preparation by the team:** a lot can happen in an iteration and it is easy to forget significant things.

- **Poor preparation by the facilitator:** making sure the meeting is well planned and well run with a clear focus means everyone's time is well spent and the team will get more benefit.

- **Assertions rather than facts:** it is important to know how people feel, but it is also important to back up that feeling with facts. For example, instead of saying that the backlog was poorly managed, it's better to know that Pete started Task 8 without knowing that Jane had already started it, because the backlog wasn't updated.

- **Dominance by a few people:** it is common for one or two dominant personalities to control an unstructured discussion and push their ideas onto the group. That means others can't contribute, and they might not fully believe in the decision.

- **Focusing on things you can't change:** the purpose of a retrospective is to work out how to improve as a team so the retrospective should concentrate on things within the team's control.

- **Trying to change too much:** especially with new teams or new projects, it is easy to find lots of things to improve. Success is more likely if there is a focus on a small number of specific things.

- **Trying to change the wrong things:** the team needs to want to make the changes, and be excited about changing them. When the team doesn't have the energy to work on an improvement, the chances are fairly high that it won't get done.

- **Treating the improvements as 'nice to have':** making your team better isn't optional, or less important than doing what the customer requests. If the changes are important they should be added to the backlog and be given a high priority.

THE ROLE OF BUSINESS ANALYSIS IN AGILE ITERATIONS

Business analysis is a critical skill set in many of the key stages of an iteration. Even in methods where dedicated business analysts are not mentioned, there are key artefacts or practices where business analysis skills and mindset can make the difference between success and failure.

Even where the team does not have a dedicated business analyst, there should be business analysis skills in the agile team. Not necessarily in each member of the team, but in enough people that the value of business analysis can be properly harnessed.

The presence of business analysis experience in agile teams can help them to keep a focus on the customer and the business needs. Seeing goals from the customer's perspective, and being able discuss the work so that it makes sense to the customer, can be essential for maintaining good working relationships and enabling collaboration.

Several of the practices in iterations require business analysis skill, particularly those relating to requirements and prioritisation. The backlog is a clear example; poor business analysis at any level can result in the wrong items being put on the backlog or in stories being split in unhelpful ways, such as functional decomposition.

Refining the backlog is a task that is often neglected or rushed, yet it is one where a business analysis approach is very important. The ability to critically assess stories, apply strong prioritisation and describe requirements in a way that reflects what is needed rather than a pre-defined solution, is extremely important. Sometimes, the customer or product owner can fulfil the business analyst role. However, this is often not the case, and even where it is possible, it is difficult to be both customer and analyst.

The contribution of business analysts

Where organisations have dedicated business analysts, there are a number of ways in which they can make an important contribution to the success of agile iterations, either as a full-time member of an agile team, or in a part-time or ancillary capacity.

Although virtually all agile methods advocate a dedicated customer representative (often called the product owner), who is preferably co-located with the development team, in practice it is often the case that this does not happen. Either the customer is not co-located or they are not dedicated, and sometimes neither is the case. Teams often look to a business analyst to fulfil this role.

Organisations that employ business analysts will also tend to develop more complex products. Navigating this complexity, particularly where there are high-level project dependencies, intangible business outcomes or strategic requirements, is a natural space to call upon a business analyst. And where the organisation is expecting the project delivery to follow agile principles, it is important that the business analysts understand agile well.

Another factor that can complicate things is where other members of the overarching project or programme team do not understand agile well. They may have come from a background of classic waterfall programme delivery and challenge some of the agile approaches. Business analysts are well placed to help re-assure them and also help the agile team know how to interact with them. This might mean changes to how the high-level requirements are described, or to how the business outcomes and high-level milestones are phrased.

Agile methods tend to be optimised for the development of code. They tend not to worry too much about the work that is required to get the backlog in order, nor to manage the integration, rollout and business readiness tasks. Many business analysts work on 'funnelling' in requirements to the backlog and ensuring that all the elements of the business change are managed.

CONCLUSION

Iterations are the core element for all agile development methods, and the role of business analysis is important to their success. The quality of the product backlog, and the ability of the team and customers to properly break down requirements to goals delivering business value are extremely important; these are areas where strong business analysis skills are needed.

NOTES

1 This is one of the original agile principles – http://agilemanifesto.org/principles.html.

2 Backlog items is the term used to describe the work that the team need to deliver within an iteration. This phrase encompasses requirements and user stories.

REFERENCES

Deming, W.E. (1982) *Quality, productivity, and competitive position*, later published under the title, *Out of crisis*. Cambridge, MA: MIT Press.

Derby, E., Larson, D. and Schwaber, K. (2006) *Agile retrospectives: making good teams great*. Dallas, TX: Pragmatic Bookshelf.

Schwaber, K. and Sutherland, J. (2014) *The Scrum guide*. ScrumGuides.org. Available from: www.scrumguides.org/scrum-guide.html [20 December 2016].

FURTHER READING

Pink, D.H. (2001) *Drive*. Edinburgh: Canongate Books.

Shore, J. and Warden, S. (2007) *The art of Agile development*. Sebastopol, CA: O'Reilly Media.

16 CONSIDERATIONS WHEN ADOPTING AGILE

This chapter covers the following topics:

- agile adoption;
- the business analyst role in an agile world.

INTRODUCTION

When agile approaches began in the early 2000s, they were mainly being applied by small teams to small, relatively simple problems and they worked really well. As the agile movement has grown and become more fashionable, teams and organisations are trying to obtain the benefits of agile for larger and more complex problems, and with larger and more diverse teams. The history in Chapter 2 clarifies that this is not how agile began. As a result, it should be no surprise that some of the recommended approaches and methods struggle when faced with large and complex problems where the adoption of agile methods can become lost or diluted if not managed or supported effectively.

Many companies who were relatively early adopters of agile found difficulties when trying to solve problems that did not align with the original intention underlying agile. To address this, they set about adapting the approaches, often with the aid of external consultants, and have now developed their own bespoke versions. This has been happening for several years and some of these bespoke methods have now coalesced into the more generic approaches that have gained popularity. The practice of tailoring and extending the methods continues, and the approaches to scale agile are not the clearly defined, well-publicised methods mentioned in Chapter 5 but bespoke adaptations created internally to address the needs of individual companies and enterprises.

Companies deciding to adopt agile practices today are comparatively lucky. Not only are the classic agile methods well understood, but there are also several new frameworks and methods available that work well on more complex or larger projects. It is also the case that organisations and businesses want to adopt agile at an enterprise level; they want to be agile organisations. This is because an agile approach to developing goods or services can realise the following benefits:

- shortened time to market of new products/services;
- adaptability to changing needs of customers;

- improved quality of products/services;
- maximised return on investment.

This chapter discusses the challenges in adopting an agile approach and how the agile business analyst can support agile transformation, as well as add value, working within and alongside agile change projects.

AGILE ADOPTION

It is difficult to be, or become, an agile project, programme or organisation as it requires a new mindset and core values. The extent of the change required to adopt agile will vary from organisation to organisation, depending upon the start point and culture. Often, organisations want the benefits that adopting an agile approach will bring, without understanding the amount of change that this will require.

Adopting agile software development

A good example concerns the adoption of agile software development. Making a statement that agile is to be adopted is far easier than doing this successfully. The adoption of agile should be considered a transformational change that encompasses all the POPIT™ elements. In other words, the agile values and principles need to be applied to the agile adoption itself, and this should be seen as a programme for change. The use of POPIT™ to analyse the changes required for adopting agile are explored in Table 16.1 below.

Table 16.1 POPIT™ analysis of agile adoption

People	The project staff will need to be familiar with the agile philosophy and principles. They will need to adopt the mindset that these encompass and will need to be able to apply the techniques. They will also need to understand the range of ceremonies and events used on agile projects. Questions such as the following will need to be addressed: Who in the organisation does agile affect? Are people trained in agile? Are they all motivated by the change or are some areas of the business, or some people, sceptical? Do experienced staff feel demotivated as they feel their previous experience is no longer valued? How do we engage with the people affected and help them through this difficult change?
Organisation	Agile requires cultural change with the adoption of concepts such as self-organising teams, empowered staff and a collaborative environment with high customer engagement and trust. Managers must become leaders and traditional project management styles will be challenged. Procurement processes may need to be adapted, and roles and responsibilities within

(Continued)

Table 16.1 (Continued)

	the software development teams and across the organisation will need to be reviewed, agreed and communicated. New roles need to be introduced and some roles removed or changed. For example, the projects will need a product owner and an agile team lead/Scrum master. When using most approaches, the business analyst role is not mentioned – everyone within the development team is allocated a developer role. Yet business analysis is needed – how is this going to be incorporated within the agile project teams?
Processes	Software development teams will need to adopt new processes that apply different tasks and a range of techniques, some new to the organisation. Existing processes that align with more linear approaches, such as those concerned with the documentation requirements of the project management office, quality assurance and control processes, and progress measurement, will need to be changed to support the adoption of agile.
Information and technology	New technological support tools such as those for continuous integration, application life cycle management, management of agile boards, and solution or product backlogs will be required and will need to integrate or work alongside existing tools. People will need to understand how the new processes will be supported using technology.

This analysis demonstrates that even when deploying change into an IT function, where agile is likely to be recognised to some degree, delivering technology or new standards is never sufficient. This is a good example of why holistic business analysis is so important.

Adopting or scaling agile

Some key factors to consider when adopting or scaling agile are shown in Table 16.2 below.

Table 16.2 Key factors for adopting or scaling agile

Organisational culture	Agile is based on management theory that values empowerment of staff and is based on trust. If an organisation has a power culture where respect is earned through authority, micromanagement is the norm when a problem arises and responses to change tend to be inflexible, then agile might not be the appropriate approach. If, on the other hand, the organisation is flexible when it comes to change and values delegation and empowerment, then agile may work well.

(Continued)

Table 16.2 (Continued)

Customer involvement	Close collaboration with customers is essential. If customers are located in a different city or country, then applying agile practices is going to be a challenge, even when using IT solutions that support collaboration. Co-located teams still face the challenge of having sufficient time with customers, which is problematic as agile development needs the customer to be an integral part of the team. If this isn't possible, agile probably isn't the best choice.
Team culture	Agile projects require a team culture whereby teams can become high performing teams: 'a one team' mentality. Some structures, such as a matrix management structure, are not suitable for using agile.
Geographic distribution	Agile works on the principle of co-located teams, so, if the team or organisation is geographically dispersed, scaling agile across the organisation can be very difficult.
Stability of requirements	If the requirements are unlikely to change during the project, a method or approach where there is an early focus on detailed requirements definition will be suitable. However, if the requirements are volatile, an agile approach is preferable as this allows the evolution of the detail during the iterative development and incremental delivery of the solution.
Team skills	Agile projects require a team of highly skilled and highly motivated generalising specialists. This means that the skills required to deliver the project outcome are available within the team. In agile teams, the team members are multi-skilled. Having a role-based organisation with independent specialist roles such as requirements engineer, developer, tester, etc., can inhibit agile development.
Business constraints	If there are a lot of business constraints that are going to restrict the effectiveness of agile adoption, then taking an agile approach should be reconsidered. For example, where procurement processes rely upon the creation of detailed requirements documentation at an early stage in the development lifecycle.
Complexity	Where a project is novel or complex, an agile approach can provide a means of testing architectural or business risks at an early stage, and changing the scope if this proves necessary. Where the problems to be addressed are extensive and involve a high degree of complexity, the relevance of an agile approach should be considered in the light of the scaling factors described above.

Adapting agile standards

In his 2009 paper 'Adapting Agile methods for complex environments', Scott Ambler introduced a model to help teams identify whether they should be considering adapting their standard agile approaches. This has evolved into the 'Software Development Context Framework (SCF)', reproduced in Figure 16.1 with permission from Scott Ambler; it can also be applied to non-software projects. The SCF identifies six factors that, when analysed, can help identify the likelihood of a project failing unless changes are made to the standard approach.

Figure 16.1 Scott Ambler's 'Software Development Context Framework'

Team Size
2 ⟷ 1000s

Geographic Distribution
Co-located ⟷ Global

Organizational Distribution
Single Division ⟷ Outsourcing

Compliance
None ⟷ Life Critical

Domain Complexity
Straightforward ⟷ Very Complex

Technical Complexity
Straightforward ⟷ Very Complex

Copyright 2013 Scott Ambler + Associates

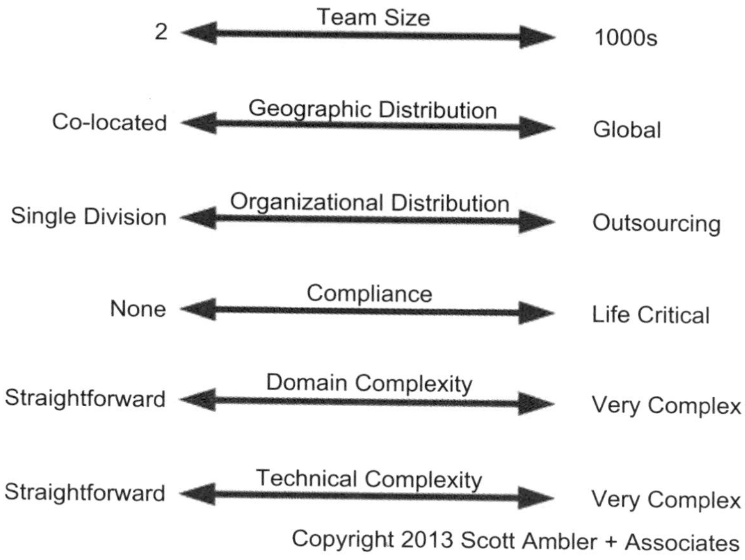

Each factor is a sliding scale. Being close to the left-hand side implies that standard agile approaches should work well; but the further to the right in any factor, the more likely it is that the methods and approaches will need to change.

Some of the scaled agile approaches described in Chapter 5, notably DA 2.0, provide a range of techniques, practices, mitigations and methods to deal with complexity without sacrificing the benefits of an agile approach. Some of these approaches utilise business analysis skills. For example, to counter the problems caused by being geographically distributed, teams can increase the amount of modelling and planning they do to reduce misunderstandings.

System of interest model

When embarking upon an agile adoption strategy it is beneficial to consider the 'system of interest' model shown in Figure 16.2. The area of interest is usually defined by an individual role or authority but could also be defined by a team or business area, for example, a chief technical officer (CTO), deciding to adopt agile development within, or across, an IT department or an agile business analyst deciding to apply agile principles and values in their day-to-day work on a business improvement project.

Figure 16.2 Levels of influence when adopting agile

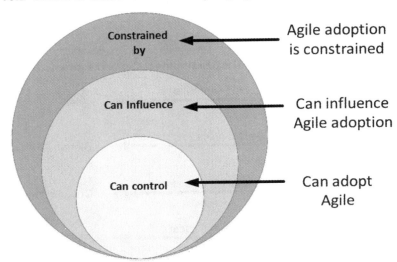

Whether the system of interest is derived from the perspective of an individual, team or organisation it is useful to understand the three elements of the model as follows:

1. **Can control**   What can the individual or team control when adopting agile? For example, a team may decide to improve how they run their iteration planning, change their estimation approach or improve the facilitation skills within the team. These things are unlikely to require permission and can readily improve the effectiveness of the team.

2. **Can influence**   What or whom can be influenced to improve the adoption of agile more widely? For example, an agile business analyst may feel hindered because others lack knowledge and understanding of agile. Spending time discussing agile may help others to see the benefits. Additionally, a manager of an IT department may be able to influence business users to work more collaboratively with development teams or influence funding for agile tools. This influence could expand the knowledge and understanding of agile, which could aid and extend agile adoption.

3. Constrained by What is it that constrains a team, individual or organisation from adopting agile more widely or scaling agile? Constraints could come from other organisations or even internal processes. Constraints need to be challenged, as they may be based on perceptions rather than reality. For example, project office process and templates that are suited to linear approaches may appear to be constraints but could be open to challenge. Real constraints, however, should be accepted and efforts applied to areas where change can occur or can be influenced.

Because the history of many agile approaches is based on small, highly collaborative teams, it can be harder to make them work where that environment is not present. The system of interest model helps to identify which areas can, and should, be challenged to help address some of the obstacles that many organisations face in wider agile adoption. Areas that may require influence or challenge include:

- organisational culture and its resistance to change;
- pre-existing frameworks that follow a linear approach;
- audit, regulatory or safety critical requirements that expect higher quality assurance;
- projects with strict contractual commitments;
- complex user environments or where there are issues with availability of end users;
- sub-contracting into a project that is run in a non-agile way;
- lack of management support or understanding of agile.

THE BUSINESS ANALYST ROLE IN AN AGILE WORLD

In this book we have discussed the importance of having business analysts who can analyse the organisational situation and understand business needs, even when the business situation is vague and ambiguous. We have explored how the business analyst can understand and adopt an agile mindset and how this can add value when they deploy their skills across multiple levels within the organisation. Business analysts are trained to explore root causes of problems, analyse problems through a business lens, recognise multiple perspectives and never assume that IT is always the solution. As Abraham Maslow commented, in his *The psychology of science* (1966):

> I suppose it is tempting, if the only tool you have is a hammer, to treat everything as if it were a nail.

As agile thinking and theory expands more widely into business systems, the need for business analysts who can readily apply the skills and approaches outlined in this book will be a key factor in organisational agility. An agile business analyst is not about **doing** agile, rather it is about **being** agile and this can only be achieved once an agile mindset is adopted.

The key characteristics that agile business analysts need to adopt are summarised in Figure 16.3.

Figure 16.3 Key characteristics of an agile business analyst

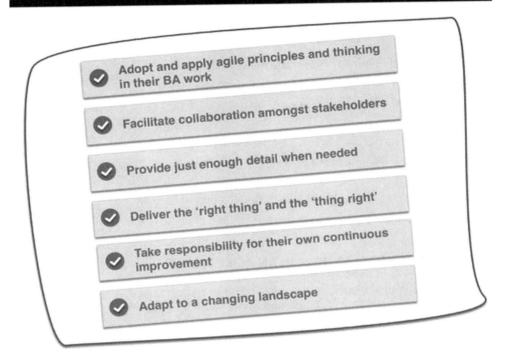

With the agile mindset firmly ingrained, business analysts can help to increase organisational agility and the success of change programmes. This requires them to work at the enterprise, programme and project levels as discussed in Chapter 3 and shown in Figure 16.4.

Figure 16.4 BA role in agile

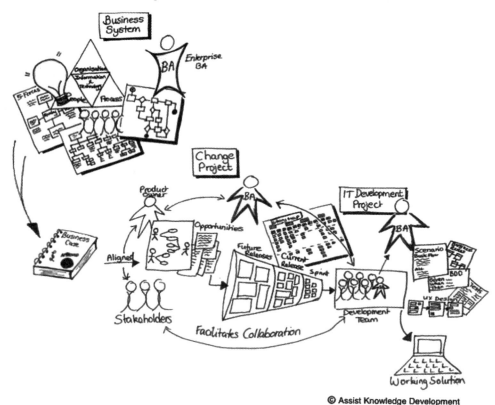

© Assist Knowledge Development

The business analyst and the product owner

Scrum has become the preferred agile development method in many organisations and this has raised the issue of the involvement of the business analyst, particularly with regard to the work of the product owner. Organisations that have not adopted Scrum, or use a variant, also report that they have a similar role to the product owner and the same issues apply.

Ken Schwaber defined the product owner role in the Scrum guide (July 2014) where he includes in his description the following:

> The Product Owner is responsible for maximizing the value of the product and the work of the Development Team. How this is done may vary widely across organizations, Scrum Teams, and individuals

The lack of clarification within Scrum regarding the business analyst role has given rise to the following two questions:

1. Can the business analyst be the proxy product owner?
2. How can the business analyst and product owner roles co-exist?

Within some projects and organisations, the business analyst may be asked to perform the role of the proxy product owner. This normally entails undertaking product owner responsibilities such as managing and prioritising the backlog, attending team meetings and representing the views of the business. This may be a temporary role or may be longer term and the business analyst covers the duties that are the province of the product owner. The reasons why a business analyst may be asked to be a proxy product owner include the following:

- product owner is overworked;
- product owner is under-skilled;
- product owner role split into product manager and product owner;
- product owner is in a different city, country or continent to development team.

While business analysts typically possess skills required of a product owner, we do not believe that the business analyst role should become the proxy product owner. Scrum is clear that the product owner is solely responsible for managing and prioritising the backlog and the work performed by the development team. We feel that the separation of responsibilities between a product owner and a business analyst operating as a proxy product owner could cause miscommunication within the development team resulting in delays to the product delivery. We believe the better alternatives are that:

- the business analyst becomes the actual product owner
- the business analyst acts as a critical friend to the product owner and the development team.

Business analysts work holistically across many business components, one of which is IT solutions. In doing this they are applying service, systems and Lean thinking. Business analysts who complete the International Diploma in Business Analysis with BCS, The Chartered Institute for IT, are trained to look beyond software solutions to define and resolve business problems. This training enables business analysts to take on the role of product owner or to be the critical friend to the product owner. Business analysts may have an IT or a business background, or, sometimes, both. However, the majority have progressed to a business analyst role because they have both logical and interpersonal skills, and a natural interest in business problem-solving. Business analysts who can offer this range of skills not only make great product owners, but are also perfectly capable of operating within an agile project team.

It appears to us that the product owner role requires business analysis skills – the skills that business analysts have been developing for over 20 years. This subject arose during an email exchange with Ken Schwaber (email conversation on 29 June 2016) regarding why business analysts often end up as proxy product owners.

This extract from the exchange is reprinted with permission from Ken:

> Over and over, I find the business people so tired of dealing with systems people that the idea of [them becoming] a Product Owner is just too much. They [the business people] don't trust or know how to talk with and direct software services, so they just delegate.

So, there is a need for skilled professionals who can support the product owner in representing the business, and who will be able to work collaboratively with the software team, and build relationships based on engagement and trust. We couldn't have put it better – and we know just the people to do this.

CONCLUSION

Although agile was originally developed with software development in mind, its values and principles apply more widely. The shift in mindset to adopt agile principles and values requires a much deeper understanding and acceptance of the need for change. The three elements that constitute agile adoption, shown in Figure 16.5, apply to the individual, the project and the organisation.

Figure 16.5 Main elements of agile

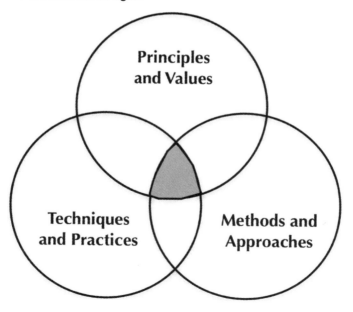

We feel that this diagram also represents what is required for the business analysis profession to adopt agile across the three levels of business analysis work. We hope this book helps all business analysts to develop their agile mindset and deliver agility in all that they do.

REFERENCES

Ambler, S. (2009) Adapting Agile methods for complex environments. IBM Rational Software. Available from: www.webfinancialsolutions.com/wp-content/uploads/2011/10/Adapting-Agile-Methods-for-Complex-Environments.pdf [20 December 2016].

Maslow, A.H. (1966) *The psychology of science*. Chapel Hill, NC: Maurice Bassett Publishing.

Schwaber, K. (2016) Email conversation, 29 June.

Schwaber, K. and Sutherland, J. (2014) *The Scrum Guide™ The Definitive Guide to Scrum: The Rules of the Game*. Available at: www.scrumguides.org/docs/scrumguide/v1/scrum-guide-us.pdf [18 January 2016].

FURTHER READING

Ambler, S. and Lines, M. (2012) *Disciplined Agile delivery: a practitioner's guide to Agile software in the enterprise*. Upper Saddle River, NJ: IBM Press.

Cadle, J. (ed.) (2014) *Developing information systems*. Swindon: BCS.

Pichler, R. (2010) Common product owner traps. Scrum Alliance. Available from: www.scrumalliance.org/community/articles/2010/april/common-product-owner-traps#sthash.4GSD4tRB.dpuf [20 December 2016].

INDEX

Adaptive Software Development (ASD) 14

agile
adoption of 259–65
alliance 13–15, 21
approaches 20–1, 73–5
boards 246–7
business analysis 25–32, 98–9, 105, 209, 265–9
business thinking 32–9
change projects 29, 213
creating solutions 17
customer collaboration 18
development 102, 118, 155, 157
disciplined 2.0 74
estimation 222–31
evolution of iterative methods 13
introduction 11
Manifesto see Agile Manifesto
methods 59–76
mindset 15–16, 24–5, 41–57
origins of 12–13
practices 21–2
responding to change 18–9
Three Pillars of 62, 249
12 principles 19–20
use cases 174
working software 17–8, 52

Agile Manifesto 2, 11, 16, 19–20, 22, 25, 31, 37, 41, 59, 161

Agile retrospectives: making good teams great (Derby) 254–5

AgileUP 21, 70

AHP (analytical hierarchy prioritisation) 132, 141

Ambler, Scott 27, 74, 101–2, 161, 263
analysis 146–7, 153
Anderson, David 21, 71

'backbone' 198–9
backlogs
explanation 209–10
iteration 210, 212, 257
and prioritisation 211–2
release 212
solutions 209–13
and stakeholders 211–2
BAM 94
BCS 268
Beck, Kent 14, 66
Bittner, Kurt 174
black box 85
Boehm, Barry 13, 224
boundaries 91
brainstorming 167
brainwriting 167
Brooch, Grady 13
burndown charts 250–2
burnup charts 252–3
business
activity models (BAM) 88–9
actors 91
agility 5–6, 8–10
analysis 256–7
architects 114
capability maps 81–2
constraints 262
epics 92–4, 211
goals 161
managers 112

process maps 87–8
process models 89–90
business analysis 25–32, 98–9, 105, 209, 265–9
Agile Manifesto 31–2
agile software projects 7–8, 25–32, 41–2, 45
and Agile teams 47–9, 102–3
landscape 4–5, 6–7
maturation of 3–4
pre-project 25–9
rationale for 2–3
and Scrum 268
within the development team 30–1
business thinking 32–9
lean 35–7, 39, 88
service 37–9
systems 32–4, 39
business use case diagrams 90–1
business use case models 90–2

change 247–8
change programmes/projects 4, 29, 29–30, 211, 213
Checkland, Peter 32
Chrysler 14
Coad, Peter 14
Cockburn, Alistair 13–14, 85–6, 126
Cohn, Mike 185, 193
collaborative working 43–6, 211
communication 43–4
competitor organisations 116
continuous improvement 49–52
Cooper, Alan 169

core agile values 6, 42
Course Organisation Systems 92
Covey, Stephen 47
Cox, Julian 84–5
critical success factors (CSFs) 79, 89, 91, 217
Crystal 14
customers 116, 118, 152, 262

DA 2.0 263
DAD 236
daily stand-ups 249–50
data architect/managers 115
de Luca, Jeff 14
decomposition
    functional 123, 126
    and goals 91, 122–6, 128–9, 201
    and hierarchy 218–9
    understanding goal levels 126–8
Deming cycle 51
Deming, W. Edwards 50–1, 235
Department for Work and Pensions (UK) 4
Derby, E. 254–5
Developing information systems (Cadle) 12–13, 84
diagrams
    context 163, 172
    use case 163, 172, 174–7
DMAIC 52, 57
domain experts *see* subject-matter experts (SMEs)
Drucker, P. F. 57
Dynamic Systems Development Method (DSDM) 7, 9, 14, 21, 67–8, 75

elicitation 146, 151, 153–8
epics 183–4
estimation
    approaches 222–3
    divide to size 228
    ordering 133, 228
    planning poker 229–31
    relative (bucket method) 227
    relative sizing 225
    techniques 224
    units 226
    up-front 226–7
    why and when 223–4

Wideband Delphi 224, 231
Extreme Programming (XP) 14

facilitated workshops 154
Farquhar, John 224
Feature Driven Development (FDD) 14
Fifth Discipline, The (Senge) 32
Fitness for Business Purpose 21
5-forces (Porter) 80
5-Ws 73
Functional Model Map (FMM) 84–7, 150–1, 159, 181

generalising specialists 61, 101–2
goals
    business 161
    and decomposition 122–6, 128–9, 201
    and functional decomposition 91, 123–6
    and iteration 128–9, 236–8
    levels 126–7
    to achieve business agility 128
    government/legal/regulatory bodies 116

Handbook of Service Science (Spohrer/Maglio) 99
Highsmith, Jim 13
horizontal view *see* business thinking, lean
human touch, The (Thomas et al) 46

IBM 13
ideas
    discussing 167
    sharing 167
Inmates are Running the Asylum, The (Cooper) 169
International Diploma in Business Analysis 268
INVEST 184, 193
iteration
    and agile 52–7, 60
    and business analysis 256–7
    evolution of methods 13
    and goals 128–9, 236–8
    introduction/explanation 233–6

layered approach 236
managing/monitoring 249–53
and modelling 84, 162, 174
non-timeboxed 248–9
and planning 238–9
product backlog refinement 244–6
progress 245–7
and requirements approach 151, 154
reviewing 253–6
and teams 239–44

Jacobson, Ivar 13, 172, 174
Japan 49
Jensen, Mary Ann 49
Jones, Daniel 35–6, 88
Just Enough, Just in Time
    and agile 56, 222, 227, 231
    and delivery 2
    and DSDM 67
    and iteration 248–9
    Lean principle of 18
    and modelling 84, 94, 161
    and stakeholders 99

Kaizen (continuous improvement) 50–1, 57
Kanban 21, 68, 71–2, 246
Kano approach 132
key performance indicators (KPIs) 79, 89, 91

Lean
    manufacturing 50, 152
    software development 72–3
    startup 73
    thinking 21, 41
Lean software development (Poppendieck/Poppendieck) 21, 72–3
Leffingwell, Den 74
LeSS (Large Scale Scrum) 75
Lightweight Methods 13, 15
Lines, Mark 74, 101–2

'Manage Course Booking' 183
'Managing the development of large software systems' (Royce) 12
manufacturing products 50
Martin, James 13, 21

Maslow, Abraham 265
Mehrabian, Albert 43–5
Mehrabian's model 43–4
micromanagement 46–8, 261
Minimal Marketable Product (MMP) 54, 153, 201–2
Minimal Viable Product (MVP) 54, 153, 201
misuse characters 163, 168, 171–2
modelling
    in an agile context 94
    BDD (behaviour driven development) 185, 192–3, 195–7
    benefits 159–61
    explanations 159, 180
    Functional Model Map (FMM) 84–7, 150–1, 159, 181
    functionality 161–3
    and iteration 84, 162, 174
    misuse characters 171
    personas 168–71
    requirements approach 146, 149–50
    scenarios 193–5
    and stakeholders 160
    system context and scope 172–8, 180–2
    techniques 82–7
    user journeys 178–9
    user stories 182–93, 197–203
    users and roles 164–8
modular business architecture 128
MoSCoW technique 5, 53, 68, 202, 212–13, 242
MOST 79, 80–1
muda (waste) 72

New York Telephone Company 13
Nexus 75
non-functional requirements (NFRs) 162, 214–16
North, Dan 196

Ohno, T. 36
OMG Business Motivation Model 33
$100 allocation 132, 141
OpenUP 21, 70
organisational agility 79–82

Out of the crisis (Deming) 50
overprocessing 36, 152
overproduction 36, 152

pair programming 22, 66
Patton, Jeff 183, 197, 198
PayPal 128, 218
PDCA cycle 51
personas 101, 103, 105, 107, 159–79, 163
PESTLE analysis 80
Plan-Do-Study-Act wheel 235
POPIT
    and agile adoption 260
    and agile mindset 53, 56
    and agile philosophy 17
    and business agility 128
    and enterprise 25, 27–8, 34, 37
    key business analysis technique 82, 87
    and modelling 184
    and requirements approach 150
Poppendieck, Mary and Tom 21, 72–3
power/interest grid 107–8
pre-project analysis 26–7
PRINCE2 68
prioritisation
    application of 137–8
    and backlogs 211–2
    decomposition 138–9, 144
    importance of 130–1, 204
    issues 139–44
    and MoSCoW framework 134–8, 140, 143
    techniques 131–4
    and timing 134
programme managers 29, 112–13
Project Management Institute (PMI) 68
project managers 113
project sponsors 112
prototyping 155
Psychology of Science, The (Maslow) 265

RACI/RASCI 44, 107–8
Rapid application development (Martin) 13

Rapid Application Development (RAD) 7, 13, 21, 67
Rational Software Corporation 13, 70
Rational Unified Process (RUP) 13, 70
Relative Mass Estimation see estimation, ordering
requirements approach
    agile requirements engineering 152–4
    business analysis 156–8
    catalogue 208–9, 213
    elicitation techniques 154–6
    and engineering 145–9, 151–2
    functional 207
    general 206
    hierarchy 216–21
    introduction 145
    itemised backlogs 209–14
    non-functional 207–8
    planning of 149–51
    technical 206
    types 205–6
resource audits 80
retrospectives 61, 254–6
risk reduction/opportunity enablement 133
Royce, Winston W. 12–3
Rumbaugh, James 13
RUP 21, 70

SAFe (Scaled Agile Framework) 74–5, 133, 184, 236
scenarios 91, 118, 155–6, 180–202
Schwaber, Ken 14, 61, 242, 267–9
Scrum
    and agile adoption 261, 267–8
    and agile working practices 24, 61–5, 98
    AND Kanban 72
    and backlogs 209–10
    and DA 2.0 74
    daily stand-ups 249–50
    development process 14
    and Disciplined Agile 2.0. 7, 9, 14
    and DSDM 68
    and iteration 242
    job and role definitions 116
    and LeSS 75

popular method 21
and roles 111
and sprint 62–4
Three Pillars of 62
and transparency 246
Scrum Alliance guide (2016) 98–9
Scrum Guide (Schwaber) 267
ScrumBan 21
Senge, Peter 32
service level agreements (SLAs) 6
Service Science theory 99
7 habits of highly effective people (Covey) 47
Shewhart Cycle 235
'shout out' approach 167
'show and tell' meetings 253–4
Sinek, Simon 5–6
Six Sigma 50, 52
skills
 generic 101
 specific 101
Soft Systems Methodology (SSM) 32–4
Software Development Context Framework (SCF) 263
software products 4, 50
software/application architects 114
solutions
 architects/designers 114
 development 19, 118
 testers 118
SPAM 192
Spence, Ian 174
Spiral model (Barry Boehm) 13
stakeholders
 and agile philosophy 18
 and analytical approaches 27
 and backlogs 211–2
 business analysis 98–9
 business and and system requirements 29–30
 categorising 103–6, 110–1
 collaborative working 97
 communication 82
 engagement 84, 106–10, 119
 external perspectives 115–16
 and modelling 160
 nature of 96–7
 and perspectives 110–15, 116–19

and prioritisation 131, 143
and requirements approach 146, 149, 151–4
understanding 44
and user stories 219
working with 97–8
stories
 and agile boards 247
 and burndown charts 250
 complex 185–6
 compound 185–7
 hierarchy of user 219–20
 mapping of 197–203
 and stakeholders 219
 writing workshops 155
subject-matter experts (SMEs) 111, 116–17
suppliers 80, 90, 107, 109, 116, 206
surveys/questionnaires 154
Sutherland, Jeff 14, 61
SWOT analysis 80–1
system of interest model 263–4

T-shaped professional 96, 99–103, 157–8
TDD 66
team leaders 118
teams
 agile 126, 247–9, 256–7
 culture of 262
 and iteration 239–44
 multi-skilled 99–103
 self-organising 46, 99
 skills of 262
 velocity 212
themes 183
Thomas, Dave 13
Thomas, P. 46
Three Pillars of Scrum 62
3Cs 188
throwaway prototypes 156
time criticality 133
timeboxing 167
Toyota Production System 35, 72
traceability 147–8
transparency 61
TUBE 66
Tuckman, Bruce 48–9
Tuckman's model 48–9

UML (Unified Modelling Language)
 activity diagram 177
 description 1
 notation 13, 91
UP (Unified Process) 21, 70–1, 236
Use Case Modelling (Bittner/ Spence) 174
Use-Case 2.0: the Guide to Succeeding with Use Cases (Bittner) 174
User Stories Applied (Cohn) 182, 193
User story mapping (Patton) 183
users
 analysis matrix 163–5
 business value 133
 interviews 154
 journeys 163
 roles 163–8
UX (user experience) 47, 162

V model life cycle 25
value chains *see* business thinking, lean
value propositions 38, 105
value stream diagram (Womack/ Jones) 88
value streams 81–2, 88
value-in-exchange 38
value-in-use 38
video conferencing 45

'waterfall' systems 12–13, 25, 60
white box 85
'whole team' concept 247
WJSF (Weighted Shortest Job First) 75, 133–4, 141
Womack, James 35–6, 88
Work in Progress (WIP) 71–2
workshops 154, 160, 167, 191
world view analysis 44, 107–8
Worldpay 128, 218
Writing effective use cases (Cockburn) 126
WSJF prioritisation technique 228

XP 21, 66–8, 72, 210, 249

Zachman's Framework 33